RECLAIMING HERITAGE

PUBLICATIONS OF THE INSTITUTE OF ARCHAEOLOGY, UNIVERSITY COLLEGE LONDON
Director of the Institute: Stephen Shennan
Founding Series Editor: Peter J. Ucko

The Institute of Archaeology of University College London is one of the oldest, largest, and most prestigious archaeology research facilities in the world. Its extensive publications programme includes the best theory, research, pedagogy, and reference materials in archaeology and cognate disciplines, through publishing exemplary work of scholars worldwide. Through its publications, the Institute brings together key areas of theoretical and substantive knowledge, improves archaeological practice, and brings archaeological findings to the general public, researchers, and practitioners. It also publishes staff research projects, site and survey reports, and conference proceedings. The publications programme, formerly developed inhouse or in conjunction with UCL Press, is now produced in partnership with Left Coast Press, Inc. The Institute can be accessed online at www.ucl.ac.uk/archaeology.

ENCOUNTERS WITH ANCIENT EGYPT Subseries, Peter J. Ucko, (ed.)
Jean-Marcel Humbert and Clifford Price (eds.), Imhotep Today
David Jeffreys (ed.), Views of Ancient Egypt since Napoleon Bonaparte
Sally MacDonald and Michael Rice (eds.), Consuming Ancient Egypt
Roger Matthews and Cornelia Roemer (eds.), Ancient Perspectives on Egypt
David O'Connor and Andrew Reid (eds.), Ancient Egypt in Africa
John Tait (ed.), 'Never had the like occurred'
David O'Connor and Stephen Quirke (eds.), Mysterious Lands
Peter J. Ucko and Timothy Champion (eds.), The Wisdom of Egypt

CRITICAL PERSPECTIVES ON CULTURAL HERITAGE Subseries, Beverley Butler (ed.)
Beverley Butler, Return to Alexandria
Ferdinand de Jong and Michael Rowlands (eds.), Reclaiming Heritage
Dean Sully (ed.), Decolonizing Conservation

OTHER TITLES
Andrew Gardner (ed.), Agency Uncovered
Okasha El-Daly, Egyptology, The Missing Millennium
Ruth Mace, Clare J. Holden, and Stephen Shennan (eds.), Evolution of Cultural Diversity
Arkadiusz Marciniak, Placing Animals in the Neolithic
Robert Layton, Stephen Shennan, and Peter Stone (eds.), A Future for Archaeology
Joost Fontein, The Silence of Great Zimbabwe
Gabriele Puschnigg, Ceramics of the Merv Oasis
James Graham-Campbell and Gareth Williams (eds.), Silver Economy in the Viking Age
Barbara Bender, Sue Hamilton, and Chris Tilley, Stone World
Andrew Gardner, An Archaeology of Identity
Sue Hamilton, Ruth Whitehouse, and Katherine I. Wright (eds.), Archaeology and Women
Gustavo Politis, Nukak
Sue Colledge and James Conolly (eds.), The Origins and Spread of Domestic Plants in Southwest Asia and Europe
Timothy Clack and Marcus Brittain (eds.), Archaeology and the Media
Janet Picton, Stephen Quirke, and Paul C. Roberts (eds.), Living Images
Tony Waldron, Paleoepidemiology
Eleni Asouti and Dorian Q. Fuller, Trees and Woodlands of South India
Russell McDougall and Iain Davidson (eds.), The Roth Family, Anthropology, and Colonial Administration
Elizabeth Pye (ed.), The Power of Touch
John Tait, Why the Egyptians Wrote Books

RECLAIMING HERITAGE

Alternative Imaginaries of Memory in West Africa

Ferdinand de Jong
Michael Rowlands
Editors

Walnut Creek, California

 **Left Coast Press Inc.**

LEFT COAST PRESS, INC.
1630 North Main Street, #400
Walnut Creek, CA 94596
http://www.LCoastPress.com

Copyright © 2007 by Left Coast Press, Inc. First paperback edition 2010.

All rights reserved. No part of this publication may be reproduced, stored in a retrieval system, or transmitted in any form or by any means, electronic, mechanical, photocopying, recording, or otherwise, without the prior permission of the publisher.

ISBN 978-1-59874-307-4 hardcover
ISBN 978-1-59874-308-1 paperback

Library of Congress Cataloguing-in-Publication Data:

Reclaiming heritage : alternative imaginaries of memory in West Africa / Ferdinand de Jong, Michael Rowlands, editors.
   p. cm. — (Critical cultural heritage series)
Includes bibliographical references and index.
      ISBN 978-1-59874-307-4 (hardback : alk. paper)
      ISBN 978-1-59874-308-1 (paperback : alk. paper)
   1. Cultural property—Africa, West. 2. Cultural property—Africa, West—Protection. 3. Memory—Social aspects—Africa, West. 4. Africa, West—History. 5. Africa, West—Antiquities. I. de Jong, Ferdinand. II. Rowlands, M. J.
      DT473.R43 2007 966—dc22 2007034207

Printed in the United States of America

∞™ The paper used in this publication meets the minimum requirements of American National Standard for Information Sciences—Permanence of Paper for Printed Library Materials, ANSI/NISO Z39.48–1992.

Contents

Illustrations	7
Series Editor's Foreword	9
Acknowledgments	11
1 Reconsidering Heritage and Memory *Michael Rowlands and Ferdinand de Jong*	13

Old Origins, New Imaginaries

2 'Taking on a Tradition': African Heritage and the Testimony of Memory *Beverley Butler*	31
3 Slave Route Projects: Tracing the Heritage of Slavery in Ghana *Katharina Schramm*	71
4 Picturing the Past: Heritage, Photography, and the Politics of Appearance in a Yoruba City *Peter Probst*	99

Materiality and Conservation

5 Entangled Memories and Parallel Heritages in Mali *Michael Rowlands*	127
6 'Enchanting Town of Mud': Djenné, A World Heritage Site in Mali *Charlotte Joy*	145
7 A Masterpiece of Masquerading: Contradictions of Conservation in Intangible Heritage *Ferdinand de Jong*	161

Recognition and Reconciliation

8 From a Glorious Past to the Lands of Origin: 185
   Media Consumption and Changing Narratives of
   Cultural Belonging in Mali
   Dorothea Schulz

9 Demystified Memories: The Politics of Heritage in   215
   Post-Socialist Guinea
   Ramon Sarró

10 Palimpsest Memoryscapes: Materializing and   231
   Mediating War and Peace in Sierra Leone
   Paul Basu

About the Contributors   261
Index   265

Illustrations

Figure 2.1	'Plato's Obelisk', Ain Shams, Cairo	47
Figure 2.2	The Bibliotheca Alexandrina, contemporary Alexandria	64
Figure 3.1	Garden of Reverence, Assin Manso	83
Figure 3.2	'Welcome to Salaga Slave Market', Salaga	85
Figure 3.3	Moru Kuala, elder of Gwollu, posing in front of the Defence Wall in his father's battle dress	88
Figure 4.1	Palace sculptures associated with local deities in Osogbo	102
Figure 4.2	Cement sculpture by Susanne Wenger and Adebisi Akanji in the Osun grove representing Obaluaye, late 1970s	102
Figure 4.3	Road clearers with Osun devotee at Osun Festival 2002	104
Figure 4.4	Osogbo Heritage Council, History of Osogbo, 1994	108
Figure 4.5	Afolabi Kayode, Osun in Colours, 2006	113
Figure 4.6	Oba Atanda Olugbena Matanmi II, early twentieth century	114
Figure 4.7	Part of the Ohuntoto Ogboni Shrine Complex, erected by Wenger, Gbadamosi, Saka, and Akangbe in the mid-1970s	116
Figure 4.8	Group of four cement figures by Adebisi Akanji in the Osun grove	118
Figure 6.1	Traditional Djenné houses	152
Figure 6.2	Masons in Djenné at work applying the yearly layer of mud needed to protect the houses	153
Figure 6.3	Fallen down house in Djenné	154
Figure 6.4	House covered in tiles in Djenné	155
Figure 6.5	Cement government building in administrative district of Djenné	155
Figure 7.1	Kankurang and one of his cross-dressed 'guardians'	163

Figure 7.2	Cartoon in national newspaper *Le Soleil*: Kankurang beating up a man who claims : 'This is not a true Kankurang. It's Modou, whose brother I disciplined yesterday'.	163
Figure 7.3	Cartoon in national newspaper 'Le Soleil'	166
Figure 7.4	Boys playing with their Kankurang	167
Figure 7.5	*Detail* by Omar Camara, oil on canvas	177
Figure 7.6	Kankurang as statuette	177
Figure 7.7	Performers with make-shift cameras	179
Figure 7.8	Performers performing as journalists	180
Figure 9.1	'Nimba' (or d'mba) masquerade, Tolkoc, 2001	225
Figure 10.1	*Handiwork of Child Combatants*, Simeon Benedict Sesay, 2000	236
Figure 10.2	Obverse and reverse of the 2004 Bank of Sierra Leone 10,000 Leone note	238
Figure 10.3	Remains of the 'Soldier Kill Rebel' monument erected by the NPRC in 1994 in Bo	243
Figure 10.4	Signboard advertising the 2003 renaming of Freetown's Congo Cross Bridge as 'Peace Bridge'	245
Figure 10.5	Illustration from *Wetin Na Di Speshal Kot: The Special Court Made Simple*, a booklet produced by the Special Court's Outreach Section in 2002 and distributed to Sierra Leonean schoolchildren	247

Series Editor's Foreword

The aim of this *Critical Perspectives on Cultural Heritage* series is to define a new area of research and to produce a set of volumes that make a radical break with routinised accounts and definitions of cultural heritage and with the existing or 'established' canon of cultural heritage texts. In a fundamental shift of perspective, the French intellectual Jacques Derrida's rallying call to 'restore heritage to dignity' is taken as an alternative guiding metaphor by which this series critically revisits the core question – what constitutes cultural heritage? – and engages with the concerns (notably the moral-ethical issues) that shape and define the possible futures of cultural heritage studies. A key objective of this series is to be of transformative value in the sense of outlining and creating new agendas within cultural heritage discourse.

This series of publications is therefore intended to provide the intellectual impetus and critical framework by which cultural heritage discourse can undergo a process of radical reflection and fundamental reconceptualisation and engage in a subsequent reconstruction of its core heritage values, practices, and ethics. Central to this project is an alignment with a wider scholarship committed to disrupting the 'Eurocentrism' that continues to underpin cultural heritage theory/practice and also with a contemporary 'politics of recognition', which is bound up in articulating new, alternative, or 'parallel' characterisations of heritage value. This commitment to produce a set of publications directed toward reconceptualising cultural heritage studies within these alternative intellectual, moral-ethical, and also grounded concerns is ultimately rooted in calls for the centring of cultural heritage discourse within a wider concern for the preservation of human dignity and human justice and to use these alternative discourses as a resource for future action in terms of creating a proactive (rather than reactive), responsive, and just future for a new critical cultural heritage studies. The individual texts in this series are regarded as building blocks in defining these new research futures.

As one of the first books in the Critical Perspectives on Cultural Heritage series, *Reclaiming Heritage* critically addresses cultural heritage theory/practice and technologies of memory-work in the specific context of West Africa. This text is ground-breaking in its radical reconsideration of cultural heritage value apropos the 'postcolonial memory crisis' and in its commitment to challenging the 'Eurocentrism' that historically has silenced, and in the contemporary context continues to obstruct, attempts to reveal 'alternative', local heritage values and to misrepresent their complex meanings. Contributors to this volume bring together new and original ethnographic case-study insights that are capable of exposing the presence of multilayered memoryscapes and reflexive engagements with (in)tangible heritages. The critical flow of the book sees contributors use 'thought pieces' and fieldwork findings to address the growing tensions between traditional 'Eurocentric/Afrocentric' 'myths of origin' and 'new' West African heritage 'imaginaries', the hybrid memory-work at play between conservation and (im-)materiality and the moral-ethical issues dominating the politics and policies of recognition and reconciliation. On this broad canvas of discussion, detailed and contextualised critiques are made on a diversity of topics, including the commemoration of the heritage of slavery in Ghana, the entangled memories at Djenné 'World Heritage' site in Mali, and attempts to mobilise heritage/memory to mediate war and peace in Sierra Leone. Ultimately, heritage as cure, as reenchantment and redemption, is rejected by contributors to this volume in favour of the need to create an alternative 'postcolonial' therapeutics and to develop hybrid technologies of memory capable of engaging the burden of memory.

Dr Beverley Butler
Critical Perspectives on Cultural Heritage Series Editor
Institute of Archaeology
University College London

Acknowledgments

How can we rethink heritage and ensure that alternative imaginaries of memory are recognised? This book examines current heritage practices in West Africa and discusses how they allow us to conceptualise heritage in a new way. The volume suggests a decolonisation of heritage through an examination of postcolonial practices.

The idea to write a volume on heritage in Africa emerged at the first European Conference of African Studies organised by the Africa-Europe Group for Interdisciplinary Studies, 29 June – 2 July 2005, London. The conference was hosted by the School of Oriental and African Studies. A number of the papers in this volume were presented at the panel Memory and the Public Sphere at this conference. Even if some of the papers could not be included, we would like to thank all the presenters and the audience for their firm engagement with the issues at stake. We wish to thank in particular the discussants Birgit Meyer and Nicolas Argenti, who gave direction to the debate and provided many valuable insights, and we acknowledge the way they have influenced the argument of this book – however surprised they may be by the final outcome.

We would also like to thank the Series Editor, Beverley Butler, for her encouragement and support throughout the editing process. We hope that this book, as others in this series, will contribute to an 'Africanist' turn in heritage.

Ferdinand de Jong,
University of East Anglia
Michael Rowlands, University College London

Chapter-opening design art is a reproduction of Bushongo embroidered raffia.

Reconsidering Heritage and Memory
Michael Rowlands and Ferdinand de Jong

Studies of memory in Africa have consistently stressed the contested nature of such practices as commemoration, remembrance, and forgetting. State ritual and personal and group recollections are inevitably situated in a politicized context. Richard Werbner speaks of a 'memory crisis': in postcolonial Africa memory is full of contradictions between the grandiosity of state ceremonialism and popular memory (cf Mbembe 1992; Werbner 1998a). The literature suggests that popular memory is genuine, whereas state ceremony and monuments are mere spectacles of the State. It is undeniable that, as a consequence of colonialism and the impact of European derived models of nationalism, the State in Africa has a tendency to monumentalize itself. Such a policy is reinforced by UNESCO and other agencies that promote heritage technologies for the production of official pasts and futures. However, in this volume we are interested in how memory attaches itself to heritage in often unexpected ways. In this context, we discover a broader principle that modern heritage and memory share a common origin in conflict and loss. Monuments, museums, and memorials are inseparable from the powerful modern moods of nostalgia and longing for authenticity as well as escalating desires for roots and origins. Thus we ask what kind of memorialising tactics and strategies attach themselves to the technologies of heritage. Which memory politics emerge in the context of such more formal institutions and which memories remain hidden and, when deliberately denied, even repressed? The aim of this volume is to examine how heritage technologies are appropriated for the recognition of past suffering and the creation of futures of hope.

Memory and the Public Sphere

Uncertainty as a recurrent feature of colonial and postcolonial states encourages us to think that people who struggle to create particular futures from particular pasts do so in a context in which the public sphere is questioned as having any moral legitimacy. Personal acts of recollection are instead realized in other forms of collective remembrance and story telling (for example, Fabian 1996) or linked to social reproduction and the protection of ethnic identity against externally perceived threat (Cole 2005). The extent to which the public sphere exists and facilitates personal and collective memory in postcolonial Africa is therefore debatable. Remembering seems to occur in opposition to the public sphere.

Citing the 'postcolonial memory crisis' in Africa, Werbner claims that memory as public practice is underdeveloped in terms of nation-building, and what little there is has been severely disturbed by violence and corruption (Werbner 1998a). An alternative and less pessimistic view has stressed that, despite atrocities and economic deprivation, personal and collective memories have been pivotal in recovering from trauma and reasserting claims to particular futures (cf Guyer 2005). Both these views raise a common question of what resources are available to form memory out of events, to create a sense of concern with the past that promotes feelings of well-being in the face of its apparent opposite as well as acting as a source of power that promotes an identity politics and claims to restitution. Both points of view tend, however, to see this in terms of personal and collective acts defined in resistance to the public sphere (for instance, Burnham 1996; Cole 1998).

At present, therefore, a tension is established between local and personal collective memories and globalising and/or state-building acts of memorialism. But such a dichotomy is questioned by the way processes of collective commemoration emerged in the twentieth century and the manner in which these processes had direct effects in colonial and postcolonial Africa, projecting a sense of place through the reification of boundaries, land holdings, the identification of sacred sites, or the preservation of vernacular architecture. Discussions of a 'politics of belonging' also stress that allocation of rights to origins fits local collective memories in ways that, although threatening and violent, do assert the connections among the State, elites, and collective memory (cf Nyamnjoh and Rowlands 1998). Recent claims have also been made to the effect that memory objectified in material culture becomes an active agent with therapeutic powers. Memory as re-enchantment merges with recent work on trauma to promise recovery from loss and denial (Antze and Lambek 1996). This view would question whether memory is different in Africa. Lambek would see the past as something more than 'remembered' or interpreted in a 'presentist' sense, as also acting as a burden on the present (Lambek 2002). Moreover, the subjectivity of the person cannot be distinguished from the public and the private aspects but carries the burden of the past in any guise. Personal and collective memory pervades the public sphere.

Technologies of Heritage

As mentioned earlier, as a consequence of colonialism and the impact of European-derived models of nationalism the State in Africa has a tendency to monumentalize itself. By this we mean something more than investment in buildings, memorials, and a general monumental architectural landscape that sets apart the city as a place of cement, glass, and steel (cf De Jorio 2006). The tendency for states to create *lieux de mémoire* that help nation-building has a wider implication of creating deliberate landscapes of memory that will act as technologies for the reification of pasts and the creation of expectable futures for their inhabitants (Handler 1988; Huyssen 2003). There is a large literature on how official urban landscapes of memory act as stages for framing myths of national identity. Although relatively underdeveloped in Africa, architectural landscapes have been encouraged by the colonial and postcolonial State (Coombes 2003; De Jorio 2006). Studies of vernacular architecture have equally stressed the *longue durée* of physical form and the ability to absorb new materials (cement, glass, and so on) and material spaces into 'traditional architecture' in order to preserve habitual ways of organising domestic and public places relating to kinship and gender norms. Although there is considerable continuity in the architectural landscape, UNESCO policy in Africa has resulted in an opposition between tangible and intangible heritage, which has privileged the idea of an authentic Africa as performative rather than monumental.

UNESCO and other agencies promote technologies for producing pasts and futures, by which we mean archives, artefacts, ritual practices, performances, and material spaces. How these technologies affect individual projects of self-realization, and in particular the intangible nature of performative culture and everyday practices, is a major theme of this volume. Thus we raise the issue of how to preserve intangible heritage and how technologies of memory affect memory (cf Nas et al. 2002). We are interested in the way, on the one hand, the material world relates to technologies that reify experiences of the past into transcending categories and forces to which individuals and groups attach themselves in terms of their everyday needs. On the other hand, we also examine how these attachments take on lives of their own and result in unexpected memory politics that tend to ignore more pressing memory issues that remain hidden and, when deliberately denied, even repressed. Therefore, we need to explore the issue of which memories are privileged and which are repressed through heritage politics.

Moreover, we need to explore how the content of particular memorialising strategies relates to the technologies that produce them and/or acts to subvert and repress them. Some will be small scale, such as family genealogies and kinship traits; others will be embedded in large-scale internationally supported projects such as heritage sites, postconflict restoration projects, and development programmes. These memorialising strategies have in common the desire to preserve. They produce technologies that select some memories and memorial artefacts for preservation and reject others. The act of curating and collecting is therefore a pivotal technological act in preserving the past to gain a future. The social effects and (mis)recognitions that these create should be understood as a politics of self-realization.

Heritage versus Memory

Heritage is increasingly thought to offer recognition, in terms of a valuation of the cultural heritage of formerly colonized and underrepresented populations. Thus the study of heritage is now receiving increased attention from anthropologists who write with approval on co-curated heritage projects (Clifford 2004). However, the anthropological interest in heritage has also raised concern about the basic assumptions of the heritage project (Hylland Eriksen 2001).

To situate the current concern with the conservation of heritage, we begin by exploring the ideological origins that underlie the globalising aims of the UNESCO world heritage policy. The most recent convention – the 2003 Convention for the Safeguarding of the Intangible Cultural Heritage – maintains the general consensus in UNESCO (that is, the 1972 Convention) that globalization and social transformation give rise to grave threats to (intangible) cultural heritage; hence the acknowledgment of a loss of cultural diversity and the need to provide normative rules to prevent this loss. The assumptions that cultural diversity is analogous to biodiversity and that there is a need for international regulations to prevent its disappearance are not seriously disputed. Only the United States and Israel refused to sign the last convention.

Although there are good reasons to assume that the preservation of cultural heritage and the practice of memory are incompatible projects, we discern a common concern in both. In the European debate on heritage in the 1980s, a tension emerged between heritage and memory as an opposition of external and internal memory. One of the GDAT debates in Manchester addressed this issue in terms of a discussion between historians and anthropologists on the propositions of Lowenthal's *The Past Is a Foreign Country* (Ingold 1996; Lowenthal 1985). A model of the past defined as 'difference' from the present formed the basis for a debate in which the protagonists basically took on either an 'historical approach' or a 'memorial approach' to the past. In the former, Lowenthal argued for the 'rise of heritage' as inevitably bound up with the rise of science, the decline of religious authority, and the establishment of meta-narratives of progress and rationality. The museum and the creation of public monumental landscapes are credited as key emblems of modernity – they provide a sense of permanence to counter modernity's experience of root-lessness, rupture, and displacement. According to Nora (1989), memory in this context is reflexively achieved through the creation of *lieux de mémoires* in contrast to a previous habitual memory that did not need to be named as such and existed in everyday ways of doing things. Heritage in this sense is therefore an expansive force built on the confidence of nation-building and sustained by a sense of loss. Heritage, archives, and museums are seen to evolve as a privileged space in which the sense of loss and disruption can be contemplated and assessed and finally cured.

In this context, we discover a broader principle that modern heritage and modern memory share a common origin in conflict and loss. Monuments, museums, and memorials are inseparable from debates about nostalgia and authenticity and escalating desires for roots and origins. Translated to an African context, the UNESCO paradigm encapsulates twin programmes around restoration, in particular, architecture, and conservation in particular measures to counter illicit trade in antiquities and art objects. However, a return to the past is always partial and incomplete. Restoring the past is insufficient without an accompanying decolonization of African history. Ann Stahl has recently documented how a writing of an African past by archaeologists includes Africa in a search of early human origins and yet excludes it in writing the archaeology of later world prehistory and history (Stahl 2004:8). Self-conscious attempts by African archaeologists to bypass colonial imaginations of African pasts and release 'hidden voices' are increasing and ever more critical of the imposition of foreign models (cf Chami 2006; Schmidt and Patterson 1996). Recent criticisms of the focus on tangible heritage favouring the restoration of monuments and landscapes (products of a Eurocentric definition of heritage) resulted in the adoption of a wider notion of intangible cultural heritage to include cultural practices and skills as well as objects and cultural spaces that communities/groups recognize as their cultural heritage. But the twin themes of restoration and conservation are essentially maintained within the wider paradigm of the archive that both restores and revitalizes heritage through formal and nonformal education.

UNESCO Heritage Politics in Africa

Archives require surveys and indexes to decide on principles of inclusion and exclusion, so it is perhaps not surprising that since the 2003 convention, over fifty national surveys of cultural patrimony have been instigated by various African states. Much of this identification has been far too late in terms of its stated aims to conserve and preserve. For instance, concerning Mali's Inner Delta region, claims have been made that over 60% of archaeological sites show traces of looting and that the number increases every year by 5% (Bedaux and Rowlands 2001). But to whom does this matter? Presumably, not necessarily to those who loot – people who may have little alternative sources of income. However, cultural loss seems in a rather unexpected way related to cultural rights. According to Article 22 of the 1948 Universal Human Declaration, economic, social, and cultural rights are indispensable for human dignity and the free development of the personality. Such rights were to be realized through a national effort and international cooperation. Associating civic rights with cultural rights was affirmed once again in the 1976 Covenant: 'The right to culture obliges public authorities to create the social and economic conditions which permit the effective exercise of this right' (UN doc 1976 A/31/111). In the same period, the question of repatriation of cultural items to countries of origin arose in general assembly debates, in particular the recognition of the removal of cultural property under colonialism. In Africa, the Banjul charter – otherwise known as the African Charter on Human and Peoples' Rights, adopted by all heads of state in 1981 – reproduces almost exactly the UN convention on the right to participate in a cultural life, including the obligation by the State in Africa to promote and protect the morals and traditional values recognised by the community.

The link of cultural rights to community rather than citizenship in Africa has the consequence of promoting an association between cultural heritage and cultural rights. It has already been pointed out that this association, which has its roots in colonial rule, has resulted in the absence of civil society in postcolonial Africa (Mamdani 1996). In our context, the implication of a failure to restore or preserve cultural heritage as the equivalent of a failure in the preservation of cultural rights has not gone unnoticed. In current political circumstances, elite associations and diaspora communities can charge the State with neglect in this respect. Whether this does any good or not, the significant point is that, in Africa, the human right to participate in culture has come to incorporate the idea that cultural identity should be explicitly tied to cultural heritage. This point happens to be very conducive to the globalisation of cultural heritage and the performance of heritage for tourism.

But it simultaneously promotes the relation of State to community in rather essentialising terms. Quite explicit cases of this situation may be seen in the way that Shona politics in Zimbabwe were tied to identification with the preservation of Great Zimbabwe. Current politics of autochthony and strangers in many parts of Africa are equally problematic in terms of the preservation of culture on behalf of local communities. Politicians increasingly need to be seen participating in 'traditions' that are usually understood as ethnic, rather than national, heritages (de Jong 2007). For it to make claims to international aid and resources, the State has the role of sustaining cultural rights, yet it remains antithetical to the translation of cultural into political rights, which adds to political tension.

Hence, there are special reasons why UNESCO has particular relevance in Africa. Post-1989 recognition of the consequences of 'weak states', institutional capacity-building, and good governance prescriptions for development aid results in a greater prominence of cultural heritage in general debates on aid and development in Africa. This prominence raises the issue of how the assumptions integrated in UNESCO World Conventions translate into policies that most weak African states have little power to negotiate. Moreover, it raises the question how such policies are appropriated by cultural elites and what their implications will be for state-society relations in postcolonial Africa. Theoretically, it raises issues with regard to how UNESCO policy affects nation-building in a space in which cultural elites, diasporas, and the reinvention (once again) of 'traditional rulers' all play a role.

Our endeavour is to translate the heritage/memory tension into another space where development/aid and nation-building are more explicit concerns. If heritage discourse focuses on discontinuity and the revitalizing of pasts, memory is constituted by a politics of remembering and forgetting that stresses repetition and continuity. We seem to be dealing, therefore, with an opposition between notions of reflexive notions of heritage and materialized pasts derived from sensory memories. We refer here to the distinctions made by Connerton (1989) and others (for example, Hirsch 1997; Nora 1989), but whereas these authors saw these distinctions as absolute social differences, we are concerned with showing how these processes operate and are triggered by one another in particular settings. We argue that memory is located in material sensory practices such as songs, performances, and photographs, *as well as* in sites where the past is conserved, mediated, and authorized.

The focused, contextualized research approach presented by the essays presented here demonstrates how material and immaterial symbols create desired memories and foci that are competed over within and without groups, in a struggle in which identity, like memory, is never fixed and completed.

In this volume, we are concerned with cultural heritage as a discursive tradition that, in an appropriately translocal manner, acts to configure power widely in Africa and yet in terms of its articulation of cultural rights has particular consequences in evoking and repressing forms of memory. In the remainder of this introduction we discuss how the various contributions feed into the debates raised.

Return to Origins

Our aim in this volume is to imagine the possibility and conditions of existence of heritages alternative to those commonly associated with the West. UNESCO's policy of defining a 'world heritage' has led to strategies of conservation and restoration that have challenged the existence of local heritage practices of preservation and transmission. But UNESCO policy is not necessarily hegemonic, and to suggest that it is attributes excessive weight to the bureaucratisation of heritage. However, we argue that the value attached to 'world heritage' is embedded in a certain imaginary of the past, in particular of a foundational assumption of cultural 'beginnings' and 'origins' that is deeply constitutive of a particular Western sense of its own historical purpose, a particular kind of historicity. We organized the volume on the implicit notion that alternative imaginaries of heritage exist in West Africa, in order precisely to contrast them to a dominant Western imagination of itself.

This book's first chapter, by Beverley Butler, is a 'thought piece', to provide a broad critical rehearsal of the conceptual, intellectual, and moral-ethical issues at stake in selected 'performative moments' of memory-work and the attendant construction of heritage imaginaries. Butler's chapter narrates the historical 'Westernization' of heritage memory and the challenges made to the so-called universal, foundational qualities of Greco-European memory and the Western, Classical, and canonical heritage genealogies as they are confronted by an 'othering' identified as an 'Africanist turn'. Butler proposes a critical reappraisal of alternative intellectual-operational 'performative moments' in the 'traditions' of African heritage.

She begins by providing a theoretical exploration of the foundation of the Western imaginary of its own beginnings, by excavating the origins of our Western heritage discourse in Classical epical traditions. Focusing on Alexandria, she demonstrates how this 'city of marble' has been claimed by a Western philosophical tradition as an extension of the Greek landscape. The destruction of its ancient Mouseion/Library has been represented as a 'loss' to the 'West', thus providing a template for our contemporary archival heritage paradigm of loss and preservation. Butler argues that the materiality of the archive and its subsequent destruction has provided a frame for the current UNESCO charter, which focuses on heritage conservation as a prerequisite for human self-realization, but she questions the legitimacy of this European legacy. In her reading of Europe's relation to North Africa, Europe's 'return' to its 'origins' in Alexandria has always been a return to imperialism. The Western claim to 'origins' necessarily involved a disinheritance of North Africans.

Postcolonial authors such as Frantz Fanon and Cheikh Anta Diop have subsequently chosen to reinherit and empower themselves through their reclamation of North Africa, the 'mother of science and culture of the West' (Butler, this volume). The landscape of ancient Egypt has thus sustained a privileged place in what have become known as Afrocentrist theses. To counter their disinheritance, Butler argues, the colonized have sought to 'take control of the violence' by therapeutic practices of possession and exorcism. Anticolonialism is thus recast as a 'psychotherapy of the oppressed' that enables colonial objects to become subjects, restoring their dignity. This suggests that the restorative programme of UNESCO should be opened up to alternative imaginations that are not necessarily based on the model of the 'Greek' archive but on other 'traditions' that have countered the disinheritance by colonialism.

The recipe (*pharmakon*) for the 'return to origins' and subsequent recovery should be rethought so as to restore dignity in postcolonial Africa. As Butler argues, such rethinking requires us to fundamentally reenvision the still-dominant Euro-Western 'traditions' of donation, reception, and inheritance and to problematize concepts of intentionality in the form of both intentional and unintentional memory-work. How, we may ask, can conventional ways of thinking about heritage as a 'legacy' of monumental architecture be reframed as a way of confronting the present? One way is to rethink the role of established, imperial institutions (Mack 2003).

Undoubtedly, another strategy is to abandon received ideas about heritage as awe-inspiring monumental architecture. The contributions to this volume present a variety of media and thus take up the task that Butler has set in the first essay. Although the monumental architecture of the Djenné mosque in Mali comes closest to the European conception of heritage, the building is constructed of mud, not marble. Mud is also the base for much of the vernacular architecture in Djenné, which is the subject of two papers. Other heritage media discussed in this volume include cotton trees, sacred groves, and masked performances. These media would traditionally not be considered 'heritage', and yet they provide the material means by which the past is represented. Alongside these heritages, more controversial and unsettling legacies are found in Ghanaian slave forts and the mass graves of the

Sierra Leone civil wars. Unexpectedly, some of the cultural legacies presented here use the modern media of photography and national television. African heritage, too, is presented through new technologies of memory.

New Heritage Projects

The possibility that new media can unleash memory-work invites reflection on their potential for engagement with other technologies of memory. How likely are monuments and memorials to resonate in the postcolony? Can these technologies be grafted on existing modes of memory and forgetting? Research on memory in Africa has so far focused on embodiment (Argenti 2006; Lambek 2002; Shaw 2002; Stoller 1995). Yet how technologies of memory reliant on the body operate in nation-states under construction is yet unclear. We may need to look at emergent technologies of memory that trigger memory-work in the postcolony. Recent studies suggest that, alongside the embodiment of the postcolonial nation in dance, music, and performance (Apter 2005; Askew 2002; Castaldi 2006), painting and graffiti have become established as new technologies of memory (Diouf 1993; Fabian 1996; Roberts and Roberts 2003). In this volume, several contributions suggest that such new technologies of memory are actually grafted on indigenous modes of remembrance that produce palimpsests of memory.

In his chapter on the Osun sacred grove in Osogbo (Nigeria), Peter Probst demonstrates how, under colonialism, the grove and its deities had become less central to Osogbo's religious life. To counter the alienation caused by colonialism, it was decided to revive the sacred grove, which then became subject to diverse imaginations. New images were to re-energize the Osun grove in a visual language appropriate to modern times. A festival was established to commemorate the Yoruba religion through sacrifices at the Osun River. But, whereas the sacred grove had exemplified the de-enchantment held characteristic of modernity, its re-enchantment as heritage opposed political factions with widely diverging positions (not unlike the struggle in Djenné, see below). Since the 1980s, the grove and the festival have become a site of polarization between, on the one hand, Christians and Muslims rejecting the festival as an expression of paganism and, on the other hand, a majority of the population embracing it as a symbol of local identity. Both factions sought to preserve the past from the changes brought by modernity, but they imagined the future differently. Probst goes on to show how their very styles of imagination differed in how the past was represented by means of photographs in Palace-issued brochures. This chapter shows how the revitalization of a sacred grove as heritage triggers the making of narratives that include those pasts in diverging imaginations of the future. Significantly, these imaginations are materialized in photography, a technology of memory grafted on the grove as an older, established way of remembering.

Probst's chapter examines how new technologies of memory interact with older modes of memory. Several other chapters examine how technologies of memory are grafted on one another. Katharina Schramm discusses how an interest in African-American financial investments has seduced the Ghanaian government into establishing the Joseph Project, to secure a steady flow of African-American tourists to a variety of memory sites in Ghana. The formal memory-scape of the slave trade as sustained by UNESCO and embodied in slave castles at the Ghanaian coast is now extended into the interior. Informal memories of the slave trade transmitted through ritual and oral tradition are now being replaced with formal technologies of memory established by the Ghanaian government. Although not completely eradicating the informal technologies of memory, the formal ceremonies and museum structures do tend to incorporate or displace the existing, local memories. Moreover, while the Joseph Project commemorates the transatlantic slave trade and represents slave markets as part of that network, the significance of these places in the history of the internal slave trade is marginalized. However, Schramm also demonstrates that the formal commemoration of the transatlantic trade feeds into local memory, and she suggests that the opposition between state-led, formal commemoration and popular counter-memory is not sustainable. Different heritage technologies effectively interact to produce a palimpsest memory.

Paul Basu, in his contribution, argues along similar lines that the production of memory in Sierra Leone has resulted in various regimes of memory that exist alongside one another, overlapping and intersecting, rather than merging into one. He examines how the Cotton Tree is a condensed national symbol represented in a number of different media, including the national Le 10,000 note. Tellingly, on the banknote, the Cotton Tree appears alongside a dove, hybridizing indigenous and foreign symbolism. In a comparable case, Basu demonstrates how the name of Bai Bureh, an important Temne warrior who resisted the British troops in the Hut Tax War, has been appropriated as a *nom de guerre* by guerrillas and how his life story has been retold in a volume entitled *Sierra Leone Heroes*, making the name available for various readings. As the Cotton Tree, the name has been used in new technologies resulting in multiple layers of co-existent yet contradictory memories. Finally, using cases of war sculpture and mass graves, Basu demonstrates how the landscape of Sierra Leone has become a memory-scape of conflict in which these layered sites of memory can also become sites of mediation.

Materiality and Objectification

That the conservation and the restoration of heritage are bound up with the attribution of origins and the imagination of futures is clearly conveyed in the chapters by Michael Rowlands and Charlotte Joy. The restoration of the monumental mosque in Djenné is controversial and has recently even led to riots on the town streets. At stake are the issues of who has the right to renovate and which materials should be used in the restoration of the mosque. The imam pursues the use of modern materials in order to adhere to a particular Saudi-financed Muslim modernity, but these materials are excluded from UNESCO's vision for a restoration that, Rowlands argues, reinstates colonial nostalgia. The materiality of the mosque's restoration is thus contested between the imam and the secular agents involved in the restoration programme; the very materiality of restoration reflects the variety of visions for the city's future. Equally contested is the restoration of Djenné's vernacular architecture, which is subject to a regulation that for most of the city's inhabitants has 'fallen from the sky'. Joy demonstrates how wide the gap is between the 'heritage elite' that has emerged in response to the heritage industry and the other inhabitants of the town. These chapters clearly convey to what extent UNESCO's conservation programme still reflects a Eurocentric heritage conception.

The restoration programme in Djenné also problematizes the distinction UNESCO makes between material and immaterial heritage. The prescriptive nature of the restoration programme encompasses the internal organization of vernacular architecture and has a direct impact on the use of space in Djenné houses. The preservation of tangible heritage conflicts with how changing kinship relations require flexible arrangements of space. Restoration of material heritage can be problematic in the sense that it objectifies social relations, assuming that social relations can, like architecture, be conserved. An analytic distinction between 'material' and 'immaterial' heritage is equally problematic in Osogbo (Nigeria), where the sacred grove and its modern architectural sculptures represent the old goddesses. As Probst demonstrates, the material heritage embodies the 'paganism' that Osogbo's Christians and Muslims reject. The very materialization of 'pagan' beliefs in sculpture triggers debate about the future of religion. And, to take yet another case: Basu demonstrates how the Truth and Reconciliation Commission in Sierra Leone has promoted the visibility of mass graves 'because they serve as recognition of the suffering of victims as well as the collective memory of the past'. However, the policy painfully brings out in the open the reality that the dead go unmourned and their spirits linger in the present. These cases suggest that the making of material heritage renders the 'intangible' into an object of reflection and need not necessarily result in the objectification of memory. In fact, it does the opposite.

This demonstrates that heritage is not, as anthropologists often assert, an objectification of memory. While heritage certainly relies on some form of objectification – material or immaterial – it is clear that heritage is always emergent. This is so because heritage is produced in a context of discourses on roots, ownership, nationalism, and a global politics of recognition. For example, the making of a Malian 'national culture' requires the objectification of local traditions in standardized formats for national television, but, as Schulz demonstrates, these objectifications are nonetheless considered 'authentic' by their performers. The objectification of heritage reconfigures 'traditions' and transforms them into formats fit for consumption by others. This transformation simultaneously lends recognition to the producers of these legacies (cf Myers 2004). In fact, as Schulz shows, the objectification of heritage is living proof of its recognition.

Objectification is also at stake when performances are classified as 'intangible' heritage, as the Kankurang masquerade recently was. This masquerade is performed in the context of initiation rites in Senegambia. Recently, the masquerade has increasingly been staged as a pastime, and this formerly fearsome mask lost its awe-inspiring authority to urban audiences. To redress this trend, understood as a 'loss' of 'tradition', elders have developed grassroots initiatives to conserve the masquerade. Alongside and in conjunction with these conservation efforts, the Gambian and Senegalese states have appropriated the masquerade as a national heritage. In 2005 UNESCO recognized the masquerade as a 'Masterpiece of the Intangible Heritage'. Ferdinand de Jong argues that this recognition of the masquerade will inevitably boost its objectification in postcards, museum exhibits, and tourist performances. Although this objectification reinforces the de-enchantment of the masquerade that many Senegalese lament, it is undeniable that the recognition of the performance as 'Masterpiece' provides the performers with great pride in their cultural heritage. The masquerade is now re-enchanted *as* heritage.

Although heritage is subjected to the politics of authentication by nation-states and international experts, performances that are 'staged' as heritage are not necessarily reduced to commodities. Of course, tourist revenues are an important incentive for African states to stage heritage, and the serving of the tourist industry is reminiscent of the domination exercized by the West when it subjected the landscape of North Africa to its gaze. As Butler reminds us, Westerners travelling to the ruins of North Africa render this landscape subject to the Western quest for 'origins'. We witness such politics of objectification in a number of articles in this volume, but such politics are monitored by those whose heritage is thus transformed into formats digestible by foreign tourists. This monitoring insures a measure of participation and brings to the heirs a form of recognition.

Recognition and Reconciliation

One of the issues discussed by Butler is how heritage can be rethought so as to provide recognition for the subaltern: how can roots restore dignity? Such a rendering of dignity is indeed experienced by the performers of the Kankurang masquerade of Senegambia. Today, the principal meaning given to the masquerade is that of a 'tradition' retrieved from destruction. Recognition of the performance seems to open up a future for a redeemed self. A similar argument is proposed by Dorothea Schulz in her contribution on the history of Mali's imagination of the nation. In contrast to the Frankfurt School scholars who argued that modernity transformed authentic traditions into commodified spectacles, she shows how contemporary Malian telespectators enjoy the broadcasting of music performances on national television, which, they feel, 'renders them their dignity'. Schulz shows how this is the latest episode in a post-independence history of nation-building. In the wake of independence, the Malian State sought to authorize itself by references to a precolonial origin. *Jeli* musicians and oral traditionalists played an important role in the nationalist project of Modibo Keita, singing praise of Mali's political class. However, the making of the Malian nation-state privileged a narrative on roots that excluded part of its population. So, when Mali's political regime was liberalized, the *jeli* orators lost their privileged treatment. In the national television programme *Terroir*, room is given to a wider variety of musical performances. The programme has triggered enthusiasm among Mali's rural communities to have their 'authentic' traditions performed on national television. Although this highly politicized process often brings out tensions between various political factions in the communities, it nevertheless serves to render what is considered by the performers as 'their own authentic tradition'. The programme *Terroir* thus succeeds in a creating a sense of national unity, not by invoking a communal past but by acknowledging the nation's cultural diversity.

Although the objectification of heritage is a pattern we discern in all contributions to this volume, such objectifications are indeed always contested. This political process is as much a process within the communities whose heritage is at stake as it is between the communities and the nation-states that they are part of. The making of heritage is a return to roots in a contemporary context in which the issues of what should be conserved as heritage and how it should be conserved are contested. The return restores dignity, but it does so in a political context of entitlement. How heritage is used to claim rights and recognition is debated by Ramon Sarró. His chapter demonstrates how a succession of political regimes in Guinea has treated political institutions among the Baga differently. Reification of cultural practice was one of the strategies employed by the French colonial regime, reaffirming the authority of 'traditional' chieftaincy. In opposition to the colonial regime, Muslim proselytizers denounced chieftaincy and the persistence of traditions associated with secret societies. These 'politics of demystification' were also pursued by Sékou Touré in order to modernize Guinea through a cultural revolution. This policy to abolish inequality and 'feudalism' profoundly changed the political relationships in Baga villages. However, in a renewed spirit of autochthony in post-socialist Guinea, the lineages that had lost many of their privileges under Touré's socialism now reclaimed their former privileges in a discourse of rights. In a context of competition for scarce resources, the lineages that lost their privileged positions reclaimed the resources that they lost under Touré. What looked like a linear narrative of 'modernization' resulting in the loss of resources returned as a claim to restore that loss as 'heritage'. The politics of heritage provide an idiom for loss and redress within a space of political entitlement.

That the production and recognition of heritage is not necessarily a redemptive process is also brought out in Basu's contribution on the war memorials in Sierra Leone. The various war memorials and peace monuments established in war-torn Sierra Leone do not bury the past but provide a multilayered memory-scape in which memories are in various ways represented, that is, re-presented. In contrast to the position that monuments are basically unsuited to established memory practices predicated on 'social forgetting', Basu suggests that monuments can trigger engagement with unfinished pasts. In fact, all the contributions in this volume demonstrate that material monuments and intangible heritage do trigger memory-work and do not thereby offer to bear the burden of memory but open up spaces for reflexive engagements. In that respect, we think that heritage and monuments in Africa can be as productive as they are elsewhere. The debate on Holocaust memorials, especially with regard to the countermonuments established by the antimonument movement, can serve as an instructive parallel case (Young 1993, 2000). The German antimonument movement posited that monuments take on the burden of memory and therefore promote oblivion. Although the antimonuments established by the artists of the antimonument movement remain committed to materiality, it is their very materiality that triggers reflection and reignites memory-work. This demonstrates that here and elsewhere, oppositions between tangible and intangible heritage, embodied and monumental memory, are not productive and need to be revisited. Our contributions suggest that hybrid technologies of heritage can bring out the burden of memory.

Bibliography

Antze, P., and M. Lambek. 1996. *Tense Past: Cultural Essays in Trauma and Memory*. London: Routledge.
Apter, A. 2005. *The Pan-African Nation: Oil and the Spectacle of Culture in Nigeria*. Chicago: The University of Chicago Press.
Argenti, N. 2006. 'Remembering the Future: Slavery, Youth and Masking in the Cameroon Grassfields', *Social Anthropology* 1 (1):49–69.
Askew, K. M. 2002. *Performing the Nation: Swahili Music and Cultural Politics in Tanzania*. Chicago: Chicago University Press.
Bedaux, R., and M. Rowlands. 2001. 'The Future of Mali's Past', *Antiquity* 75:872–76.
Burnham, P. 1996. *The Politics of Cultural Difference in Northern Cameroon*. Edinburgh: Edinburgh University Press for the International African Institute, London.
Castaldi, F. 2006. *Choreographies of African Identities: Négritude, Dance and the National Ballet of Senegal*. Champaign, IL: University of Illinois Press.
Chami, F. 2006. *The Unity of African Ancient History: 3000 BC to AD 50*. Dar Es Salam: African Books Collective.
Clifford, J. 2004. 'Looking Several Ways: Anthropology and Native Heritage in Alaska', *Current Anthropology* 45(1):5–30.
Cole, J. 1998. 'The Uses of Defeat: Memory and the Political Morality in East Madagascar.' In *Memory and the Postcolony: African Anthropology and the Critique of Power*, R. Werbner (ed.), pp. 105–25. London: Zed Books.
———. 2005. 'Foreword: Collective Memory and the Politics of Reproduction in Africa', *Africa* 75(1):1–9.
Connerton, P. 1989. *How Societies Remember*. Cambridge: Cambridge University Press.
Coombes, A. E. 2003. *History after Apartheid: Visual Culture and Public Memory in a Democratic South Africa*. Durham, NC: Duke University Press.
de Jong, F. 2007. *Masquerades of Modernity: Power and Secrecy in Casamance, Senegal*. Edinburgh: Edinburgh University Press for the International African Institute.
De Jorio, R. 2006. 'Politics of Remembering and Forgetting: The Struggle over Colonial Monuments in Mali', *Africa Today* 52(4):79–106.
Diouf, M. 1993. 'Fresques murales et écriture de l'histoire: Le Set/Setal à Dakar', *Politique Africaine* 46:41–54.
Fabian, J. 1996. *Remembering the Present: Painting and Popular History in Zaïre*. Berkeley and Los Angeles: University of California Press.
Guyer, J. I. 2005. 'Postscript: From Memory to Conviction and Action', *Africa* 75(1):119–23.
Handler, R. 1988. *Nationalism and the Politics of Culture*. Madison: University of Wisconsin Press.
Hirsch, M. 1997. *Family Frames: Photography, Narrative and Postmemory*. Cambridge, MA: Harvard University Press.

Huyssen, A. 2003. *Present Pasts: Urban Palimpsests and the Politics of Memory*. Palo Alto, CA: Stanford University Press.
Hylland Eriksen, T. 2001. 'Between Universalism and Relativism: A Critique of the UNESCO Concept of Culture'. In *Culture and Rights: Anthropological Perspectives*, J. K. Cowan et al., pp. 127–48. Cambridge: Cambridge University Press.
Ingold, T. (ed.). 1996. *Key Debates in Anthropology*. London: Routledge.
Lambek, M. J. 2002. *The Weight of the Past: Living with History in Mahajanga, Madagascar*. New York: Palgrave Macmillan.
Lowenthal, D. 1985. *The Past Is a Foreign Country*. Cambridge: Cambridge University Press.
Mack, J. 2003. *The Museum of the Mind: Art and Memory in World Cultures*. London: The British Museum Press.
Mamdani, M. 1996. *Citizen and Subject: Contemporary Africa and the Legacy of Late Colonialism*. Princeton, NJ: Princeton University Press.
Mbembe, A. 1992. 'Provisional Notes on the Postcolony', *Africa* 62(1):3–37.
Myers, F. M. 2004. 'Ontologies of the Image and Economies of Exchange', *American Ethnologist* 31(1):5–20.
Nas, P. J. M., et al. 2002. 'Masterpieces of Oral and Intangible Culture: Reflections on the UNESCO World Heritage List', *Current Anthropology* 43 (1):139–48.
Nora, P. 1989. 'Between Memory and History: *Les lieux de mémoire*', *Representations* 26 (Spring):7–25.
Nyamnjoh, F., and M. Rowlands. 1998. 'Elite Associations and the Politics of Belonging in Cameroon', *Africa* 68(3):320–37.
Roberts, A. F., and M. Nooter Roberts. 2003. *A Saint in the City: Sufi Arts of Urban Senegal*. Los Angeles: UCLA Fowler Museum of Cultural History.
Schmidt, P., and T. Patterson. 1996. *Making Alternative Histories: Practice of Archaeology and History in Non-Western Settings*. Santa Fe: School of American Research Press.
Shaw, R.. 2002. *Memories of the Slave Trade: Ritual and the Historical Imagination in Sierra Leone*. Chicago: Chicago University Press.
Stahl, A. 2004. *African Archaeology: A Critical Introduction*. Oxford: Blackwell Publishing.
Stoller, P. 1995. *Embodying Colonial Memories: Spirit Possession, Power and the Hauka in West Africa*. London: Routledge.
Werbner, R. 1998a. 'Beyond Oblivion: Confronting Memory Crisis.' In *Memory and the Postcolony: African Anthropology and the Critique of Power*, R. Werbner (ed.), pp. 1–17. London: Zed Books.
———. (ed.). 1998b. *Memory and the Postcolony: African Anthropology and the Critique of Power*. London: Zed Books.
Young, J. E. 1993. *The Texture of Memory: Holocaust Memorials and Meaning*. New Haven, CT: Yale University Press.
———. 2000. *At Memory's Edge: After-Images of the Holocaust in Contemporary Art and Architecture*. New Haven, CT: Yale University Press.

'Taking on a Tradition': African Heritage and the Testimony of Memory

Beverley Butler

> To take on a tradition, then, and what is most powerful and gripping within it, one must affirm and contest not only the arguments and claims of tradition but traditional ways of making arguments and claims, of claiming authority, producing evidence, and gaining conviction, traditional modes of receiving and reading the tradition. Hence it is necessary not only to take a critical stance toward the tradition but to adopt a performative strategy with regard to it. Whereas Derrida's texts thus analyse traditional philosophical issues and concepts in order to reveal something untraditional within them, they also perform traditional critical gestures in order to invent other, unprecedented gestures from within them. (Naas 2003: xix–xx)

Derrida's strategy of 'taking on a tradition' has obvious implications for the domain of cultural heritage and cultural memory.[1] Written as a 'thought piece', this first chapter deploys this strategy to provide a broad critical rehearsal of the conceptual, intellectual, and moral-ethical issues at stake in selected 'performative moments' of memory-work and the attendant construction of heritage imaginaries. The critical contribution of this chapter is to narrate the historical 'Westernisation' of heritage memory and the challenges made to this discourse as it is confronted by an 'othering' identified as an 'Africanist turn'. Thus my objective in this paper is to use Derrida's critical framework in order to return to selected 'performative moments' within the 'tradition' of African heritage, and, in a further connectivity with Derrida – who, as a Sephardic Jew born in Algeria, has his own North African origins – to, more specifically still, engage with the North African landscapes of Egypt and Algeria. Historically, the myth and memory of both these contexts have a potent place within the 'Euro-Western' imagination, and yet they have reemerged to occupy an equally powerful position within anticolonial and postcolonial discourse and latterly within the lexicon of deconstruction.

What has emerged is a concern to address what Derrida refers to as the 'testimony of memory' as, first, a means to draw out the tension between memory-work and narrations of heritage that focus on monumental, material heritage (especially in terms of the violences inherent in the European creation of 'public' heritage culture) and the need to critically address the 'performativity' (ibid.) of tradition in order to go beyond tangible/intangible binaries and, second, as a means to engage in alternative intellectual-operational projects bound up in 'untraditional' philosophical and ethical concerns of new contemporary global constituencies. These ways of addressing Derrida's 'testimony of memory' in turn allow us to move beyond Classical traditions of Aristotelian memory concepts, Platonic theories of repetition (cf memory as 'rediscovery'), and an accompanying Kantian cosmopolitics. By way of contrast, such engagement maps Freud's 'disturbance' and 'othering' of memory and the 'epistemological violences' of deconstruction in order to address alternative, uncanonical experiences of African 'tradition'. The aim, therefore, is to address new connectivities vis-à-vis cultural transmission and to locate alternative 'heritage' discourse and marginalised memory-work. Of note, too, is that the particular intellectuals/activists featured in this chapter all have subversive attitudes toward 'reading' literary texts and a preoccupation with oral and memorising practices. Underpinning the chapter is a need to apprehend more clearly 'heritage memory' as a 'performative moment', a space of uncanny encounter with ancestors and as a destabiliser of temporalities.

'L'Afrique du Nord': Alexandria and Algeria As Memory 'Recovery'

> [O]ur tradition . . . our history gave us not only a set of received views and classical themes but a particular concept of the concept of history, a particular tradition of thinking tradition. (Naas 2003:xvii)

Derrida's critical strategy of 'taking on a tradition' begins with an insistence on the 'duties' and 'responsibilities' of intellectuals and practitioners to deconstruct the 'heritage' by returning to the 'testimony of memory' and to 'origins' and 'founding concepts' (Derrida 2002:3–4). Thus in this first section

I move between the North African landscapes of Alexandria and Algeria to critically return to selected classical-canonical 'performative moments'. As Derrida makes clear, the seductions of this Classical genealogy are linked to the desire to legitimate 'one single pure origin' and to lay claim to a number of founding concepts that, he reiterates, constantly go 'back to Greece and back to this Greek origin' (ibid.:23). As such, the 'West's' or Occidental modernity's 'retrospective reference to Greek memory' and the 'West's' use of the ancient past – especially the Greco-Roman past and its characterisation as the 'childhood age of philosophy' – provide resources to legitimate modern institutional identities and practises (ibid.:5–6).

In particular, I emphasise the manipulation and memory-work at play, most notably, in terms of how Greek-Roman myth and memory as founded on an elite 'Western' literary epic-philosophical tradition of homecoming have been mobilised historically by European powers. Fundamental to orthodox narratives are the act of cultural transmission synonymous with the Renaissance 'arts of memory' and the recovery and the translation of Classical texts (cf Yates 1992). The ongoing 'legacy' of this 'Greco-European memory' is uncovered by Derrida in terms of his dubbing UNESCO an 'archive of this heritage', as is the institution's grounding in Kantian cosmopolitics (Derrida 2002:3–4). The archive itself (as 'philosopheme') (ibid.) emerges as the core technology of memory in the articulation of a shift between memorising-cultures and literate societies and as underpinned by a twin desire to give 'substance' to memory (to inscript, objectify, and thus create 'material memory' (cf Kwint et al. 1999) and to secure a metaphysical diagnostic capable of reviving a spiritual sense of well-being, health, and redemption.

Alexandria, 'Capital of Memory'

> [A]fter Alexander had conquered Egypt, he was anxious to found a great and populous Greek city there, to be called after him . . . [A]s he lay asleep he dreamed that a grey-haired man of venerable appearance stood by his side and recited . . . lines from the *Odyssey*. (Plutarch, *Life of Alexander* 1973:282)

The intimacies of the preceding scenario with the myth-historical 'birth' of Alexandria – both the city and its legendary 'universal' archive – are acute; I examine this 'event' as my first 'performative moment'. As Derrida reiterates, any act of 'taking on a tradition' requires engaging in 'not only the philosophical but the literary tradition that begins with the epic poetry of Homer' (Naas 2003:xxiii).[2] Derrida's point here is to open the European 'epic tradition' to 'other' uncanonical readings.

Alexandria's epic birth, as recounted by Plutarch, begins with Alexandria being revealed to Alexander the Great in a dream; his mentor, the philosopher Aristotle, is said to have appeared before Alexander guiding the hero to what was to become Alexandria's famous promontory: the Isle of Pharos. Alexander's map or guidebook was Homer's *Odyssey*. This famous ancient epic account of an heroic homecoming was subsequently positioned as the city's founding text, an act that bestows on Homer the accolade of the city's 'architect' in the epic visionary sense (Plutarch 1973:282). Thus Alexandria was afforded a 'legendary' status with the city's birth located at the pivotal moment between myth and history and between the oral and literate traditions. Accompanying this epic drama of the city's foundation were further 'preludes' and 'heroic precedents' accomplished by Alexander – which Derrida dubs the 'sure signs' of a tradition (Naas 2003:48–49) – that accentuate the 'predestined' nature of the city's creation (Polignac 2000a:33). Plutarch includes here Alexander's pilgrimage to Siwa Oasis and his consultation with the Oracle of Zeus-Ammon. The Oracle subsequently legitimated both hero and city. Not only was Alexander 'proclaimed son of god' and thus conferred with 'divine origin', but his project of 'world conquest' was endorsed, which drew him further East (ibid.:33).

Of a long line of inventors and promoters of legend spanning both ancient and modern worlds who have subsequently engaged in 'reviving and reformulating' Alexandria's myth and memory, it is, however, those of the 'West', as self-appointed heirs of the 'Greek' tradition, who have dominated the scene from the Renaissance memory-retrievalism onward and whose 'monolithic transmission' (Jacob and Polignac 2000:18) of Alexandria's legacy into modernity claimed possession of Alexandria's foundational dramas and its motif of homecoming as part of the 'West's' own odyssey and ancestry – that is, its epic search for origins, for an ancient homeland, and, crucially, for metaphysical roots. A privileged 'Western' genealogy and literary philosophical tradition has thus imposed itself on the city, affording modernity's so-called universal histories to claim possession of Alexandria's myth and memory as exclusively 'Western' concerns and to see the city as, distinct from the rest of Egypt and Africa, an extension of the Greek landscape and tradition. This myth-historical 'birth' and accompanying desire to stage modernity's march of civilisation/conquest in the footsteps of Alexander also saw the 'Westernisation' of Alexandria's potent lexicon of 'signs and images' (Polignac 2000b:212) and its 'ready canon' of 'myths and icons' (Halim 2002:5), which, in turn, established a number of personas, archetypes, ancient identities, and templates to be revived and emulated by Western modernity and provided resources by which the West's identity and memory-work can be managed, mediated, and manipulated and claimed as 'self-objects' (cf Kohut 1978).

A claim is thus made to the monumental heritage of this iconic, marble city,[3] which with its *public buildings* and *urbanised public space* is regarded as an ancient model ripe for emulation within Euro-Western tradition. Alexandria has even been dubbed an 'ancient Manhattan' owing to its grid system (see La Riche 1998). Similarly, Alexandria's potent characterisations as the New Athens and as the 'meeting point of East and West' are used to lay claim to the city's foundational values – as the 'birthplace' of cosmopolitanism, universalism, and the scene of intellectual, humanistic philosophical inquiry and as civilising project (see Klibansky 2000; Polignac 2000b).

Archival Memory: 'Redemptive Formula'

Significantly for Derridean 'readings', it is Alexandria's ancient archive – the Mouseion/Library – that, as Strabo and other ancient authors make clear, emerges at the locus point of the city and its mythologisation (Polignac 2000a).[4] It is the ancient Alexandrina's acts of literary translation that are credited with placing 'Alexandria at the birth of our world' (Errera 1997:138) and that cast the city as 'one of the great wombs of western literature' and as the 'memory of the world' (Polignac 2000a:42). This particular line in cultural transmission has canonised and subsequently universalised a certain tradition as the cultural 'norm'; this is a tradition synonymous not only with the possession of tangible, monumental heritage in the public sphere but also with the fixing or objectification of memory as written culture. Thus 'the text' and 'the book' are valourised over oral, memorising traditions (ibid.).[5] Crucially, here at the Alexandrina, Homer's epics became archived and annotated as fixed texts (ibid.).

Adding to these dramas, Alexandria as odyssey and as homecoming is underpinned by a trauma of origin and myth of redemption. It is the destruction of the ancient Mouseion/Library that, with some paradox and great effectiveness, secures its status as phoenix-like institution (Findlen 2000:176). The event is read by the 'West' as the traumatic loss of an ancient ancestor and this reading embeds the institution, like the city itself, in an entropic poetics of melancholy, nostalgia, and loss. This tradition has been sustained and reworked by modern writers such as Cavafy, Forster, and Durrell, the last of whom dubbed Alexandria the 'Capital of Memory' (1986). This tradition also generates the redemptive urge that gives birth to the repetitive desire to rebuild the Alexandrina 'on the ruins'. What has become broadly known as the 'Alexandria project' (Butler 2001a; 2001b; 2003; 2006a; 2007) became bound-up mythologisation that 'to write was to return' (Foucault quoted in Errera 1997:138), thus positioning Alexandria and its archive as sites of renewal and rebirth.

In this respect, the ancient Alexandrina, as the casualty of what is understood as an originary act of iconoclasm, is canonised as the icon from which the traditional heritage paradigm of loss and preservation establishes its roots (Lowenthal 1985:109). This tradition in turn is underpinned by an Aristotelian memory-model in which heritage, as are the archive and memory, is imagined as 'container-like' and as a 'nonrenewable resource' subject to entropy. Notably, it is this same Aristotelian model that continues to be universalised through UNESCO and given a cosmopolitan thrust as 'world heritage'. The demise and subsequent sacralisation of the Alexandrina paradigm see the institution take on qualities of the eternal ancestor and acquire its 'Platonic dimensions'. The Alexandrina paradigm is internalised within popular, 'collective memory', and by these means reemerges as the 'universal', iconic image/model[6] of the 'Museum/archive' (as transcendental subject), which is subsequently characterised within Platonic tradition of memory as 'rediscovery' and subject to the repetition and mobilisation of 'archetypes' and 'templates' (Butler, 2001a; 2001b; 2003; 2006a; 2007). Thus the ancient model becomes the 'real' museum/archive, with individual museums and archives regarded as part of its mirrorings and thus as 'pale reflections' of the original (Bettelheim 1989:143).[7]

Between Memory and History: Immigrant Odyssey

The psychological seductions and the empathetic identifications that have become essentialised parts of the Alexandria project and the 'West's' ancient coding of the birth of the Alexandrina can be unpacked further as synonymous with an 'acting out' of a wider 'universal' drama of 'individuation' in which the West's traumatic act of separating out from the 'Greek' childhood/homeland (personified in the figure of Alexander the Great, who as ancestor-hero charts out this odyssey) sees the ancient Alexandrina (as ancestor-archive) positioned as both a 'refuge' and an 'asylum' for the ancient 'Greek' exiles and diaspora by their modern claimants (Bazin 1967:6). Such an account of the Museum/archive, therefore, legitimates and fixes the 'Greek' immigrant odyssey as point of origin for the universal pathway of history. Not only does this 'traditional' account of origins co-opt the Museum/archive into a teleological trajectory, but also 'mankind's' desire for a cyclical, repetitive ritualism synonymous with an earlier 'primitive' state of being is simultaneously recovered and preserved in the Museum/archive's transcendental qualities. The need to take 'refuge in intemporal spheres' is regarded to be of great importance and imbues the Museum/Alexandrina with its other-worldliness (ibid.:6). The essentially 'diasporic nature of the archive' thus positions the institution 'outside time'

(Rapaport 2003:78). Not only does the archive emerge as a synonym for a return to origin/ancestor, but it is also invested as a means to manage, mediate, and potentially redeem traumatic loss and reinstate collective memory. As a diagnostic tool, the archive is argued to respond to 'mankind's' [sic] struggle to live in 'history' (see also Eliade 1991 [1954]).

Derrida similarly diagnoses a clear identification of 'trauma in the archive' and explicitly cites 'the archive of Alexandria' as Western civilisation's 'paradigmatic' example (Rapaport 2003:77). He subsequently locates the role of the archive at the break between memory and history and as a place where destabilised, failed memory – or memory-in-exile – is rehoused (ibid.:76). Such acts of empathetic identification, although couched in utopian terms, are subject to a more distopic urge (often bound up in a narcissistic, colonising trope), and, as Derrida argues further, the presence of 'archival trauma' and 'archive-violence' also has led to the ordering of the world into categories of the 'Civilised and the Barbarian', thereby laying down the origins of the 'Clash of Civilisations' thesis that has resurfaced to predominate in politics today (see Said 2001).[8] This traditional narrative gives further significance to the motif of 'rehousing memory-in-exile' by linking it to the dynamic of 'war trauma'. It is significant, too, that the motif of the archive or culture as a cure for 'war trauma' and the associated impulse to build 'on the ruins' persists – not least in UNESCO's own duty to the wider UN Charter's commitment to postwar reconstruction, to peace-keeping strategies, and writ larger still to nothing less than the 'survival of humankind' (see www.unesco.org). In this context, the rhetorics of the museum as a secular shrine and the contemporary devotional public performances of the 'heritage crusades' (Lowenthal 1996) emerge. The archive is also canonised as the West's privileged medium for reflecting on the human condition and to address the issue of 'what it is to be human' (cf Bazin 1967; Butler 2006a).

Algeria: The 'Romanisation' of Tradition

> In much the same way that Napoleon's 1798 invasion of Egypt engendered the first painstaking, systematic study of society, so the 1830 invasion of Algeria unloosed a veritable swarm of surveyors, geologists, geographers, archaeologists, botanists, zoologists, painters, and protosocial scientists who sized up and took the measurements of the Barbary Coast recently become *l'Afrique du Nord*. (Prochaska 1990:31)

As Prochaska asserts (above), the act of 'taking on a tradition' in terms of the broader European creation of 'L'Afrique du Nord' witnessed a repetition of technologies and techniques by which France's entry into and occupation of Algiers in 1830 mirrored Napoleon's 1798 invasion of Egypt (ibid.). Explored as a 'performative moment', the French invasion of Algeria in 1830 can be further exposed as a repetition in which Napoleon Bonaparte sought to emulate Alexander the Great's ancient conquests. Accompanying this 'performance' is the manufacture of 'sure signs'[9] (Mitchell 1998). The atemporal quality of such mythologisation is strategic in offering a means to contemporarily recast the violences of the Egyptian and Algeria campaigns as a repeat of Alexander's 'benevolent colonialism', his role as 'liberator,' and within the moralising cosmopolitical project of the ancient 'civilizing mission'(Wood 1997:235).[10] This modern 'colonising' project and the 'event' of occupation were thus templated within a broader 'tradition' in which the production of key documents or 'descriptions' saw Europeans view North Africa as their lost archive now undergoing recovery and as increasingly subject to the scrutinies of multiple modes of 'Orientalism' (cf Said 1978), in which Egyptology, archaeology, and the heritage, museum, and public culture were to play a decisive part.[11]

The projects of 'colonising Egypt' (Mitchell 1998) and 'making Algeria French' (Prochaska 1990) are thus bound up in the activities of 'savants', who as key agents of appropriation, were sent to survey and to archive in encyclopaedic fashion the land, monuments, and objects; Even the 'natives' were 'pictured', named, bounded, and rationalised for the Euro-Western gaze. What is important to stress here is how the literatures implicated in the repossession of heritage and tradition are bound up in the reworking and repetition of memory in conjunction with 'new' technologies of representation and memory-work, not only in order to produce self-legitimating narratives but also, as we shall see, to disinherit locals and local memory. The 'recovery' of 'heritage memory' is, however, inextricably linked to military violence. For example, not only were the French 'savants' based in camps with military troops, but the bloody 'event' of the bombardment of Algiers was staged as a public spectacle for 'tourist' consumption. As Mitchell details: 'In 1830 entrepreneurs from Marseilles had converted a steamer into a floating hotel and taken tourists to watch the city's [Algiers'] bombardment and occupation by the French. (Thus from its opening act of violence, European colonisation of the Middle East began to involve the new tourist industry)' (Mitchell 1998:57).

Classical and Roman archaeology were likewise vital new technologies of representation and memory-work concurrent with colonisation. While Europeans claiming Alexandria's tradition and heritage positioned themselves as the 'New Greeks' and/or 'philhellenes', the specific strategy in terms of the colonisation of Maghrebian North Africa saw European nations exploit the Classical period further as they 'presented themselves as the natural and direct inheritors of the Romans' (Mattingly 1996:50). The task of 'emulating Rome' (ibid.:53) once again saw memory-work complicit in the strategies by which 'substance', both physical and metaphorical-moral, was given to colonising projects. The 'performance' by European nations of a return to (what they laid claim to as) their ancient ancestors/ancient 'self-group' was given authenticity and legitimation by the simultaneous 'rediscovery' of monumental and archaeology evidence.

Here intimacies of archiving impulse, memory-recovery, and militarism reemerge. The French in both Algeria and Tunisia employed the army on archaeological work. It was thus 'the activities of the special mapping units' that resourced the 'excavations and recording of inscriptions' combined with the 'individual efforts of many soldiers and officers' who typically volunteered their 'free time' (ibid.:54). Again, the motif of empathetic identification with an ancient self-group persists and is bound up in the ability to feel 'at home/origin' and in the sense of well-being inherent in gaining protection from the close proximity of ancestors. As Mattingly argues, it was 'comforting for the French and Italian armies on campaign' to discover 'traces of the earlier penetration of the Roman legion into the same spaces' (ibid.). The 'same basic sentiment' is repeated in European narratives that stress 'the desolation and emptiness of the modern [North African] landscape' in contrast to the newly 'excavated' and 'reconstructed' 'Roman ruins' that 'punctuated...almost every step' (ibid.:53). Writ larger still, this drama of 'emulating Rome' is dominated by a return to Imperialism; as Mattingly continues: 'In the heyday of European Imperialism . . . many aspects of modern colonial government aped Roman titles and Institutions (such as the use either formal or informal) of the title Preconsul for many governors' (ibid.). Examples can also be found of Roman mausoleums being 'rededicated' in order to pay 'homage on behalf of the French Foreign legion' (ibid.). Similarly, 'victorious French generals were compared to legendary Roman commanders' (ibid.). Thus from 'different perspectives' these monuments can be regarded as 'either wonderful symbols of European civilization or [as] propagandist monuments of an alien government' (ibid.:52–53).

Crucially, too, the European privileging of the 'written text' reemerges, this time in the form of Latin epigraphy, which is acknowledged as 'the key tool employed in the setting of the academic agenda for Romano-African studies' (ibid.:51).[12] Not only are such 'texts' used to legitimate the European presence and ancestry, but the exclusionary nature of this trajectory meant that 'until Maghgrebi scholars themselves learned Latin, they were effectively locked out of the study of Roman Africa. By controlling the study of the written sources, the French were able to exacerbate the cultural distance from the

Romans felt by the Berber and Arab populations' (ibid.:51–52). Mattingly adds: 'Following standard European Orientalist thinking [see Said 1978], it was the mission of the coloniser to educate Africans about their own cultural heritage' (Mattingly 1996:52). This strategy was bolstered by the assertion of modern European heirs of a return to a model of 'benevolent Roman rule'. Archaeological evidence was used to support the thesis that 'once the initial trauma of conquest had passed, life under Roman rule was viewed as overall a positive experience, bringing a higher degree of civilization to the region but also allowing native talents to flourish within the Roman system' (ibid.:56).

The European reclamation of tradition is therefore subject to a concomitant force of disinheritance. Once again, the privileging of the powerful European immigrant underpins this force; thus 'colonial discourse strove to disinherit the North African peoples of their cultural history, by ascribing to immigrants all the positive achievements of Roman Africa and by portraying the African either as passive receptors of superior culture or as nomadic and lawless people incapable of self-government' (ibid.). This Orientalist impulse thus asserted 'the "otherness" of North Africa (Arab and Berber speaking, with its Islamic culture and its tribal and nomadic societies)' (ibid.).

'Disturbance of Memory'

The culture of colonialism has given rise to the emergence of a complex trajectory of memory-work operating across colony and metropolis that is narrated in terms of the 'objects'[13] taken from North Africa for both display and study in Europe and subsequently North America. Yet again, this trajectory of memory-work can be seen within a framework of ancient to modern emulation; from the Ptolemies of Alexandria, to the Romans, to Napoleon's generals, the public parade of imperial trophies has been heavily ritualised before objects were archived or exhibited on public display.[14] African and Egyptian cultural treasures continue to fill the Alexandrina museum/archive's modern heirs – notably, the Louvre, the British Museum, and the Altes Museum. Occidental modernity, however, becomes increasingly preoccupied by a 'memory crisis' at 'home' and simultaneously invests in a certain paradox in which colonial museological object-work serves to 'authenticate' artefacts 'repossessed' in the colonial territories, displaying these for public consumption in the Western metropolises at the same time as modernity's own metaphysical feelings of inauthenticity see *lieux de mémoire* fill cultural-historical landscape as markers of a 'loss of origins' (Maleuvre 1999:59).

In the case of visitors travelling to the Orient and North Africa, the experience draws out further contradiction. As commentators reiterate, the model or template for the colonial imagination is premised on the ability to 'picture' the world and subsequently to put one's faith in the 'reality of reconstruction' and in 'new' technologies hailed as 'mechanical mirrors of truth' (Mitchell 1998:27) However, just as Derrida diagnosed 'archival trauma', one can locate a rupture explained as a 'contradiction between the need to separate oneself from the world and render it up as an object of representation, and the desire to lose oneself within this object world and experience it directly; a contradiction which the world exhibitions ... and their clear distinction between visitor and exhibit, were built to accommodate and overcome' (ibid.). Flaubert, for example, visiting Cairo in 1850, gave an account of the shift from consuming literary-pictorial texts in the metropolis to literally visiting Egypt. He records his 'initial bedazzlement' at the 'bewildering chaos of colours' and the 'visual turmoil' before him (ibid.:21). Flaubert's response was, however, to resist the 'disorder' he experienced by subsequently 'recovering one's self possession as expressed in pictorial terms' and engaging in a process by which the 'world arranges itself into a picture and achieves a visual order' and is stabilised thus 'in accordance with the laws of perspective' (Flaubert in Mitchell 1998:22). Flaubert is subsequently able to reiterate his observation that 'one *re*discovers here much more than he discovers' (ibid.).

Parallels can be made here with Freud's theorisation of a 'disturbance of memory' (Freud 1984). Freud uses his account of achieving his 'long-cherished dream to visit' that seminally 'Greek' icon, 'the Parthenon', in 1904 (Rojek 1997:56) as a means to analyse how his literal confrontation with the Acropolis – which had previously existed for Freud only as a literary landscape (and as such had been repressed as an 'object of the imagination') – brought about a 'disturbance' capable of accessing the unconscious (Freud 1984 [1936]:443–56). Crucially, Freud's biographers/critics have linked this 'disturbance' to Freud's and psychoanalysis's wider destabilisations of the dominant 'Greek' identity/ psyche to a project of 'othering' that offered the possibility of accessing repressed identities, notably of both 'Jew' and 'Egyptian' (Forrester 1994; Raphael-Leff 1990). Likewise, Freud is responsible for 'inverting' dominant Eurocentric memory-work in order to profile the dynamics of forgetting, trauma, and mourning and for refuting the concept of objects as analogues of memory (cf Forty and Küchler 1999).

The need for European powers to overcome such 'disturbances' required them to bring order to North Africa in terms of creating 'a world reframed'. Not only were cities such as Cairo rebuilt to emulate 'exhibition-like cities in Europe' (Mitchell 1998:17), but also the unfamiliar 'chaotic' structures of local villages were subject to destruction and reorganisation in order to resemble the 'careful layout of the exhibition ... within which activities could be organised, controlled, and observed' (ibid.). The violent change wrought by the creation of 'public culture' on the European model within North Africa threatened local rituals and traditions of well-being. One can draw out a legacy here, too, in terms of UNESCO's 'enframing' of 'world heritage sites'. As critics have argued, from the first international salvage campaign at Abu Simbel to the recent revival of the Bibliotheca Alexandrina, the creation of 'public culture' on the European model continues to exert a destructive violence on local landscapes (see Butler 2003, 2007; Hoggart 1978).

Disrupting 'Greek' Memory: 'Voice of the Third World'

> Derrida has been interested in the ways language is used not only to *say* something but to *do* or *perform* it, in the ways it is used not simply to talk about the world but to engage in it. (Naas 2003:xxi)

> From Paris, from London, from Amsterdam we would utter the word[s] 'Parthenon! Brotherhood!' and somewhere in Africa or Asia lips would open '...thenon!...therhood!' It was a golden age... We did not doubt they would accept our ideals, since they accused us of not being faithful to them. Then indeed, Europe could believe in her mission: it had Hellenised the Asians and created this new species, the Greco-Roman blacks. (Sartre in Fanon 2004 [1961]:xliv)

> [W]hen the colonised hear a speech on Western culture they draw their machetes or at least check to see they are close to hand. (Fanon 2004 [1961]:8)

Derrida's strategy to critically 'take on a tradition' argues the need not only to address the 'testimony of memory' but also to mobilise the 'openings' and 'fissures' that 'disrupt [traditional] memory' in order to remodel these as part of a fundamental reconceptualisation of 'tradition' (Derrida 2002:9). Similarly, this forms part of attempts 'to locate something within it that the tradition has itself never been able to make its own' and to apprehend heritage and tradition as a subversive memory-space in which 'performance' is bound up in action and in the 'unexpected' emergence of 'another event' (Naas 2003:xxx).

With this in mind, in this section I explore how the myth and memory of North Africa so potent within the 'Euro-Western' imagination reemerges to occupy an equally powerful position within anticolonial and postcolonial discourse. Moreover, this anti/postcolonial context is marked by the emergence and the articulation of new relationships across North and South, amid the traumatic 'birth' of new nations as they come into force via acts of decolonisation and partition and as confronted by the reemergence of narcissistic, neocolonial ambitions in the global arena. Crucially, too, this period witnessed the 'birth' of UNESCO as a redemptive formula on the ruins of World War II.

Acropolis versus Mumbo-Jumbo

In a critical return to the Algerian context, I focus on Frantz Fanon. I take Fanon as a liminal figure positioned between two major intellectual-political traditions: that of 'third world' anticolonialism and that of the French Academy. Fanon's engagement with the former francophone activist-intellectuals saw him engage with the strategies of 'negritude', 'nativism', and 'afrocentrism'. Additionally, his position within contemporary French philosophical and literary circles shows how his interests in revolutionary Marxism and psychology were further influenced by existential philosophy. His work – notably *The Wretched of the Earth* (2004 [1961]) – brings these two trajectories into debate. Sartre's now famous preface to this work highlights his crude though effective reductionism of the binary choice available to anti-/postcolonial cultural revivalism: the emulation of Europe versus the search to define 'native' tradition. The preference of the 'native', Sartre presumed, is to reject the 'Greek' tradition: 'In their shoes, you might say, I would prefer my [mumbo-jumbo] *zars*[15] to the Acropolis' (Sartre in Fanon 2004 [1961]:liii–liv). What emerges in Fanon's text, however, is a call to go beyond such inversions of Western heritage models and to radically alter the codes by which to 'take on a tradition'.

Fanon's text can be regarded as an alternative 'performative moment' capable of issuing a challenge to European traditions of donation, reception, and the 'inheritance' by exposing them to alternative strategies of memory-work, representation, and cultural transmission synonymous with 'another event' emerging from colonialism: that of decolonisation. Fanon's text is regarded as a new epic for a new age and has been famously dubbed the 'Bible of Decolonisation' and the 'Handbook of revolution' and is a text celebrated by Che Guevara, Malcolm X, and Steve Biko, among many others (see Bhabha in Fanon 2004 [1961]: xvi-xvii; Young 2001:281). Interestingly, this text, which, as we shall see, vehemently rejects the emulation of European models, has emerged as a template or model for revolution and decolonisation. Positioned as the 'voice of the Third World', Fanon's work has been hailed as 'the founding analysis of the effects of colonialism upon colonised peoples and their cultures' and 'a revolutionary manifesto of decolonisation' (Young 2001:119–20).

Fanon's negative rejectionism of the Euro-Western 'cult of the leader and of personalities' (Sartre in Fanon 2004 [1961]:xlvii) annunciates a rejection of the desire to walk in the footsteps of the ancient Greco-Roman ancestors, thus signalling that European humanism's 'claims to be universal' have failed (ibid.). This rejection of the desire to walk in the footsteps of the Greco-Roman ancestors is underlined in Fanon's assertion that there are 'better things to do than follow in Europe's footsteps' (Fanon 2004 [1961]:236). From reading Fanon's text, Sartre argued that a reversal of positions between coloniser and colonised is taking place under decolonisation. Just as Freud perceived the 'Acropolis' as a 'performative moment' of 'othering', Sartre draws out, in Fanon's text, an even more subversive 'othering' of Greco-European 'objects', 'icons', and 'templates'. Sartre underlines that Europe has used these as 'lifebuoys'; thus 'the Parthenon, Chartres, the Rights of Man' were resources for European well-being and for legitimating Europe as 'the subjects of history' (Sartre in Fanon 2004 [1961]:lix–lx). From reading Fanon's text, Sartre also argued a reversal of positions. He adds to the list of European 'icons' not only 'the swastika' (ibid.) but also visions of those destined to 'rot in the camps' (ibid.:lxii) as essentialised parts of Europe's cultural repertoire, and he also reiterates that 'Europe is doomed' (ibid.:xlviii). The recognition that 'we know now what they ['the lifebuoys'/'traditional values'] were worth' sees a recast Europe as a 'shipwreck' that now 'leaks like a sieve' (ibid.). This realisation prompts Sartre to acknowledge the shift of agency from First to Third Worlds: 'In the past we made history, and now it is being made of us ... decolonisation has begun' (ibid.).

Fanon's own text critically rehearses the alternative strategies open to the 'Third World'. In what follows, I first pursue Fanon's attachments, and divergences, with the 'negritude', 'nativist', and 'afrocentrist' movements. Writ large, these movements, synonymous with francophone intellectual-activists such as Césaire, Senghor, and Diop, defined a positive strategy that, as Fanon crystallised, have the intent of inverting the European models of tradition. He states: 'Following the unconditional affirmation of European culture came the unconditional affirmation of African culture' (Fanon 2004 [1961]:151). One key example of the literary-political project of 'writing b[l]ack' in epic style is Fanon's former mentor Césaire's *Notebook of a Return to My Native Land,* which has been described as an attempt 'to reappropriate the negative ['racial'] term and give it a positive meaning' (Philcox quoted in Fanon 2004 [1961]:248). Although Fanon's chapter 'On National Culture' outlines a more complex and subtle position on 'tradition', Fanon does critically assess the contributions as well as the limits of such projects (Fanon 2004 [1961]:145–80).

Fanon's initial assertion is that Europe provoked this strategy of anti/postcolonial reappropriation of tradition not only by repeatedly 'placing white culture in opposition to other noncultures' but also by its impulse to impose itself on the 'colonised country's present and future' and to 'distort', 'disfigure', and 'destroy' 'the past of the colonised people' (ibid.:149–50). He argues that 'Europe's' 'leadership of the world' positioned 'native' populations in 'shadow of its monuments' and via colonial appropriation 'bursts boundaries of space and thought' (ibid.:235). 'The concept of negritude, for example, was the affective if not logical antithesis of that insult which the white man had leveled at the rest of humanity', and this 'alone proved capable of lifting taboos and maledictions' (ibid.:150). He reiterates that this genre of negritude represents on the part of black and third-world activist-intellectuals an 'historical obligation to racialise their claims' (ibid.:152). He adds that this 'reaction was one of self-regard and celebration' (ibid.:151), bound up in 'rediscovering one's people' and is a project that 'finds a safe haven in a refuge of smoldering emotions' and also 'places a certain emphasis on traditions and customs' (ibid.:154–55). The strategy also promised a pan-African agenda with the U.S. African diaspora 'quick to claim common ties and identical lines of thought' (ibid.:151).

Fanon shows some sympathy with the intent: 'This passionate quest for a national culture prior to the colonial era can be justified by the colonised intellectuals' shared interest in stepping back and taking a hard look at the Western culture in which they risk becoming ensnared . . . Fully aware they are in the process of losing themselves and consequently of being lost to their people, these men work away with raging heart and furious mind to renew contact with their people's oldest, inner essence, the farthest removed from colonial times' (ibid.:148). This quest, as Fanon sees it, is 'guided by secret hope of discovering beyond the present wretchedness, beyond this self-hatred, this abdication and denial, some magnificent and shining era that redeems us in our own eyes and those of others', and he adds: 'They must have been overjoyed to discover that the past was not branded with shame, but dignity, glory, and sobriety' (ibid.).[16] This search for dignity is linked further by Fanon and the Front de Libération Nationale (FLN) to political demands that targeted colonialism's denial of the idea of a historical Algerian past[17] and with the call to action: 'When the colonised intellectual writing for his people uses the past he must do so with the intention of opening up the future, of spurring them into action and fostering hope . . . [one] must take part in action' (ibid.:167).

Making Algeria Algerian

In the context of Algeria, the 'nativist' movement also became the particular inspiration for a subversive 'return' to ancient identities, landscapes, personas, and, problematically, 'racial' stereotypes, too. Like colonialism before it, nativism permeated archaeological discourse and debate and also the aspirations of decolonisation. Thus Algeria's myth and memory formally 'hijacked by

European interests' now served as a resource for 'native resistance' (Mattingly 1996:57). Thus, while 'European scholars maintained the thesis that the Africans were rebellious, ungovernable troublemakers, the antithesis was to make them freedom fighters and partisans, seeking to throw off the burden of alien rule' (ibid.). A new template reminiscent of Said's 'triumphant ideology' predominates (Said 1983). This search for and empathetic identification with acts of ancient 'native resistance' made parallels between ancient 'revolts' and 'acts of armed resistance' (Mattingly 1996:56) and 'cultural resistance to Rome' and the 'liberation and nationalist movements of the twentieth century' (ibid.:57). The ability to mobilise memory and identity was profiled as a strategy of 'reinheritance' (ibid.).

The problematic aspect of such a strategy is bound up not only in the 'espousal of an authentic ethnic identity' and a belief in 'pure' indigenous cultural traditions but also in the 'danger' of replacing 'one distorted view of ancient colonialism with another equally doubtful formulation' (ibid.:59). This complex situation has led to what Mattingly refers to as a 'splendid irony' (ibid.) revolving around 'complaints about the historicity of the postcolonial perspective, while refusing implicitly to question the underlying basis of the orthodox view' (ibid.:58). The concern here is that the identities chosen to re-inherit and empower are themselves 'a projection of a crude contemporary stereotype onto the Roman African past' (ibid.). Such interventions have, however, empowered Maghrebian scholars to subsequently shift their attention to other periods, notably that of Islamic archaeology following independence. Difficulties still persist in terms of a complex impasse vis-à-vis 'taking on a tradition', which concerns a contested cosmopolitics in which Roman Africa has become adrift in a 'postcolonial limbo' (ibid.:62).[18]

Afrocentrism's Return to Egypt

> For us, the return to Egypt in every domain is the necessary condition to reconcile African civilization with history . . . it will play the same role in rethinking and renewing of African culture that Ancient Greece and Rome plays in the culture of the 'West'. (Diop 1992:149)

Motifs of the 'reclamation' of ancient identities and personas underpin one of the most resonant 'returns' made to North African/Egyptian origins, that of the Senegalese historian and political activist Cheikh Anta Diop. Diop saw his work bound up in agendas of both decolonisation in Africa and Pan-Africanism. In his 'return to Egypt', Diop asserted a connection between contemporary sub-Saharan black African culture and the ancient Egyptian

Pharaonic culture, which he understood to be a black African civilisation (Diop 1992:163). Emulation of and empathetic identification with ancient personas is crystallised in Diop's characterisation as the Black Pharaoh or Pharaoh of African Studies. This 'return' was an act that would bring about the renewal, rebirth, and regeneration of African culture. The death of African culture, Diop believed, was enacted by European scholars who strategically exiled Africa from its place in world history (ibid.:149). The reclamation or repossession of this heritage took the form of a symbolic return. Diop's thesis asserts that everything starts in Egypt – Egypt is thus positioned as the distant, forgotten, or repressed mother of science and culture of the West: a teacher to Greece in its infancy – a culture Diop believed owed everything to its encounter with Egypt (ibid.:163).

Figure 2.1 'Plato's Obelisk', Ain Shams, Cairo (photograph: Beverley Butler)

The endeavour to reclaim an earlier layer of memory and a more originary origin than that of Greco-European memory argues a reversal of the flow of the donation, reception, and inheritance of tradition. A specific link is made between this thesis and an ancient academy that once stood in Old Heliopolis, Cairo. For Diop and others, this prominent centre of science and religion, which, significantly, was in existence before the Alexandrian Mouseion/Library, is pivotal in proving that the flow of universal knowledge came from Egypt to the rest of the world (ibid.:299). The site, once home to some iconic 'needles', now boasts only one such column, known as 'Plato's obelisk' (ibid.:149). Diop and other authors claim that ancient scholars, including Plato (hence the name of the obelisk), Strabo, Solon, Pythagoras, Thales, and Eudoxus to name a few, either visited or were initiated at Heliopolis (ibid.). Also, according to this thesis, these philosophers came to ancient Heliopolis to 'learn' wisdom from black African culture: an historical 'fact', they argue, that Herodotus and other ancient authors took as common knowledge (ibid.:300).

For Diop and others writing in this genre, Old Heliopolis is reinvested as the place for the regeneration of contemporary African culture – both in terms of the African continent and the African Diaspora. Diop stated that black African memory was traumatised not only by racist Western scholars exiling Africa from world culture, history, and philosophy but also as a result of the historical experience of slavery (ibid.:113). He believed that the psychological impact of this 'exile' and its associated trauma needed to be addressed: to lose one's history was to lose one's soul and to risk a disintegration of self and self-group (ibid.). An alternative mode of memory-work was advocated via attachments and identifications made between modern black African culture and ancient Egyptian Pharaonic culture. Part of the training of initiates at Heliopolis involved the practice of the 'strengthening of the soul'; Diop believed that this activity was an apt prescription for the contemporary African (ibid.:299–300). Heliopolis was thus privileged by Diop as the place for internal psychic restoration and, as he understood it, memory recovery (ibid.:13).

The central tenets of Diop's work continue to be reworked and revived by other authors in new cultural and political contexts (see, for example, Mbeki 1998).[19] The landscape of ancient Egypt has thus sustained a privileged place in what have become known as Afrocentrist theses (Howe 1998). Critics yet again argue that by simply inverting the traditional Western model in order to make claims for a superior African origin has led to a failure to problematise the pseudoscientific, essentialist, and transhistorical notions of 'race' on which the thesis resides (ibid.:215–75). As Howe comments, picking up on the title of

Bernal's (1987) book: 'Black Athena is just as wrong as White Egypt' (Howe 1998:9). Perhaps to offer an antidote, Egypt has also provided a point of inspiration for the recent articulation of a thesis of 'travelling cultures' that privileges and intellectualises the fluidity of routes over the obstinacies and fixities of roots (see Clifford 1997 on Ghosh).

Colonial Trauma

To return to Fanon's alternative theorisations: His chapter 'On National Culture' ultimately recasts the desire to 'return to a Golden Age' as a 'painful, forced search'. Fanon argues that 'seeking to stick to tradition or reviving neglected traditions is not only going against history, but against one's people'(Fanon 2004 [1961]:179). This he asserts leads 'native intellectuals' to a 'dead end'. He similarly seeks to reject the 'spiritual' or 'metaphysical principle' of cultural authenticity' and 'do away' with notions of ethnic or 'racialised' cultural specificity' of 'the African "tradition"' (ibid.). He also problematises the concept of authenticity by arguing that 'revivalism' sees traditional culture evidently 'transformed in the process' (ibid.:174).

For Fanon, the question of memory-work and cultural transmission requires him to psychologise the character of colonialism and decolonisation. Fanon thus analyses the 'symptoms' he witnessed in Algiers.[20] He subsequently typologises 'the colonist as an exhibitionist' and attacks the 'narcissisms and ostentation of Europeans', which, he argues, are made manifest in Europe engaging in a 'permanent dialogue with itself' (ibid.:237). This context, Fanon argues, is host to the psychic wounds of slavery (ibid.). More fundamentally still, Sartre argues that 'in psychiatric terms' the effect of colonialism has left the Algerian people 'traumatised. For life' (Sartre in Fanon 2004 [1961]:li) and is symptomatic of a wholesale 'cultural and psychic genocide' (see Bhabha in Fanon 2004 [1961]:xxviii). Not only are colonialism and, more explicitly, the colonised body sites of 'traumatised memory' but also the war of liberation declared to be a 'breeding ground for mental disorders' (Fanon 2004 [1961]:182–83). Fanon's clinical insights into the 'pathology of the tortured and that of the perpetrator'[21] similarly lead him to uncover the mutual 'dehumanization' of this context and to define a 'pathology of the entire atmosphere in Algeria' (ibid.:216–17). Taking an alternative, though complementary, perspective Sartre asserts: 'France has become a neurosis' (Sartre in Fanon 2004 [1961]:lxii). Fanon argues further that the context of colonialism/decolonisation 'disregards human memory' by 'radically negating deep down what others have done to us' (Fanon 2004 [1961]:216–17).

Personae of Stereotypes

Underpinning what Fanon describes as this 'psycho-affective predicament' is the 'overdetermined' nature of memory and identity-work (ibid.:148). The concept of the 'psycho-affective' first appeared in Fanon's previous text, *Black Skin, White Masks* (1986 [1952]), which takes as its focus the analysis of racism in 1950s metropolitan France. Here he argues that the 'black', 'colonised', and 'native' body is encountered by Europeans as an archive of negative images and 'personae of stereotypes' (Fanon 1986:116). This 'performance' is one in which 'the white man's eyes' calls forth his 'other', who is characterised as being 'battered down by tom-toms, cannibalism, intellectual deficiency, fetishism, racial defects' (ibid.). The 'other' is likewise marked as a source of 'infection' and 'pollution' (ibid.). The emphasis on memory as embodiment climaxes in Fanon's prayer end: 'O my body, make of me always a man who questions!' (ibid.).

Similarly, in *The Wretched of the Earth* he argues that 'colonialism forces the colonised to question: *Who am I in reality?*' (Fanon 2004 [1961]:182). The question, however, is mired by what Bhabha crystallises as the 'colonial condition of life-in-death' (Bhabha 2004:xxxvi). As Fanon insists elsewhere, as a culture of 'absolute evil' colonialism forces the native to undergo 'dehumanisation' and 'alienation' (Fanon 1967 [1964]:34–35). By these means the native becomes an 'object-man', 'phantom-like' and thus 'reduced to the state of an animal' amid the 'struggle to keep alive' (Bhabha 2004:xxxix). Fanon likewise 'conceives of the colonised – body, soul, culture, community, history' – in a process of 'continued agony' and 'social death' (ibid.).

A key consequence is that the colonised are therefore 'devoid of public voice' and excluded from sites of collective memory and identity-work. Thus there emerges the 'native' preoccupation with 'tradition' and increasingly with what Fanon calls 'supernatural safeguards' (Fanon 2004 [1961]:19–20). The strategy of 'reviving awesome old myths' and 'meticulous rituals' is part of an attempt at seeking protection. Similarly, 'possession by djinns, by Zombies, and by Legba, the illustrious god of voodoo' and the intensification of the cults of 'vampirism', of the 'zars, the loas, [and] the Saints of Santeria', are, Fanon argues, bound up less in 'religious' and 'sacred dimensions' and more in their capacity to be 'turned into a weapon against despair and humiliation' (ibid.). Fanon sees these supernatural worlds as offering a 'template' by which the colonised can 'take control of their violence' (ibid.).

This situation leads to a 'native' world increasingly abound with 'terrifying myths' and populated by 'leopard men, snake men, six legged dogs, zombies … animalcules, [and] giants that encircle the colonised with a realm of taboos, barriers, and inhibitions' and 'magical superstructures' (ibid.:18–19). Fanon argues that the 'fear' conjured by 'the atmosphere of myths and magic operates [as] an undeniable reality' and acts as 'a secret sphere of "identification"' within 'underdeveloped countries' (ibid.). The native's 'collective sphere' thus falls 'exclusively within the realm of magic' and is paradoxically experienced as an 'ego-boosting' ritual both *despite* and *because of* the fact that, as Fanon makes clear, 'the fear of Zombies' and their like is 'more terrifying than [that of] colonists' (ibid.).[22] Here 'tradition', the past, the ancestors, ghosts, and the 'supernatural' are coexistent forces that act on the colonised to see through their demands. The 'role of dance, ritual, of sacred places', and of 'exorcism' open up as alternative spaces that are at once violent and therapeutic (ibid.). The psychological effects and 'psychoses' inherent in this context, as Sartre points out, lead to a situation in which 'personality dislocates like dementia' (Sartre in Fanon 2004 [1961]:liii) Fanon similarly argues that such 'performances' or 'symptoms' climax in a 'splitting' that yet again paradoxically 'ensures the stability of the colonised world' (Fanon 2004 [1961]:20). For Fanon, however, to 'squander' physical power 'in trances ending in exhaustion' is a 'lost' opportunity for the 'native' to channel such action into 'liberation'. The struggle for survival and also the struggle to 'be human' in the process of decolonisation – this 'epic', Fanon argues, is 'played out on a difficult day-to-day basis, and the suffering involved far exceeds that of the colonial period' (ibid.).

Psychotherapy of the Oppressed

According to Fanon, 'liberation' can be 'achieved only through the destruction' of what he terms 'colonial compartmentalism' (a form of 'Manichaeism') and working through the 'double-temporality' of the 'Third World' (ibid.:180). He reiterates that the '"new humanism" of the Third World cannot properly emerge' until this spatial/ temporal strategy is 'at an end' (ibid.:55). Perhaps the most controversial part of Fanon's text is the imagery of destruction and advocacy of violence of which Sartre is said to have 'fanned the flames' (Bhabha in Fanon 2004:xxi). Also controversial is the insistence that the 'only true culture' left open to the wretched of the earth is that of 'making a revolution' (Sartre in Fanon: 2004:11). Sartre clarifies Fanon's identification of the origin of violence with that of the colonist. He thus see the colonised acts of violence in terms of a deadly act of repetition,: 'Their violence [is] ours on the rebound' and is 'reflecting back at us . . . from a mirror' (Sartre in Fanon 2004 [1961]:li). The new forword to *The Wretched of the Earth* sees Bhabha argue further that the process of colonisation/decolonalisation 'results in a process of depersonalization that creates a sense of bodily memory and a violent corporal agency' (Bhabha in Fanon 2004 [1961]:xxv). Fanon's meditations, 'On Violence', the first chapter of *The Wretched of the Earth*, similarly sees this 'bodily' aspect of his intellectual approach related to the 'native's' 'dream to dislocate the world' and to 'blow the colonial world to smithereens' (Fanon 2004 1961]:6). In short, Bhabha asserts that 'the colonised acquire a visceral intelligence dedicated to the survival of body and spirit' (ibid.).

Again with much pathos and paradox, Fanon argues violence to be a 'psychotherapy of the oppressed' (ibid.:41). The role of violence within anticolonial discourse and activism is therefore recast as a potent act of memory-work and as an alternative, 'redemptive formula' based on the 'ideology of regenerative violence' through 'physical struggle' (ibid.). The issue of the identity of the coloniser and the colonised being inextricably linked to the latter's exploitation and based on an originary colonial violence reemerges. Fanon famously argues that it is only 'by becoming a subject of violence that the dehumanised colonised subject becomes a subject for the first time; violence functions as a kind of psychotherapy of the oppressed' (ibid.). Here violence offers a 'primary form of agency', a performative strategy of 'creating a presence' and a reclamation of personhood as the 'subject moves from nonbeing to being, from being an object to a subject'. Using the body as a resource to act on colonial power, to demand human justice under the threat of violence, operates as a form of 'poison-cure'.

Restoring Dignity

The ultimate outcome of Fanon's strategisation is to create a 'national culture' as it 'takes shape through struggle' (ibid.:97). While Fanon emphasises that 'national consciousness [is] nothing but a crude empty shell' (ibid.), his focus is to inscribe a plan of action beyond narrow-minded nationalism. Of note is that Fanon sees an emergent 'new model of nation and citizenship' linked to the creation of public culture. He asks: 'Without the rights of representation in the public sphere, can the subject ever be citizen in the true sense of the term?' Away from colonial compartmentalism, he argues the need to 'enrich consciousness' and 'restore dignity to all citizens, furnish their minds, fill their eyes with human things, and develop a human landscape for the sake of its enlightened and sovereign inhabitants' (ibid.:144). Here Fanon envisages an alternative mode of cultural transmission, a 'new 'psycho-affective' realm, 'a place of social and psychic mediation where citizen and individual develop and grow' (ibid.:40).

The reclamation of a 'national stage' and of 'global equity' requires the creation of a 'postcolonial consciousness based on a "dual emergence" of national sovereignty and international solidarity' (ibid.:179–80). Rejecting narratives of 'pan-Africanism', Fanon insists that 'national consciousness is the highest form of culture' (ibid.). Arguing that attention needs to be given to the specific operational and existential needs of national culture, he reiterates that 'nationalism . . . is alone capable of giving us an international dimension' and further that 'it is in the heart of national consciousness that international consciousness establishes itself and thrives' (ibid.). The denial of national realities and national differences, he argues, is a mistake, as is the belief in a 'universality' without addressing the 'racism' that pervades this dynamic. Similarly, Fanon reiterates how 'formal-citizenship' and 'equality' cannot be critically understood without addressing colonial and neocolonial power structures (ibid.).

Storytellers, Memorising Cultures

Here, too, one can crystallise more clearly the role of heritage, cultural transmission, and memory-work in Fanon's vision. Rejecting both the '*zars*' and the 'Acropolis' and in a return to epic narratives and the recuperation of memorising culture, Fanon identifies the Algeria storytellers as the vanguard of both revolution and tradition. He narrates the transformation of this genre: 'From 1952–53 on, its [Algeria's] storytellers, grown stale and dull, radically changed both their methods of narration and the content of their stories. Once scarce, the public returned in droves. The epic, with its standardised forms, reemerged. It has become an authentic form of entertainment that once again has taken on a cultural value. Colonialism knew full well what it was doing when it began systematically arresting these storytellers after 1955' (ibid.:174).

For Fanon, the epic 'arouses forgotten muscular tensions and develops the imagination' (ibid.) and is underpinned by the immediacy of memory-work: 'Every time the storyteller narrates a new episode, the public is treated to a real invocation . . . The present is no longer turned inward but channeled in every direction. The storyteller once again gives free rein to his imagination, innovates, and turns creator.' Of crucial importance to Fanon is that the storyteller 'searches for new models, national models, apparently on his own, but with the support of his audience . . . it has become part of the action in the making or already in progress' (ibid.:174–75). Fanon talks of the 'same eagerness' that is emergent in the 'fields of dance, song, rituals, and traditional ceremonies' as creativity 'starts to diversify' and 'energises culture' (ibid.).

End-Game: Mimicry versus New Man

> It is the question of the Third World starting a new history of Man . . . which will not forget Europe's crimes . . . For Europe, for ourselves, and for humanity, comrades, we must turn a new leaf, we must work out new concepts and try to set afoot a new man. (Fanon 2004 [1961]:239)

Fanon's conclusions outline a subversive form of 'othering' under the banner of 'the Last shall be the first' (Fanon 2004 [1961]:50). He argues for a 'new structure of society' and a search for 'new concepts' (ibid.:235–36). While intent on keeping in memory 'Europe's crimes', he rejects what he refers to as 'useless laments', 'sickening mimicry', and the 'grotesque' and 'generally obscene emulation' of Europe (ibid.). He reiterates: 'Do not ape Europe' and calls for his reader to 'stop envying Europe' and to 'stop fearing it', arguing that the 'native intelligentsia' must take part in a 'radical restructuring of human society' and 'must not be content to define itself in relation to values which *preceded* it' (ibid.).

Having characterised Europe as a 'Sleeping Beauty' (ibid.:62), Fanon calls for an end to 'the supremacy of white values', to an Enlightenment universalism that for Fanon amounts not only to 'abstract universal values' but also to 'massacres' and an 'avalanche of murders' (ibid.:236). The humanist 'tradition' is relegated to another of Europe's 'outmoded games' (ibid.). Having declared that the 'European game is finally over', he argues that 'we must innovate, we must be pioneers' and 'tense our muscles and our brains in a new direction' and 'look for something else' (ibid.:239).

That the 'native intelligentsia' no longer 'stood sentinel on duty guarding the Greco-Roman pedestal' (11) reminds one of what Sartre in a previous text referred to as the 'strip-tease of our [Europe's] humanism' (Sartre 2001:150–51): Therefore, although cautious of the presence of 'new international institutions', notably the World Bank and the IMF (one could add UNESCO), which Fanon argues have taken on 'the feel of the colonial ruler', it is the redemption of 'humanism' and of the 'human condition' that ultimately preoccupies him. He demands: 'Let us endeavour to invent a man in full, something which Europe has been incapable of achieving . . . For Europe, for ourselves and for humanity, comrades, we must make a new start, develop a new way of thinking, and endeavour to create a new man' (Fanon 2004:239).

Derrida As Greekjew Egyptian

> Hieroglyphs and pyramids, Thoth and Isis, colossi and Sphinx: Egypt repeatedly returns to haunt Derrida's writing... Egyptian motifs regularly appear at important moments in the texts. What is the place of 'Egypt' in deconstruction? Is there any sense in insisting on Derrida, greekjew or jewgreek, as North African, analogically 'Egyptian'? (Bennington 1992:97)

> Metaphysics – the white mythology – which reassembles and reflects the culture of the West: the white man takes his own mythology . . .the scene that nevertheless remains active and stirring, inscribed in white ink, an invisible design covered over in the palimpsest. (Derrida 1982:213)

Metaphysical Destabilisations

The postcolonial critic Robert Young characterises 'poststructuralism' as both the 'symptom and product' of 'a single historical moment' – not that of 'May 1968' but the 'Algerian War of independence'. The 'echo of the violence of Algeria', he insists, has been responsible for a 'form of epistemological violence' (Young 2001:412) that has been 'playing itself out in an insurrection against the calm philosophical and political certainties of the metropolis' (ibid.). Not only does Fanon's work feature in this legacy, but the rupture of the philosophical and political 'calm' has specific intimacies with deconstruction and a shared interest in the concomitant 'rupture' in the donation and reception of the 'white mythologies' and in the transmission of tradition.

'Deconstruction's' intimacies with Algeria are therefore more than Derrida's biographical origins; they extend further to define Derrida's 'return to North Africa' and the deconstuctionist lexicon of objects and personas. The above-rehearsed 'Egyptian motifs' and figures such as that of the 'Zombie' are returned to in order to harness their subversive potential (Bennington 1992). Thus there is a refusal to position 'Egypt' and 'Africa' in traditional archival/museological terms as the 'objects' of therapeutic mediation that enables the West to accede to its own subconscious and give a public account of its subjectivity (cf Mbembe 2001:3). Rather, this strategy is intended to short-circuit the usual logic of distinction to provoke an anxious encounter as a third space (see Collins and Mayblin 2001). In a complex schema (or nonschema as Derrida might have it), 'Egypt/Africa', like 'deconstruction' itself, are staged liminal 'sites'/'nonsites', a 'beyond', a 'between', and a 'beneath', and an 'undecided' that is always enigmatic and therefore never fixed (Bennington 1992:116; see also Derrida 1996).

Acknowledging the intellectual 'debts' to Levinas (1987), Derrida fixed his own liminal position as 'greekjew': an 'Egyptian' writing 'from the margins' defines his intellectual task of employing deconstruction to confronting Western 'logos' culture with its own fears, distress, confusion, and blindness with regard to the nature of its own origin (Bennington 1992:97). Moreover, the key dramas that Derrida seeks to return to in order to 'unfix' them are the foundational episodes apropos 'taking on a tradition'. It is here that alternative connectivities in the transmission of the 'Greek gifts' of Western metaphysics are mobilised.

Return to Egypt

Derrida's return to what has been described as the most 'exemplary scene of giving and receiving, writing, and reading, in the history of philosophy' (Naas 2003:xxiii) necessitates a return to Plato's text *Phaedrus*. This text, considered by many as *the* foundational 'performative moment' in the Western philosophic-metaphysical tradition, centres on Socrates' ('who famously never wrote anything' [Collins and Mayblin 2001:26]) recounting the myth of the 'invention of writing' as a means to argue that 'speech is superior to writing' (see Collins and Mayblin 2001:26–29; Derrida 1996:65–74). As Naas reiterates, for Derrida *Phaedrus* is 'a dialogue which gives us a tradition by establishing its own modes of reception, legacy, and inheritance' (Naas 2003:xxiii).

Derrida's 'reading' of Plato's text begins with a repetition of the myth of the 'invention of writing' in which the liminal figure Theuth (in his guise of inventor) visits Egypt in order to exhibit 'his arts' before the Egyptian king Thamus (Plato quoted in Derrida 1996:75). As Derrida explains: 'When it came to writing, Theuth said, "This discipline (*to mathema*), my king, will make the Egyptians wiser and will improve their memories (*sophoterous kai mnemonikoterous*): my invention is a recipe (*pharmakon*) for both memory and wisdom"' (ibid.). Here Derrida chooses to 'freeze the scene' before the point at which the king makes his 'decisive' moment – his rejection of the 'invention of writing' – as a means to crystallise the analogy between this moment and the 'rejectionism' at the heart of the 'pronouncement on writing' made by Western metaphysics (ibid.:75-76). For Derrida, the king's words of reply to Theuth speak for the Western metaphysical position: 'Those who write will stop exercising their memory and become forgetful. They'll rely on the external marks of writing instead of their internal capacity to remember things'. The 'inauthenticity' of writing is pursued further by the king: 'You've discovered a pharmakon, not for true memory . . . you offer your students a mere appearance of it, not the reality . . . they'll carry the conceit of wisdom, instead of being really wise' (ibid.:102). As a consequence, it is therefore fixed that 'writing is poison' and that Theuth attempted to put into circulation a poisoned gift (see Collins and Mayblin 2001:31).

Derrida argues that this 'decisive' moment is synonymous not only with 'the doctoring of philosophy' (Derrida 1996:xxiv) but also with the doctoring of 'the reception of the tradition itself' (Naas 2003:xxiii). Once again, Derrida argues that the privileging of the traditions of the white mythologies seeks to 'legitimate some works, exclude others, and to decide what is worthy of being passed on' thus eliciting (now) 'orthodox' patterns of transmission and 'modes of disinheritance' (ibid.).[23] In response, Derrida's return to *Phaedrus* is made in order to 'unfix' the metaphysical certainties that accompany the 'birth' of writing/metaphysics by drawing out a key emblem of deconstruction; the 'play of undecidability', which he identifies in this and in other foundational 'moments' of Western philosophy/origins (see Collins and Mayblin 2001:32 for a discussion). He reiterates that writing, like the archive and metaphysics itself, will always be an index of the West's mourning for the authenticity of speech (Derrida 1974:141–42). It is this traumatic break – the West's rejection of writing – that (again *despite* or *because* of its obvious 'inauthenticity') reinvests the archive/writing (and potentially metaphysics and its 'objects', too) as the model and medium of redemption.[24] In this particular case, Derrida invests Theuth as a figure of 'undecidability' and creatively conflates the latter's identity with that of the Egyptian god Thoth (Derrida 1996:85–94).

Return to Heliopolis

With more depth, in a strategic 'recovery' of the figure of the Egyptian god Thoth, Derrida is able to revisit the landscape of Heliopolis. This is undertaken to draw out an alternative archival 'mythos' and a destabilising cosmopolitics capable of blurring 'Western'/'non-Western' heritage traditions. Part of Derrida's strategy is to keep Plato's visit to Heliopolis (which Diop saw as pivotal to the 'Afrocentrist' thesis) as a great 'undecided' event in Western metaphysics (ibid.:85 ft. 15). This is achieved by recovering from among Thoth's multiple identities as 'limen' and 'mediator' his role as 'scribe and bookkeeper of Osiris' and his intimacies with Heliopolis and archival memory (ibid.:91).

Thoth takes his position as 'Master of the books' and with some mystical potency as 'master of divine words' (ibid.). With echoes of the genre of the 'tree fetish' and the 'Lady of the Tree' as the repressed originary objects of the archival imagination/cultural transmission, Thoth has a 'female counterpart' at Heliopolis, Seshat, meaning *she-who-writes* and who takes the position of 'Mistress of libraries' (ibid.). As counterparts, their duties are defined thus:

'She marks the names of the kings on a tree in the temple of Heliopolis, while Thoth keeps account of the years on a notched pole' (ibid.). Crucially, Thoth is also a presence in 'the scene of the Last Judgement', and, as such, 'in the underworld, opposite Osiris, Thoth records the weight of the heart-souls of the dead' (ibid.). It is the confusion of cosmopolitan identities, their co-existence and mixture, that attracts Derrida and encourages him to harness the potential of both Thoth and Heliopolis for further metaphysical 'unfixing' and philosophical 'destabilisation'.

Pharmakon

Derrida's preoccupation with the subversive potential sees him further recast 'Egypt' as *'pharmakon'*. As a cosmopolitical object, the *'pharmakon'* is synonymous not only with the concept of the 'poison-cure' and of the 'recipe' but also, traditionally, with 'receptical' or 'space' (see Naas 2003:1011). Derrida subsequently 'unfixes' the orthodox genealogies in order to 're-envision' their performativity in terms of a 'place or medium of transfer, transition, and translation' sympathetic to the 'archive of another' and to those on the 'margins' (Derrida 2002:13). Here, yet again, a gesture is made toward an alternative model or template of 'heritage performance'; again one can draw out the 'psych-affective', private-public, and indigenous-metropolitan trajectories, the connectivities of human-object, of inconsistent temporalities, and the presence of agency in terms of the force of ongoing hybridisation. The need surfaces to understand 'heritage performance' as 'poison-cure' and 'recipe', that is, not only to identify 'heritage/archival trauma' and its potentially curative properties but also to apprehend the shades, contradictions, and paradoxes in between.

Conclusion: Global 'Heritage Performance'

> Deconstruction was founded on the 'problem of the status of a discourse which borrows from a heritage the resources necessary for the deconstruction of that heritage itself'. (Derrida 1978:282, quoted in Young 2001:418)

> We would have to rethink not only our own relationship but the very temporality and identity of tradition itself and, thus, the very identity of who, as its inheritors or disciples, are given to taking it on. (Naas 2003:xxiii)

In conclusion, I combine a return to my focus on 'heritage memory' and 'heritage performance' with Derrida's call for UNESCO to 'reenvision heritage' for contemporary global constituencies (Derrida 2002). Derrida's insights, as do those of Freud, Fanon, and others featured in this chapter, offer a means by which to radically alter the schemas to 'take on a tradition' and to make new connectivities between written texts and oral transmission. Commenting on Derrida's concerns, Naas argues that 'more than a 'simple duality' or a 'simple opposition between accepting or rejecting tradition as our own' (Naas 2003:xviii) any reconceptualisation of heritage needs to address the *re-enactment* of tradition and its gestures' (ibid.:xxix). Within this process of 'taking on a tradition' is the inevitability that tradition will be 'repeated and interrupted, performed and transformed', and subject to the emergence of 'unprecedented gestures from within' (ibid.). At stake, therefore, is the very 'nature of translation' and the *'way* [tradition and memory are] . . . transmitted' (ibid.). Not only does Derrida empower us to 'suspend' and 'interrupt' such transmission and (as outlined in earlier sections) to 'find resources for reading it against itself', but he also argues that, at the *'moment of reception*, the moment of donation or presentation, when time itself is given and received, one begins to catch a glimpse of both the incredible power of the tradition, its way of recuperating the most heterogenous and marginal elements, *and* its great fragility, its vulnerability to the very gestures of reception that make it' (ibid.:xviii–xix).

The apprehension of the 'incredible power' and 'vulnerability' of tradition is bound up further in the fundamental way in which deconstruction 'problematises the concept of "intention"' (ibid.). A central feature here is the 'atemporality' of heritage memory and tradition's 'unique relationship to time' (ibid.: xxix). Thus the 'horizon for donation and reception of any legacy' is inevitably subject to 'a radically unknown future for that legacy', which Derrida refers to as a 'messianicity without messianism' (ibid.). The decision to act makes an exception of the subject and is thus event-like; performed within what Derrida calls the 'spectral' and within the structure of undecidability, the decision is not given but comes as a surprise yet must be taken. Reframed as the 'othering' of memory and transmission, a revelatory moment takes the form of recognition 'that it [tradition] has already from the beginning been other than itself' (ibid.:xx). In a radical reversal, Derrida argues the performativity of tradition is such that 'it is always the other who signs, who authorises us or gives us the power to speak, who leaves us with a tradition or history to work with or against, who situates us with a name, place, or time'. He reiterates: 'We are always preceded' (ibid.:xvii).

UNESCO and New Global Constituencies

The dynamics described above define the complex, hybridised nature of dominant and alternative heritage discourse and memory-work in the contemporary global context. A more detailed return to Derrida's 'deconstructionist' 'reading' of UNESCO addresses this broader context. Derrida reiterates the need for UNESCO to make a conceptual and moral-ethical 'break' with its historical, cultural, and metaphysical preoccupations with 'Greek memory' and 'Greek origins' (ibid.:40). He further argues that UNESCO's origins are bound up in an Occidental ontological tradition whose violences have 'displaced', 'among others', 'Egyptian, Jewish, Arabic' memory' (ibid.). Derrida's point is that UNESCO – like philosophy itself – does not have 'one sole memory' but, again, needs to recognise that 'even at origin, in its Greek moment, there was already some hybridization, some grafts, at work, some differential element' within UNESCO's foundational philosophies (ibid.).

It is this hybridising force that Derrida sees as UNESCO's subversive dynamic, revealing as it does how the organisation necessarily participates in an 'othering' of its foundational values. Derrida's appeal is for the mobilisation of 'another model' that, 'while keeping in memory this European, Greek philosophy, and the European history of philosophy, take[s] into account that there are events, experiences, and alternative philosophies which cannot be reduced to this origin'. He does however, insist on the need to displace and 'reenvision' some foundational concepts. In contrast to Fanon, Derrida highlights the concept of 'nation' and UNESCO's commitment in its Convention (the organisation's 'performative text') to the 'rule of nation' for particular concern. Derrida argues that, in the age of 'post-nation', a 'new ethics' and 'new internationalism' are needed that are capable of 'open[ing] up UNESCO's logic and its existence' as a truly 'world institution' (ibid.:74). Derrida subsequently sums up this strategy in terms of a moral-ethical 'debt', 'duty', 'response', and 'responsibility' toward 'the archive of another', to 'difference', and to the simultaneous 'opening-up the self-validating aspect of the institution to the "voice of the other"' (ibid.:23) and to a remodelled future institutional cosmopolitics committed to creating a 'democracy-to-come' (ibid.:40).

Furthermore, Derrida's broader discussions of cosmopolitanism and hospitality reiterate the 'concrete stakes of the situation' by drawing on examples of cultural and ethnic conflict in Bosnia and Kosovo and ongoing struggles in Algeria and Israel/Palestine (ibid.:27). He subsequently characterises these and other conflicts as 'ones whose formulations call into question the very concepts defining human organisations and relations embodied in UNESCO's constitution' (ibid.).[25] By connecting these agendas of heritage and tradition further to embrace refugee and asylum rights and critical reflections on amnesty, truth, and reconciliation, Derrida argues that these connectivities are an integral part of his moral-ethical project of 'restoring . . . heritage to dignity' and creating a 'just' future (Derrida 2004:5). Here is located the potential means by which those who remain 'exiled' outside the realms of institutional-archival hospitality – the archive's originary constituency – can seek to access an archival 'refuge-home'. Derrida underlines the point that UNESCO is the fundamentally privileged place – or more strongly, the 'only place' possible – for truly developing these issues in the contemporary global context (Derrida 2002:2).

Burden and Weightlessness

Taking the project of reconceptualising heritage beyond UNESCO's door demands a more radical intellectual-operational change. It requires more than just a 'break' in the assumption that all 'heritage memory' is located within the Occidental historiographic tradition that begins with a Classical 'Golden Age' of ancestor-origins that is subsequently redeemed via new 'arts of memory' and accompanying textual technologies in the post-Renaissance period. Modernity's various 'memory crises', whether caused by the metaphysical trauma of modernity's loss of 'authenticity/origin' and/or the literal displacements wrought by industrialisation, are subsequently narrated in a revival and objectification of memory bound up in the (fragile) faith placed in *lieux de mémoire* (see Maleuvre 1999). Moreover, whether it is 'crises of representation' that emerge in the wake of the moral-epistemological trauma and genocidal murder of the Holocaust or the 'memory boom' that ensues, the dynamic of memory-work thus succumbs to, among other factors, Freudian 'disturbances', Derridean 'unfixing', and the 'epistemological violences' (cf Algeria and others) that 'break' with a Euro-Western genealogy and that ultimately expose the 'real' within the global arena.

This realpolitk in turn demands a reworked 'heritage memory' that represents more than a Halbwachsian model of collective memory and goes further than adding to the narrative the technologies and connectivities of postmemory that are emerging to define themselves (Crane 2000). Likewise, it is too easy to characterise heritage in the global context as exclusively bound up in the export of Euro-Western 'memory crises', for example, as located in UNESCO's heritage programmes, and to dismiss 'heritage' simply as the monumentalisation of Occidental 'bad faith', again now an export commodity for manipulation on a global scale by 'top-down' power-blocs in 'emergent nations' and/or 'failed states'. The appetite for heritage and tradition in the search for 'culture-as-cure', 'refuge', and 'transformational magics' sees heritage, whether in contemporary Madagascar (cf Lambek 2002 or contemporary France (cf Bourdieu et al. 1999), understood as bound up in the weight of the past and in social suffering. It is the radical ambivalence of heritage – its terrors and its claim to restore human dignity – that requires us to explore the possibility of a new ethics of 'heritage humanism'.

'Africanisation of Tradition'

Elsewhere, a colleague and I sought to articulate what we termed an 'Africanist turn' in heritage discourse (Butler and Rowlands 2006). Here, one could offer, for example, a certain 'Africanisation' or 'indigenising' force vis-à-vis UNESCO's 'global strategy', which has provoked an 'othering' in terms of the inscription of 'cultural landscapes', the authentication of 'masterpieces of intangible heritage', and the rescue and distribution of archival heritage in UNESCO's Memory of the World Programme (see www.unesco.org). In this transformation, UNESCO has given recognition – however problematic – to the 'archives of another' (Derrida 2002:86). Perhaps one could go to another extreme and counter the historical 'Westernisation' of tangible heritage by recasting every ethnography dealing with non-Western cultural transmission as a 'heritage performance' and, yet again, problematically, as evidence of 'parallel heritages' (see Butler 2006a; 2006b).

What we sought to do, however, was not only to apprehend a context that was marked by narcissistic, colonising acts of empathetic identification carried out in the name of global health but also to engage with alternative 'sympathetic magics' operating across North and South, which are responsive to the 'humanisation' of heritage contexts/discourse. These alternative performances insist on a critical revival of the core heritage meditation on the human condition – of 'what it is to be human' – and require of the heritage critic more knowledge of human-object worlds and greater understanding of 'ourselves/others' as transformed by objects/events/performances/environments. What one might call a certain 'heritage animism' comes into play in strategies – historical and contemporary, local and global – to 'stabilise' the 'ancestors' (their atemporal agency positioning them as neither alive nor dead). The underlying demand here is that the 'ancestors' gain justice and are 'justly remembered'. This particular flow of the 'Africanisation' of the West gives recognition to a certain vision of 'one-world' ancestry (Butler and Rowlands 2006).

As part of this vision, one may also attempt, for example, to assert the necessity of human beings expressing themselves through the medium of storytelling as a key focus of identity, memory-work, and meaning-making in 'heritage performance' and as a fundamental resource of asserting the 'dignity of self'. Similarly, as extra-discursive and extra-textual objects as fetish, pharmakon, and as good/bad gifts (that is, capable of absorbing and removing pollutions from the past; cf Parry 1986) occur with the performative force of a promise, they open the possibility of whatever comes to pass without in any way guaranteeing it. Thus, the 'Africanist turn' is taken precisely in order to subvert the Freudian theme of internalised memory and identity as fixed in a particular trajectory. A Western subjectivity is deemed to be confronted by an exteriority: the world of objects and things that instills an agency for good or bad purposes depending on context.

Thus, understanding the power of 'objects' and 'ancestors' (in their various tangible/intangible and hybridised forms) to define a future allows a certain pathway toward surrendering the notion of a controlling centre of meaning and prioritises the call of the 'archive/memory' of 'another', not least those that now occupy the category 'of the wretched of the earth'. This relates to the need to develop an understanding of these dynamics of othering vis-à-vis 'canonical' and 'uncanonical' sites, spaces, collections, performances, and field-work contexts. One potent dynamic concerned with the 'testimony of memory' can be seen to reside in the objects of memory contained within the (so-called) world archives/museums that mimic the Alexandrina as ancestor-institution. Examples of such objects were displayed as part of the British Museum's 'Museum of the Mind'; many of them were ethnographic objects from Africa, reconceptualised as synonymous with a 'memory... constantly on the move' (Mack 2003:149).

One may argue that both intended and unintended memory-work may arise from such potent collections. To pursue a more 'unexpected' intervention of such 'memory constantly on the move' pertinent to this chapter, one could point to the 'performative moments' of heritage revivalism currently effecting a disturbance to the landscape of Alexandria. Not only has the contemporary city been witness to a joint project between UNESCO and the Egyptian government to revive the ancient Mouseion/Library 'on the ruins' of what is claimed to be its ancient counterpart (Butler, 2001a; 2001b; 2003; 2006a; 2006b; 2007), but accompanying this 'event' are ongoing underwater excavations in the Bay of Alexandria. The latter acts of excavation and memory-work have seen archaeologists confronted with the 'unexpected' in the form of thousands of finds strewn on the seabed. The director of the excavations commented: 'At the first glance the chaos was incomprehensible' (Empereur quoted in La Riche 1998:52). In all this messiness, two iconic landscapes – Alexander's 'Greek city' and the landscape of Heliopolis – were among those found merged, mixed beneath the Mediterranean. This 'disturbance' and the revelation that ancient Alexandria was 'less Greek and more Egyptian' (ibid.) than previously thought remerged to 'break' the fixity of exclusive claims to narrate the Egyptian/African landscape and in so doing opened up heritage memory

Figure 2.2 The Bibliotheca Alexandrina, contemporary Alexandria (photograph: Beverley Butler)

to the testimony of discrepant cosmopolitics. Similarly, this identification of alternative cosmopolitical heritage discourse delineates the critical basis from which to apprehend diverse heritage imaginaries in historical and contemporary African settings. In the chapters that follow, these imaginaries are particularised in terms of West Africa.

Notes

1. As Naas states, 'taking on the tradition [is] . . . another way of glossing "deconstruction"' (Naas 2003:xix). Derrida's purpose in 'taking on *the* tradition' – *the* tradition being a genealogy bound up in the ongoing 'legacy' of 'Greco-European memory' and in 'themes of tradition, legacy, and inheritance in the Western philosophical tradition' (ibid.:xviii) – is his attempt to go beyond the concept of the '"singular" inheritance' claimed by such a 'Greek' metaphysical tradition in order to apprehend new strategies of 'taking on *a* tradition' in the sense of giving recognition to 'another tradition' (the traditions of the 'other') (ibid.:xix).
2. Derrida also refers to 'a constant return to Greek philosophy, particularly Plato and Aristotle' as well as the Homeric epics (Naas 2003:xxiii)
3. Not only does the ancient Alexandria monumentalism include the Pharos Lighthouse (one of the Wonders of the ancient World) but also the Ptolemies royal palaces site (synonymous with the seductions of Cleopatra, Mark Anthony, and Caesar), the Serapeum (the famous temple complex), and Alexander's Tomb feature within this vision (see La Riche 1998).

4. Built in the third century BCE by Ptolemy Soter, the Mouseion/Library has been cast as an 'enigma' (Abbadi 1990:15). Although little is known about the institution, it is best understood as a composite of a Temple of the Muses, a 'universal' library, a philosophical academy, and a planetarium. The ancient Alexandrina brought together texts, learned men, and artefacts in an attempt to fuse 'Greek' heritage with the Aristotelian project of acquiring 'universal' knowledge (ibid.).
5. Pre-Alexandria memory-work is argued to be a scenario in which poets and others would appeal to 'external memory aids', that is, the gods and the muses, who mediated between the human individual and the recall of epics (cf Perniola 1995).
6. A paradox here is that no image of the Alexandrian archive survives.
7. It is here, too, that the myth holds in tension its initial expression as a literary, metaphorical/metaphysical project of retrievalism and acts of material objectification from the Renaissance onward. Thus the Alexandrina emerges as a 'template' in the West for its archival institutions (and is subsequently mapped into its colonial possessions) (Butler 2006a).
8. Currently dominated by the dichotomy, Islam and the West (cf Said 2001).
9. These included Napoleon Bonaparte's visit to Siwa Oasis in Alexander's footsteps (Mitchell 1998).
10. Significantly, too, Bazin identifies in French attempts to colonise Egypt the central position of the Institut d'Egypt established by Bonaparte's savants in Cairo, which as a research institute, museum, and academy contains the core elements of the Alexandrina paradigm (Bazin 1967:191)
11. See Layton et al. (2001) on archaeology as an 'archival' technology.
12. As Mattingly argues: 'The former French territories in the Maghreb have yielded over 60,000 latin texts, and, indeed, the importance of French North Africa in the development of Latin epigraphy as a discipline cannot be overestimated (1996:51)
13. And also the exhibition of peoples, for example, in World Expositions (cf Coombes 1994 and Greenhalgh 1988).
14. That is, both Alexander the Great and the Ptolemies pursued projects of decorating Alexandria with objects taken from both inside and outside Egypt (see La Riche 1998).
15. Earlier translations of Fanon's text use the derogatory reference to 'mumbo-jumbo'. More recent versions use the term '*zars*' to describe a genre of spirits identified in particular with North African cultures. For a discussion, see Philcox in Fanon 2004.
16. This has similarities with the metaphor of 'return to darkness', which is threatened to happen to the colonies 'if the colonist were to leave' and would lead to the 'natives' regression 'into barbarism, degradation, and bestiality' (Fanon 2004:149).
17. Besides announcing the beginning of the revolution against French colonialism, the FLN's Proclamation of 1 November 1954 listed grievances and goals, including the extraordinary demand for the abrogation of 'all edicts, decrees, and laws . . . denying the history, geography, language, religion, and customs of the Algerian people' (Naylor 2000:5–6).
18. As Mattingly further details: 'In present-day Algeria, the civil war between the government and Islamic fundamentalist groups makes archaeological fieldwork impossible to carry out, while at least one archaeologist has been dismissed from

post and publications impounded in warehouses as government policy vacillates between conciliation of Islamic groups and repression of its critics, armed or otherwise.... Algeria is an extreme and alarming case, but it illustrates the real dangers of allowing the theoretical basis of Roman Africa to drift in a postcolonial limbo. Unless Roman Africa is adopted (or reinherited) by North Africans as part of their own history and culture, it seems to me that there is little hope for the long-term health of the subject' (Mattingly 1996:62).
19. The South African President Mbeki pursues an Afrocentrism in selected political speeches – for example: 'To perpetuate their imperial domination over the peoples of Africa, the colonisers sought to enslave the African mind and to destroy the African soul ... The beginning of the rebirth of our continent must be our own rediscovery of our soul, captured and made permanently available in the great works of creativity represented by the pyramids and the sphinxes of Egypt, the stone buildings of Axum and the ruins of Carthage and Zimbabwe, the rock paintings of the San, the Benin bronzes and the African masks, the carvings of Makonde and the stone sculptures of the Shona ... In that journey of self-discovery and the restoration of our own self-esteem, without which we would never become combatants for the African renaissance, we must retune our ears to the music of Zao and Franco of the Congos and the poetry of Mazisi Kunene of South Africa, and refocus our eyes to behold the paintings of Malangatane of Mozambique and the sculpture of the Dumile Fine of South Africa' (Mbeki 1998:299).
20. Fanon argues that 'all political leaders should be psychiatrists' (Young 2001:277)
21. Again, these are accounts of case-study interviews with patients, entitled Colonial War and Mental Disorders (Fanon 2004:181–219).
22. The Zombie also appears from a different perspective in Sartre's preface when he accuses European's of creating 'Zombies' in terms of the dehumanisation of colonised peoples – that is, 'you have turned [them] into the zombie' (Sartre in Fanon 2004:xiviii).
23. The excluded 'other' includes the disinheritance of mothers and daughters as based on the template of 'Pharmarcia and Khora' (Naas 2003:xxiii–xxiv).
24. Derrida, for example, takes up the motif of the 'hieroglyph' as an equally potent 'model' to express the co-presence and co-existence of 'origin', 'writing', 'archive', and 'difference' (Derrida 1996:85–87; see also Bennington 1992:116; Collins and Mayblin 2001:33).
25. These factors, which have gone largely unproblematised within mainstream cultural heritage studies, are, however, mirrored in calls by postcolonial theorists, activists, and others for the conceptualisation of a 'new humanism' and of a more universally applied Human Rights culture, no longer tied to what has been identified as another of the most oppressive filters within the global arena – that of Western liberalism (see Butler 2006a).

Bibliography

Abbadi M. 1990. *Life and Fate of the Library of Alexandria*. Paris: UNESCO Publishing.
Bazin, G. 1967. *The Museum Age*. J. Cahill (trans.). New York: Universe Books.
Bennington, G. 1992. 'Mosaic Fragment: If Derrida Were an Egyptian ...'. In *Derrida: A Critical Reader*, D. Wood (ed.), pp. 97–119. Oxford: Blackwell.

Bernal, M. 1987. *Black Athena: The Afroasiatic Roots of Classical Culture and the Fabrication of Ancient Greece*. London: Verso.

Bettelheim, B. 1989 [1956]. *Recollections and Reflections*. Harmondsworth: Penguin Books.

Bhabha H. 2004. 'Introduction'. In F. Fanon (ed.), *The Wretched of the Earth*. New York: Grove Press.

Bourdieu, P., et al., 1999. *The Weight of the World: Social Suffering in Contemporary Society*. Palo Alto, CA: Stanford University Press.

Butler, B. 2001a. 'Egypt: Constructed Exiles of the Imagination'. In *Contested Landscapes: Movement, Exile and Place*, B. Bender and M. Winer (eds.), pp. 303–18. Oxford: Berg.

———. 2001b. 'Return to Alexandria: Conflict and Contradiction in Discourses of Origins and Heritage Revivalism in Alexandria, Egypt'. In *The Destruction and Conservation of Cultural Property*, R. Layton and J. Thomas (eds.), pp. 55–75. London: Routledge.

———. 2003. '"Egyptianizing" the Alexandrina: The Contemporary Revival of the Ancient Mouseion/Library'. In *Imotep Today: Egyptianizing Architecture*, C. Price and J-M. Humbert (eds.). London: University College London Press.

———. 2006a, 'Heritage and the Present Past'. In *The Handbook of Material Culture*. Sage Publications: 463–79.

———. 2006b, '"Three Concepts" – Hospitality, Cosmopolitanism and Human Dignity: Re-conceptualising Heritage Futures', *Archaeologies: The Journal of the World Archaeological Congress*. AltaMira Press.

Butler, B. 2007. *Return To Alexandria –An Ethnography of Cultural Heritage Revivalism and Museum Memory*. Walnut Grove, CA: Left Coast Press.

Butler, B., and M. Rowlands. 2006. 'The Man Who Would Be Moses. In *A future for Archaeology*, R. Layton, R. Shennan, and P. Stone (eds.), pp. 97– 107. London: University College London Press.

Césaire, A. 1983. *Notebook of a Return to a Native Land: The Collected Poetry*, C. Eshleman (trans.). Berkeley and Los Angeles: University of California Press.

Cleere, H. 2001. 'Uneasy Bedfellows: Universality and Cultural Heritage'. In *Destruction and Conservation of Cultural Property*, R. Layton, P. Stone, and J. Thomas (eds.), pp. 22–29. London: Routledge.

Clifford, J. 1997. *Routes: Travel and Translation in the Late Twentieth Century*. Cambridge, MA: Harvard University Press.

Collins, J., and B. Mayblin. 2001. *Introducing Derrida*. London: Icon Books

Coombes, A. 1994. *Reinventing Africa: Temples of Empire: The Museum and Its Publics*. New Haven, CT: Yale University Press.

Crane, S. A. (ed.). 2000. *Museums and Memory*. Palo Alto, CA: Stanford University Press.

Derrida, J. 1974. *Of Grammatology*, G. C. Spivak (trans.). Baltimore: John Hopkins University Press.

———. 1985. *Margins of Philosophy*, A. Bass (ed.). Chicago: University of Chicago Press.

———. 1996. *Archive Fever: A Freudian Impression*. E. Prenowitz (trans.). Chicago: University of Chicago Press.

———. 2002. *Ethics, Institutions and the Right to Philosophy*. P. Pericles Trifonas (trans.). New York: Rowman and Littlefield Publishers.

Derrida, J. 2004. *On Cosmopolitanism and Forgiveness*. London: Routledge.
Diop, C. A. 1992. *Great African Thinkers: Cheikh Anta Diop*, I. Van Sertima (ed.). New Brunswick: State University Press.
Durrell, L. 1986 [1957–1960]. *The Alexandria Quartet*. London: Faber and Faber.
Eliade, M. 1991 [1954]. *The Myth of the Eternal Return: Or Cosmos and History*, W. R. Trask (trans.). Princeton: The Princeton/Bolligen Series in World Mythology.
Errera, E. 1997. 'The Dream of Alexander and the Literary Myth'. In *Alexandria 1860–1960: The Brief Life of a Cosmopolitan Community*, R. Ilbert and I. Yannakakis with J. Hassoun (eds.), pp. 128–44. Alexandria: Harpocrates Publishing.
Fanon, F. 1967 [1964]. *Toward the African Revolution*, H. Chevalier (trans.). New York: Monthly Review Press.
———. 1986 [1952]. *Blacks Skin, White Masks*, C. L. Markmann (trans.). London: Pluto Press.
———. 2004 [1961]. *The Wretched of the Earth*, R. Philcox (trans.). New York: Grove Press.
Findlen, P. 2000. 'The Modern Muses: Renaissance Collecting and the Cult of Remembrance'. In *Museums and Memory*, S. A. Crane (ed.), pp. 161–78. Palo Alto, CA: Stanford University Press.
Forty, A., and S. Keuchler. 1999. *The Art of Forgetting*. Oxford: Berg Publications.
Forrester J. 1994. '"Mille e tre": Freud and Collecting'. In *The Cultures of Collecting*, J. Elsner and R. Cardinal (eds.), pp. 224–51. London: Reaktion Books.
Freud, S. 1984 [1936]. 'A Disturbance of Memory on the Acropolis'. In *On Metapsychology*, A. Richards (ed.), pp. 443–56. London: Penguin Books.
Greenhalgh, P. 1988. *Ephemeral Vistas*. Manchester: Manchester University Press.
Halim H. 2002. 'On Being an Alexandrian'. In *Al Ahram Weekly*, April 11–17, No. 581:5.
Hoggart, R. 1978. *An Idea and Its Servants: UNESCO from Within*. London: Chatto and Windus.
Howe, S. 1998. *Afrocentrism: Imagined Pasts and Imagined Homes*. London: Verso.
Jacob, C., and F. Polignac. 2000. The Alexandrian Mirage. In *Alexandria, Third Century BC: The Knowledge of the World in a Single City*, C. Jacob and F. Polignac (eds.), pp. 14–19. Alexandria: Harpocrates Publishing.
Klibansky R. 2000. 'A Return to Athens via Alexandria?' In *Alexandria, Third Century BC: The Knowledge of the World in a Single City*, C. Jacob and F. Polignac (eds.), pp. 217–30. Alexandria: Harpocrates Publishing.
Kohut H. 1978. *The Search for the Self*. New York: International Universities Press.
Kwint, M., et al., 1999. *Material Memories: Design and Evocation*. Oxford: Berg Publications.
Lambek M. 2002. *The Weight of the Past: Living with History in Mahajanga, Madagascar*. Basingstoke : Palgrave Macmillan.
Levinas E. 1987. *Collected Philosophical Papers*, A Lingis (trans.). The Hague: Nijhoff Publishers.
La Riche, W. 1998. *Alexandria: The Sunken City*. London: Weidenfeld and Nicholson.
Lowenthal, D. 1985. *The Past Is a Foreign Country*. Cambridge: Cambridge University Press.
———. 1996. *The Heritage Crusade and the Spoils of History*. London: Viking.
Mack, J. 2003. *The Museum of the Mind*. London: British Museum Press.

Maleuvre, D. 1999. *Museum Memories: History, Technology, Art*. Palo Alto, CA: Stanford University Press.
Mattingly, D. 1996. 'From One Colonialism to another: Imperialism and the Magreb'. In J. Webster and J. Cooper, *Roman Imperialism: Post-Colonial Perspectives*, pp. 49–70. Leicester: Leicester University Press.
Mbeki, T. 1998. *Collected Political Speeches*. New York: New Sign Books.
Mbembe, A. 2001. *On the Postcolony*. Berkeley and Los Angeles: University of California Press.
Mitchell, C. 1998. *Colonising Egypt*. Berkeley and Los Angeles: University of California Press.
Naas, M. 2003. *Taking on the Tradition: Jacques Derrida and the Legacies of Deconstruction*. Palo Alto, CA: Stanford University Press.
Parry J. 1986. 'The Gift, the Indian Gift and the "Indian Gift"', *Man* (ns) 21 (3): 453–74.
Perniola, M. 1995. *Enigma: The Egyptian Moment in Society and Art*, C. Woodhall (trans.). London: Verso.
Plutarch, 1973. 'The Life of Alexander'. In Plutarch, *The Age of Alexander*, I. Scott-Kilvert (trans.), pp. 252–334. London: Penguin Books.
Polignac, F. 2000a. 'The Shadow of Alexander'. In *Alexandria, Third Century BC: The Knowledge of the World in a Single City*, C. Jacob and F. Polignac (eds.), pp. 32–42. Alexandria: Harpocrates Publishing.
———. 2000b. 'A Myth Reborn'. In *Alexandria, Third Century BC: The Knowledge of the World in a Single City*, C. Jacob and F. Polignac (eds.), pp. 212–16. Alexandria: Harpocrates Publishing.
Prochaska, D. 1990. *Making Algeria French: Colonialism in Bone 1870–1920*. Cambridge: Cambridge University Press.
Rapaport, H. 2003. *Later Derrida: Reading the Recent Work*. London: Routledge.
Raphael-Leff, J. 1990. 'If Oedipus Was an Egyptian'. In *International Review of Psychoanalysis*, P. Okasha (ed.) (17):309–35.
Rojek, C. 1997. 'Indexing, Dragging and the Social Construction of Tourist Sites'. In *Touring Cultures: Transformations of Travel and Theory*, C. Rojek and J. Urry (eds.), pp. 54–74. London: Routledge.
Said, E. W. 1978. *Orientalism*. New York: Pantheon Books.
———. 1983. *The World, the Text and the Critic*. Cambridge, MA: Harvard University Press.
———. 2001. 'Clash of Definitions'. In *Reflections on Exile and Other Literary and Cultural Essays*, E. W. Said (ed.), pp. 569–93. London: Granta.
Sartre, J.-P. 2001. *Colonialism and Neocolonialism*. London: Routledge.
Wood, M. 1997. *In the Footsteps of Alexander the Great*. London: BBC Publications.
Yates, Frances A. 1992. *The Art of Memory*. Harmondsworth: Penguin.
Young, R. 2001. *Postcolonialism: An Historical Introduction*. Oxford: Blackwell.

Slave Route Projects: Tracing the Heritage of Slavery in Ghana
Katharina Schramm

The history of the transatlantic slave trade, stretching over a period of more than 300 years, has profoundly influenced contemporary social and economic relations on a global scale. The trade as well as the economic system it supported fueled the capitalist development in Europe and the Americas while at the same time marking the beginning of the import-dependency of Africa (cf Williams 1964). Chattel slavery, as it was practised on the American plantations, rested on the racist ideology of white supremacy that is still very much alive today.[1] On the African continent, slavery existed for an even longer period, alongside the transatlantic network as well as independent of it. In royal armies and courts as well as in agriculture, slaves constituted a major workforce. Especially after the abolition of the transatlantic slave trade and the huge surplus in slaves resulting from it, many slaves were incorporated into their African masters' families. Although they were granted access to some privileges (such as the right to marry, to acquire wealth, and so on), their slave status meant that they and their descendants were denied full political power in traditional government.

Because of this complexity, the effects of slavery also vary tremendously – be they in social, psychological, and economic terms or with regard to current political subject-positions. As a result, there have always been many different ways of dealing with the slavery past in different times and places – ranging from silence and denial to collective identification with motifs of resistance, for example.

In the past decades, the rather fragmentary and flickering resurgence of the slavery topos in very heterogeneous settings has given way to a remarkable rise in public references to slavery and the slave trade on an almost global scale.[2] Thus, the triangular trade between Europe, Africa, and the Americas has become a key issue of international heritage initiatives, such as those led by UNESCO and ICOM (the International Council of Museums). African governments have also 'rediscovered' the history of slavery as a marketable asset to promote their burgeoning tourist industries.[3] At the same time, localized collective and individual memories of the slave trade and slavery (both in Africa and transatlantic) continue to exist – sometimes in accordance with official heritage-discourse, at other times in contestation to it.

This chapter focuses on recent efforts of representing the history of slavery in Ghana. In my analysis, I regard official and popular memories as intrinsically connected to each other. I am interested in the politics of heritage and memory that unfolds at their interface. The correlation between heritage and memory has often been theorized in the strictly oppositional terms of (state) memorialism versus (popular) counter-memories (cf Bodnar 1994; Werbner 1998; to some extent Cole 2001). While the notion of counter-memories opens up opportunities for a thorough critique of nationalist ideologies and the regimes of power associated with it, it also tends to proclaim the authenticity of local voices as against the manipulative force of the state and other hegemonic institutions. The question that remains underexposed in this interpretative scheme concerns the areas of overlap and interpenetration between different levels of discourse. In the context of the slave route projects that are discussed here, these relationships are far from static. Memory that is marginalized in one setting can become part of a dominant rhetorical strategy in another and vice versa. Official commemorative rituals may feed on images derived from popular memory and the other way round. In addition to these considerations, one also needs to examine the strategic adaptation of locally existing memories to national and transnational narratives. Such adaptation is practiced not only by dominant agents but also by 'ordinary people', who in the process are still able to maintain these 'other stories' that are frequently termed counter-memories.

In other words, what I am interested in is the very dynamics between the streamlining of a complex history into *one* particular narrative on the one hand and the continuous and palimpsest-like shining through of alternative meanings and interpretations of the past on the other. In particular, I look at the process by which the northern Ghanaian slave sites that are historically connected to the African slave trade are nowadays being incorporated into a transatlantic interpretative scheme and thereby turned into destinations for

African American travelers. I explore how local history is being adapted to existing images of the transatlantic slave trade, as they are mediated by national and global agents.

In my analysis, I focus on two heritage projects that play a role in the recent upsurge of interest in the northern slave sites. Those are, on the one hand, the UNESCO Slave Route Project and, on the other hand, more prominently, the so-called Joseph Project, which has been initiated by the Ghanaian Ministry of Tourism. I look at the specific heritage conceptions that underlie those initiatives and ask how they are put into practice. My discussion begins with a few remarks on a particular event, Panafest 2001, where the discursive re-evaluation of the northern Ghanaian slave sites began to take shape.

Going Up North: The Background to Contemporary Representations of the Slave Trade

Panafest is one of the most important cornerstones of the Ghanaian tourism industry. Taking place under the twin motto 'The reemergence of African civilisation: Uniting the African family', this biennial festival attracts visitors mainly from the African Diaspora. In August 2001, as part of a so-called Pre-Panafest pilgrimage, a delegation of African American festival participants came to the northeastern Ghanaian border town of Paga. Here, they visited the Pikworo slave camp at Paga-Nania, 'the site of the genesis of slave trade in the Gold Coast', as it was stated in a newspaper comment.[4] This was the first time that a visit to a northern slave site featured as part of the official Panafest itinerary.

Efua Sutherland, who had written the original Panafest proposal, had envisioned the event as a pan-African historical drama festival, devoted to a thorough examination of the slave trade as a key episode in the history of African people – both in the Diaspora as well as on the continent. She singled out her hometown, Cape Coast, located on the shore of the Atlantic Ocean, as the major festival venue. Here, the violent history of the transatlantic slave trade is epitomized by the imposing structure of Cape Coast Castle and Dungeons. The castle, which has been designated by UNESCO as World Heritage Site,[5] stands symbolically as one of the last points of contact for enslaved Africans before they were taken away from the continent to work on the plantations of the New World.[6]

Since the first international edition of Panafest in 1992, the number of African American visitors to Ghana has grown considerably. This development needs to be viewed in light of the emergent Ghanaian tourism industry, which is an important sector of the national economy, ranking third after the production of cocoa and gold. Huge efforts are being made to turn Ghana into a prime tourist destination in the West African subregion. Given the high concentration of slave trade relics in the form of European fortifications along the Ghanaian coast line, African American heritage or 'roots' tourism is singled out as the most important niche market in this sector.[7]

For the majority of people from the Diaspora who are coming to Ghana, the slave trade does indeed serve as the key point of historical reference that motivates their journey. The experience of the slave sites may provide a sense of emotional catharsis to those who are seeking to link up with their African past. This experience, however, is not achieved independently of the infrastructural and representational parameters that are provided by the tourist industry: Destinations are being created by identifying sites and making them accessible – both in physical and narrative terms. In the resulting pilgrimage, tourism's commercial and commemorative aspects are therefore always closely intertwined.[8]

Thus it comes as no surprise that by the mid-1990s, communities outside Cape Coast overtly began to claim their own share in the history of slavery and the slave trade. International initiatives such as the UNESCO Slave Route Project have helped to raise the public awareness that the slave trade had not only affected the coastal areas but had also relied on a network of slave routes that stretched far into the interior. The powerful imagery of gangs of slaves being marched down to the coast has for a long time served as a key icon of visual as well as performative representations of the slave trade. It can be found in the exhibition 'Crossroads of People, Crossroads of Trade' at the Cape Coast Castle, and it is also central to a number of theatrical performances that narrate the story of the slave trade.[9] Yet, for quite some time, most Diasporan visitors did not venture on the trip to the northern part of Ghana.[10] The time limit of organized tours rarely exceeds fourteen days, and itineraries are tight even without tourists' travelling the 900 km up north. Besides, the bulk of investments in tourism infrastructure has for a long time concentrated on the south, thus further cutting the already deprived North from economic upswing.

To counter this trend, from 1996 onward the USAID-sponsored 'Community-Based Ecotourism Initiative' has attempted to develop small-scale tourist programmes in which the northern relics of the slave trade feature as 'attractions' alongside the opportunity to experience 'beautiful scenery' and 'unique architecture' or 'traditional drumming and dancing'. These initiatives, however, address mainly the target group of European and American backpackers and students, and not so much the more affluent African American heritage tourists, who are mostly middle-aged and of a middle-class background, expecting a higher standard in terms of accommodation, food, and so forth. The 2001 visit of the African American delegation to Paga-Nania therefore marked a new trend in heritage tourism in Ghana, which has since gained ground. Efforts are now being made to incorporate northern slave sites into the framework of pilgrimage tourism and thereby to offer them to a Diasporan audience. As a senior officer of the Ghana Tourist Board commented enthusiastically on the Panafest-event:

> [When] it comes to marketing the slave-trade heritage, northern towns such as Paga have a lot to offer. (. . .) Beyond the subliminal spiritual significance [of the pilgrimage] lies the economic potential. (. . .) Northern Ghana's linkage with the Trans-Atlantic slave trade is too strong to be taken lightly. From Sandema to Yendi, Gwollu to Nalerigu the landscape is replete with relics. (Akpabli 2001)

What is striking in this statement is the fact that all the sites that are mentioned, including the Pikworo camp in Paga, are primarily connected to the slave raids of the Zabarima-traders Babatu and Samori in the late nineteenth century. By that time, the transatlantic slave trade had already been abolished for a few decades; the British slave-trading activity officially ceased in 1807, France followed in 1848, and Brazil, which was reluctant to abolish the lucrative business, was forced to do so in 1852. Even though the official abolition did not lead to a complete halt in slaving activities but rather resulted in an increase in illegal slave exports in some areas, the eventual ending of the institution of slavery in the Americas also marked the end of the transatlantic slave trade.[11] In the British colonies, this was done in 1834, in the United States in 1865, and finally in Brazil in 1888. By then, the industrial revolution had changed the face of the Euro-American economy, and the major European powers began their scramble for Africa in order to facilitate direct colonial exploitation. However, the inner-African slave trade went on for a longer period. In Asante and the Northern territories of the Gold Coast, laws on the emancipation of slaves were passed as late as 1908, with the institution of slavery still operating illegally at least up to 1928 (cf Perbi 2004:193, 205).

Although the slave sites in Northern Ghana are primarily related to the slave raids of the late nineteenth century, the earlier transatlantic slave trade had made its impact here, too. Mossi and Hausa traders operated in those areas long before Samori and Babatu entered the historical stage (cf Der 1998). After its defeat against the Asante Empire in the eighteenth century, the Dagomba kingdom was forced to pay an annual tribute of 2,000 slaves to Asante. While some historians claim that the majority of those slaves were retained in the Asante army (cf Ward 1966), others maintain that a great number were sold to European traders along the coast, from where they continued to be shipped overseas (cf Boahen 1992). Nevertheless, in the areas that were affected, such as the ones mentioned by the representative of the Ghana Tourist Board (Akpabli 2001), this earlier history fades before the more recent experiences of the raids of Samori's and Babatu's troupes, whose captives were fed mainly into the African slave market.

In my interviews with groups of elders in a number of villages in Ghana's Upper Eastern, Northern, and Upper Western Regions, it turned out that some people's memory of those slave raids was still very vivid.[12] There were various stories about family members who had been captured but managed to escape and return, and about others who had been finally displaced. Sites of resistance against the slave raiders were known and were often connected to shrines with great spiritual significance. In a similar vein, some spirits of the enslaved were said to still be able to cause havoc and misfortune in affected families and needed to be appeased through sacrifices or special funeral arrangements. All these incidents were related to the more recent experience of slave raids that lay only one or two generations away from the narrator.

In the official representations of the history of slavery in northern Ghana, as they are presented by the Ghana Tourist Board via local tour guides, this fact is either downplayed or ignored. Even though Samori and Babatu are acknowledged as the main agents of the slave raids, it is regularly stated that all captives were taken down south, and eventually to the coast. Cape Coast and Elmina Castles, the most well-known relics of the transatlantic slave trade in Ghana, are frequently mentioned as the slaves' final destination. This version of history is compatible with a certain strand of Afrocentric interpretations of the past, which follows a Manichaean logic of black victimhood (in some contexts coupled with resistance) and white agency in inflicting atrocity. The following incident is indicative of this ideological position. During my fieldwork, I was told by several employees of the Ghanaian Ministry of Tourism about a white American Peace Corps volunteer at Pikworo camp who helped in the restoration and presentation of the site. Her presence provoked fierce reactions on the part of members of an African American tour group who accused her of appropriating *their* history: 'This is my home. Who are you to tell me about this history?'[13] Similar reactions are known from African Americans at the coastal slave dungeons, where a sense of ancestral presence is often generated among Diasporan visitors (cf Bruner 1996; Schramm 2004a). To them, just as to the local populations around the northern slave sites, the past is not closed yet; the spirits of the enslaved are still roaming, so to speak. But they address different pasts altogether, even if these pasts can be said to have been violent and painful in both cases. The attempted fusion of these strands of memory and practices of commemoration into one narrative is indicative of a particular heritage conception that tries to cut out ambiguity and tension. Yet, as the conflict at Pikworo indicates, this strategy, while working in some contexts has serious limitations in others. In the following sections, I discuss these dynamics further by looking at the two heritage initiatives that are most influential in the current discourse on the slave trade in Ghana.

The Slave Route: Preserving the Memory of the Slave Trade for Humanity

The UNESCO international project 'The Slave Route' was launched in 1994.[14] Based on the assumption that the slave trade 'is barely present in humanity's collective memory and history books', the project aims at breaking that silence and according the (transatlantic) slave trade its proper place as 'the greatest tragedy in human history' (Diène 1998:1). The stated aim of the project is it to arrive at 'a kind of collective catharsis to move things from tragedy to life' (ibid.). Thus, through its commemoration, the experience of the slave trade as 'the ultimate symbol of violence' ought to be turned into a guarantor for 'lasting peace' among the nations (Mayor n.d.:4). Three areas are listed as main fields of activity: scientific research, education, and, last but not least, cultural tourism.

To facilitate the research component of the project, several conferences were hosted by UNESCO that brought together an international scientific committee comprising historians, archaeologists, anthropologists, economists, museum workers, and artists. Funding has been made available to identify and preserve relics of the slave trade on the three continents involved – Africa, the Americas, and Europe (lately including the Indian Ocean islands).[15] Museums have been encouraged to mount exhibitions on the slave trade – the Ghana National Museum, for example, now hosts a permanent display on the slave route. In addition to these motions, the Slave Trade Archives Project was inaugurated in 1999 as part of UNESCO's 'Memory of the World' programme, with the aim of keeping the existing written documents on the slave trade for posterity. The educational projects pursued with the help of UNESCO involve the revision of school books and the provision of new learning materials, such as films and comic books that should inform children on the historical atrocity of the slave trade.

The most visible aspect of the project is that of cultural tourism. Here, just as in the educational project, the results of scientific research ought to be made accessible to a wider audience. The act of remembrance, restricted to the identification, preservation, and eventual display of slave-trade related locations, items, and stories, is linked to development concerns that are most pressing to the contemporary societies that still suffer from the impact of the slave trade, especially in Africa and the Caribbean. Through tourism, much-needed revenue should be generated and investments in local economies should be encouraged. However, great emphasis is put on the demand that this endeavour should take place with constant awareness of the sensitive nature of the slave trade. For example, it is stated in the Accra Declaration on the WTO-UNESCO Cultural Tourism Programme 'The Slave Route' that the project should be carried out in such a way that the 'political, social, cultural, moral, and spiritual values of the populations concerned' (Accra Declaration 1995) not be violated.

Yet who are the populations concerned? Whose values need to be respected, and how is this to be achieved? The encompassing nature of the slave trade (both in terms of time frame and spatial scope) impinged on buyers as well as sellers, Africans as well as Europeans, blacks as well as whites, those who were taken away as well as those who remained in Africa – yet all these groups were affected in different ways and hold different, and often conflicting, historical memories. Whereas enslavement, the Middle Passage, and plantation slavery constitute central memorial *topoi* in the black diasporic public sphere, they are much less acknowledged among Europeans or white Americans. In a similar vein, in Africa itself, there is a heavy public silence with regard to the history of slavery and the slave trade (cf Schramm 2006).

It is this silence that is being addressed by the WTO-UNESCO declaration when it requests local populations to 'enhance their awareness of the cultural heritage of the slave trade' (Accra Declaration 1995). But, as the situation in Ghana suggests, silence does not necessarily mean a complete lack of awareness; on the contrary. For a long time, slavery has been a very significant constituent of social and economic life. Today, many families, especially in the Ghanaian South have members who are descendants of former slaves. Although there is no reference to slave descent in the daily interactions of people, it becomes a major factor in struggles for power and can be a cause of violent chieftaincy disputes. Besides, there is a huge difference in perception of the slave trade between the southern and northern parts of the country and between such groups that were mainly victimized and those who profited. Consequently, as Emmanuel Akyeampong has argued, 'to bring slavery and its legacy within the realm of public discussion threatens national integration in recently independent countries' (2001:1). Because of that complex situation, the memory of slavery remains often confined to private knowledge or to nonverbal means of discourse such as ritual practices and spirit landscapes that have become remarkably transformed by the insecurity and disorder that came about with the slave trade (cf Shaw 2002). These processes indicate that the history of the slave trade is not just a thing of the past to be put on display for educational purposes. It cannot be sufficiently grasped by a cultural heritage approach.

In recent years, UNESCO has made several attempts to move away from its previous focus on monuments, since this definition of heritage tends to privilege a Eurocentric perspective and furthermore to freeze the past in monumental time-scope, clearly set apart from the present (cf Herzfeld 1991). New emphasis has been put on the concept of cultural landscapes, which represent the 'combined works of nature and man' and exemplify their interrelation. Moreover, the focus on 'intangible heritage' has become a promising new direction in the heritage conceptions of museum workers and cultural politicians alike – oral histories, religious practices, and a diversity of values are viewed as important aspects of World Heritage that deserve special protection. UNESCO has mounted an entire new programme on the concept of intangible cultural riches. In this framework, 'intangible heritage' is defined as part of a living culture that entails a strong link with the past through its transmission and constant recreation from generation to generation. It is said to provide communities and groups with a sense of identity and continuity in the face of the homogenizing forces of globalization.[16] The objective of all these initiatives is in line with the UNESCO policy of promoting human rights and sustainable development. From this perspective, 'diversity' appears as a value in itself through which tolerance and mutual respect can be achieved.[17]

The 'Slave Route', just like the 'Silk Route', which was the focus of a previous UNESCO initiative, is presented as one such cultural landscape. The UNESCO standards for the recognition of such formations as World Heritage imply the notions of 'outstanding universal value' and representativity (UNESCO 1999). Consequently, the memory work that the project attempts to stimulate addresses the whole of humanity, thereby potentially erasing all differences between victims and perpetrators, or rather between their descendants and their varying political and emotional positions toward that history. Of course, owing to the inherent complexity of the slave trade(s) and slavery institution(s), any easy dichotomy fails to grasp the various interrelations and entangled histories that make the slave trade an important aspect of contemporary reality (cf Gilroy 1993; Thornton 1998). The UNESCO approach, however, does not give sufficient credit to this contemporary relevance either. The fact that the Slave Route is presented on the same conceptual and institutional level as the Silk Route, which has had a completely different impact on economic, sociopolitical, and cultural relations, indicates a distinctive heritage approach on the part of UNESCO, whereby history is treated as a cultural asset and not so much as a powerful political force. This is not to say that the attempt to bring the issue of the slave trade to light and to encourage its public recognition (and that of its victims) is wrong from the start; on the contrary. Yet the problem that remains unresolved is that which is also faced by many of the Truth and Reconciliation Commissions that have recently sprung up in the aftermath of so many instances of political violence: Truth and justice do not always go hand in hand; reconciliation is not always desired by all parties involved; and forgiveness is not easily achieved (cf Holiday 1998).

The UNESCO outlook misses another important element in the contemporary politics of representation associated with the slave trade – namely, the formation of specific group identities and the (re-)construction as well as contestation of strict community boundaries alongside its commemoration. For example, the demand for repatriation and reparations, as voiced by many Diasporans who actually come to Ghana, moves the significance of the past from the symbolic to the concrete. At the same time, it is a source of ongoing tension – not only within the heterogeneous group of the travellers themselves but also between Ghanaian and Diasporan as well as Euro-American stakeholders. Those dimensions are not entailed in the UNESCO approach.

The Joseph Project: Reaching Out to the Diaspora

The second official narrative that I want to examine in more detail, the so-called Joseph Project, also attempts to create a memorial community, but from a quite different perspective. Not humanity per se is being addressed here but rather the racialized black 'family' that ought to come together and reconcile under the prophetic sign of the biblical story of Joseph (Genesis 37:1–50, 26).[18] By making those explicit references to the notion of an African (black) family, the Joseph Project partly leans on the discursive tradition of radical pan-Africanism. Its wider purpose, however, is more connected to the attempt of the Ghanaian state to raise its international profile as well as to its domestic party politics.[19] Inaugurated in 2003, the project is the outcome of a personal initiative by the then Ghanaian Minister of Tourism, Jake O. Obetsebi-Lamptey. At first sight, it falls in line with a number of other programmes that were all put in place by the previous NDC-government.[20] Panafest and Emancipation Day, the most visible of these programmes, have, in the words of the Minister himself, 'become magnets to draw attention to Ghana as the gateway for African self-rediscovery and spiritual awakening' (Programme 2005). Yet the Joseph Project proclaims to go further than that – and thereby attempts to dissociate itself from too close an association with the NDC-regime. In 2007, the 200th anniversary of the British abolition of the transatlantic slave trade coincided with the 50th anniversary of Ghana's independence, and the association between abolition and independence was clearly made. Consequently, the Joseph Project combines notions of pilgrimage, commemoration, and cathartic healing with the celebration of African excellence and the appeal to the Diaspora to contribute to the continent's economic advancement.

Even though calls to 'come home and invest' have been voiced from the very beginning of the homecoming-drive, the biblical framing of the project gives it a remarkable twist that distinguishes it from previous endeavours to reach out to the Diaspora. First of all, the explicit Christian bias reflected in the name of the project has been harshly criticized by Ghanaian neotraditionalist groups such as Mission Afrikania (cf De Witte 2004) and other pan-Africanist organizations and individuals, who perceived it to be a deviation from the ideal of African self-reliance. They preferred a more 'African' name and demanded a clear distinction from any European references. Partly in reaction to those criticisms, the overarching ceremonial framework is now called 'Akwaaba Anyemi', a linguistic creation made up of two Ghanaian languages, Twi and Ga, which can be translated as 'Welcome Sibling'.

However, despite these changes (made strategically, in order not to offend the sensibilities of potential visitors), the narrative of Joseph remains the keystone of the entire project. Hence Joseph, the favourite son of Israel, who was sold by his own brothers into slavery, only to later forgive them and save his family from starvation, is turned into a role model for African Americans. The slavery past is reinterpreted as a tragedy that can nevertheless be turned into the basis for a meaningful future. History appears as destiny: 'Now do not be distressed or blame yourselves for selling me into slavery here; it was to save lives that God sent me ahead of you' (Genesis 45:5).[21]

On the homepage of the Ghanaian Ministry of Tourism, this passage is reinterpreted as follows:

> We must . . . gather . . . strength from [the slave trade] and lay to rest the disturbed spirits of our ancestors who have never known peace. (. . .) Those of us who believe in the promise of God to Africa, take our hope from the story of Joseph in the Bible. For we believe that God loved Joseph and yet saw him cast into the hell of slavery and brought out in triumph. (Jake O. Obetsebi-Lamptey)[22]

Contemporary African Americans are called on as the 'true Josephs' whose responsibility lies in supporting their African brothers (and sisters). Yet, whereas the biblical Joseph took his family to Egypt, the land of the slaveholders, the 'Josephs of today' are called on to return home, that is, to come to Africa, and Ghana in particular. The Joseph Project promises to offer long-term perspectives for repatriation, as, for example, through visa exemptions for members of the Diaspora.[23] However, its main feature is annual pilgrimages along the Slave Route. In one of my interviews with the then Minister of Tourism, he stated:

> The same way you go to Mecca – at the end of it you are supposed to get to salvation, you've been through it, so now you are closer to heaven. So when you've been through all this, you should come out of it with a real feeling of self-value and a rediscovery of self.[24]

The pilgrimage is designed as a circle, emphasizing its cathartic symbolism. It starts from the (in)famous slave castles along the coast, 'hallowed memorials of an agonized past' (Programme 2005), then stretches into the interior, up north, before returning to the coast.

Assin Manso

After passing Cape Coast and Elmina, the first stage of the journey is Assin Manso, a town that, according to W. E. F. Ward, served as one of the largest eighteenth-century slave markets (Ward 1966:88). Ward's book *The History of Ghana* and his reference to Assin Manso as the 'great depot' through which the Asante sent their slaves down to the coast, is regularly used by tour guides as proof for the status of Assin Manso as a major slave market. This use of the written word is quite telling with regard to the dynamics of representation that I am discussing here. Writing, even by a British historian, is often regarded as an authorization of oral tradition(s). Yet such scholarly verification is not the only source by which a historical narrative is inscribed onto a place: Performative aspects and active spatial reformations are as important in this meaning-making process.

In 1998, Assin Manso was re-inscribed onto the map of African-diasporic historical imagination through the reburial of two slave ancestors (one from Jamaica, one from the United States) as part of the Emancipation Day ceremony. A central aspect of the iconography through which Assin Manso asserts its status as an important pilgrimage site is the existence of the Nnonkonsuo (or Slave River). Here, it is claimed, slaves took their last bath on African soil before being marched down to the slave castles of Elmina and Cape Coast along the coast.[25] Since the initial event, Diasporan travellers have come every year to the river to establish a closer linkage with their ancestors (cf Schramm 2004a).

Under the new umbrella of the Joseph Project, the whole site underwent some radical transformations. The area around the river and the graves has been fenced, and entrance fees are imposed. A 'Garden of Reverence' has been laid out, complete with a 'Hall of Prayer', a 'Wall of Return', where each visitor can etch his or her name (for a fee), and a 'Meditation Lawn'. The outer walls of the reverential garden have been decorated with scenes from the times of the slave trade: the northern raids, the punishments, the bath in the river, the selling to the Europeans, and, not to be omitted, a replica of the technical drawing of a slave ship, black body squeezing against black body, the whole design laid out with a perverse sense of economic efficiency. From the inside, the same wall serves as a portrait gallery of pan-African heroes: W. E. B. DuBois, Frederick Douglass, Kwame Nkrumah, and others look down at the visitors and remind them of their achievements. Two sides of a medal: The pain and suffering of the ancestors appear as the prerequisite for the eventual resurrection of their descendants. The commemoration of the traumatic past is thus literally turned into a celebration of the future.

However, the local population is now almost excluded from the site.[26] Formerly, the area around the river was regarded as a sacred grove, and because of that it was also separated from its surroundings. No farming activity was allowed, and access to it was limited to ritual experts who would sacrifice to the river God. With the recent developments, those local religious associations

Figure 3.1 Garden of Reverence, Assin Manso (photograph: Katharina Schramm)

have given way to a new notion of sacred space that is linked to the memory of the transatlantic slave system. As Barima Kwame Nkyi XII, paramount chief of the Assin Traditional Area, stated: 'During our festival, we went to the river to sacrifice. Now we are doing that during Emancipation Day'.[27] However, during Emancipation Day 2005, when the reverential garden was first opened to the public, the townspeople of Assin Manso were rigorously kept out of the enclosed area until the delegations of African Americans, local dignitaries, and governmental representatives had finished their rounds. When they were eventually allowed in, even they suddenly viewed the site through the lens of the 'tourist gaze', detached from their everyday social experience and consciousness (Urry 1990:2). Walking across the 'Meditation Lawn', they searched for signs of the Diasporan presence, appreciating the new ceremonial architecture and studying the inscriptions on the wreaths that had been left by the various delegations. Their curiosity was directed at a site that now symbolically 'belonged' to somebody else, even though the community is supposed to benefit economically from the revenue generated through pilgrimage tourism.[28] The ambiguity that had characterized the Nnonkonsuo as a sacred space that could accommodate a multiplicity of meanings, *including* the promise of catharsis and emotional uplift for Diasporan travellers, has now given way to a seemingly unequivocal, monumental historical representation.

Salaga

Similar developments are to be expected for the slave sites that are located further north and form part of the pilgrimage route. At Salaga, one of the principal slave markets of the nineteenth century (cf Akurang-Parry 2001; Der 1998; Johnson 1986), a large visitor reception facility is under construction. At present, the market site is used as a filling station, and the only hint at its former significance is a recently erected signboard that says 'Welcome to Salaga slave market'. The big Baobab tree to which slaves used to be chained fell in a storm in 1970. Nineteen years later, it was replaced by a younger tree that now provides some shade at the edge of the market. To the Ministry of Tourism, however, this replacement is not sufficient: 'If Salaga was really such a great centre for slavery, I don't believe it was just one tree to which the slaves were chained. So we want to plant a few full-grown Baobab trees to indicate that this was the place where the trading went on'.[29] Plans exist for the area to be cleaned up and fenced, with benches being provided for the tourists to rest.

Today, there is still a vivid memory of the time when the town was a striving market centre, where slaves were sold alongside cattle, horses, salt, and, most

Figure 3.2 'Welcome to Salaga Slave Market', Salaga (photograph: Katharina Schramm)

importantly, kola nuts. On request, visitors are taken to an old woman whose father used to keep slaves himself. She still owns the shackles with which, according to her, only 'stubborn slaves' were chained.[30] I was told that African Americans would 'give her money and valuable things' just to hear her story.[31] The significance of the fact that she is a descendent of a slave dealer fades before the strong perception that Salaga, even though a site of denigration and suffering for the people who were sold here, could indeed be the missing link for those who are searching for their roots.

The 2005 weblog of Kwadwo Fodwoɔ Gyase, an African American traveller to Ghana, documented his return-journey, which also took him to Salaga:

> Here is Salaga. Where mothers are torn from children and children sold from mothers. The paths WE took to arrive here are too numerous to name. (...) The Path. What paths lie ahead for those of US who return to walk this sacred earth in body and in spirit? In face of the uncertainty that comes with reflecting on days not yet here, i am comforted by knowing the Ancestors are indeed walking with me. i know they have lead me to this place ... calling my hands, heart, and mind to do the fertile work that needs to be done: Healing, awakening, inspiring, restoring, bringing together, building, uprooting, destroying, and avenging – all for Our people, Afrikan people.[32]

At first sight, his perception of Salaga (and the routes by which it is connected to other slave sites, such as Paga, Saakpuli, and Assin Manso) appears to be in line with the transatlantic interpretation offered by the Ministry of Tourism. The commemorative community that he rhetorically constructs is one that encompasses all African people, just as references to the 'African family' are characteristic of the official rhetoric. But whereas the Ghanaian government, through the Ministry of Tourism, opts for a reconciliatory tone that supposedly does not offend anybody, the addressees of Gyase's report are located in the Diaspora and belong to a specific political grouping to whom the notion of 'avenge' (against the 'white death bringers', ibid.) is intrinsically connected to the promise of 'healing'.[33] This radical turn is certainly not intended by Ghanaian tourism officials (who have an interest in attracting a broader group of tourists, including Europeans and white Americans), but it can partly be seen as a consequence of the highly emotional presentation of the slave route. Though dominant, the transatlantic narrative is far from being harmonious and homogeneous and rather opens up new fields of conflict that are not easily contained.

When Gyase invokes the ancestors as a guiding force in his search for roots and a future 'path', he refers to those who were enslaved and shipped away. If one looks at the memories of the people who were affected by the slave trade on the continent, a very different picture emerges that defies any such straightforward relationship with the formerly enslaved.

Internal Routes, Entangled Relations

From Salaga, slaves were taken in different directions down to the Asante-kingdom or into Togoland, by then a German colony. Some of the slaves stayed in the area, which today results in very complex kinship ties. Slave masters could have many wives, including slaves, some of whom in their turn remarried after slavery was abolished. Today, the descendants of those different relationships may consider one another as relatives. For example, my host in Bolgatanga one day related to me that his grandmother had been sold as a slave in Salaga and got married to his grandfather only after she had regained her freedom. Referring to a friend of mine, whose family originates in Tamale (not far from Salaga), he told me that Abdul and his brothers were the great-grandchildren of his grandmother and her former master and that they belong to the former master's family. When I asked Abdul about this story, he confirmed by saying, 'yes, we call him our grandfather!'.[34] Whereas the relationship of those two families was characterized by respect, my host's grandmother's family rejected her children's descendants when one of them went to Burkina Faso to 'trace his roots': 'They said: "Who are you? Our daughter was taken away, so we don't know [what happened to her]. Who are you to say you are her child?" There was no dowry paid, the customary rites have not been performed, so they didn't accept him'.[35] The violent abduction of their daughter did not lead them to openly embrace her offspring; on the contrary.

Thus, while the descendants of former masters and slaves often share a given social space, there does not seem to exist a 'victim's tale' or a sense of solidarity with those who, in the terminology of contemporary public discourse, lost their home and try to recover it. Gyase's and other African Americans' expectations about the unequivocal guiding power of the ancestors are not necessarily mirrored by the experiences (and interests) of their African counterparts.

In official discourse, the entire history of internal displacement, reconnection, and rejection is not made the subject of discussion but is completely ignored. Instead, places such as Salaga are presented exclusively within the transatlantic framework. Thus, on the homepage of the Ministry of Tourism, under the caption 'Salaga Slave Markets and Wells', one reads: 'Over the last five years, Ghana's historians and archeologists have been carrying out a major project to identify the "Slave Route": those areas where captives were hunted *and the routes by which they were marched to the coast*'.[36] The coast, and by association the slave ship, become the only points of reference through which a linkage with the Diaspora is established. The suffering of the slaves is given new meaning by the return of their American descendants. Present-day internal divisions, as they exist in Ghana along the line of slave descent, are either ignored or denied through an oversimplified notion of slave incorporation. This narrative strategy is employed in order to construct firm boundaries between those who suffered and those who gained, which again form the backbone of the image of black racial solidarity to which the Joseph Project explicitly refers.

The Motif of Resistance

Just as the pilgrimage is carried out in a circle, history is also being presented as a circle in which rupture and fragmentation give way to healing and harmony. Yet, as the quotation from Kwadwo Fodwoɔ Gyase has indicated, not everybody who is addressed by the Joseph Project fully shares this view. Even if there is a general trend to portray the history of the slave trade as one of black victims and white perpetrators, there are also instances in which African Americans express bitterness and anger about the fact that they were sold by their 'own brothers and sisters'.[37]

Within the representational framework of the Joseph Project, this accusation is responded to by a strong emphasis on the motif of defiance. Gwollu, a town that was under siege by the troupes of Samori Touré, is among those

Figure 3.3 Moru Kuala, elder of Gwollu, posing in front of the Defence Wall in his father's battle dress (photograph: Katharina Schramm)

places that are singled out as sites of resistance. Here, the townspeople erected a defense wall that could not be surmounted by the slave raiders. Nearby, a museum structure has been put up with the help of the Canadian High Commission. Plans exist for community members to donate items, such as weapons and war dresses that are still in possession of individual families, to be exhibited in the museum. Whereas the secretary to the Gwollu chief was very positive about this move and said that everybody would be happy to donate, the people who actually own the things were more than reluctant to agree to the museum plans.[38] To most of them, those objects were sacred and linked historical memory with religious connotations. One old man told me that his father's war dress, with which he had fought in battle, was still highly spiritually charged. Before putting it on, he had to perform a sacrifice, and this obligation also applied to his descendants when wearing it. When I asked him if he would be prepared to give it away, he answered: 'No, we need it to protect ourselves! When in the night the need arises, how am I going to get it?'[39] The idea of a museum display, where objects and their history would be carefully stored away and put in a showcase for tourists to see, is not viable for those who consider them as part of their family inheritance and who believe in the spiritual power of the ancestors.[40]

Another site of resistance is Sandema, where people were able to defeat Babatu's troupes. Today, the weapons that were seized in that battle are kept inside a shrine (*fisa*), whose resident spirit, so it is said, had supported the townspeople and led them to victory. Until today, Builsa people commemorate Babatu's defeat in one of their dances, which is performed during festival time. This motif of resistance, even though it lies outside the transatlantic frame of reference, nevertheless coincides with important diasporic memorial tropes, such as the references to Maroon societies or the Underground Railroad. The historically differentiated resistance is currently being transferred to a more general level, opening up the space for a number of interpretations. The recounting of Babatu's defeat as it is offered in the dance performance or in the stories surrounding the *fisa*-shrine emphasize local agency and can therefore be usefully accommodated in the dominant narrative of a black commonality (facing an enemy from the outside). Still, the answer to the question of European involvement, as it was given to me by a group of elders at the *fisa*-shrine, reveals a greater historical complexity, denied in official discourse: 'There was no relationship between the raiders and white people. During that time, the white people were not among the raiders. But when they came, they were against slave raiding and slavery (*yom tere*)'.[41]

In other contexts, however, especially among the younger generation, the idea of white people as not only slave traders but raiders has recently become part of the transmission of oral history. TV images (for example, derived from the screening of *Roots* on Ghana's national station, GTV), fragmented schoolbook knowledge, and the various media reports on cultural events involving Diasporan participation provide a combined source for the refashioning of oral traditions in the context of tourist representation.[42] Moreover, local authorities in the affected communities have also adopted the dominant discourse in order to tap the economic potential expected from heritage-tourism. For example, during a durbar that was performed on the occasion of Emancipation Day 2004, the paramount chief of the Gwollu Traditional Area, Kuoro Buktie Limann, gave a speech in which he demanded reparation for the slave trade from 'countries who benefited from the trade'.[43] Such statements help to turn the transatlantic theme into a kind of self-fulfilling prophecy: The fact that people come and want to hear a particular story, in combination with the actual staging of the pilgrimage, gives it credibility – at least in its own, limited scope.

The outlook of the Joseph Project is one that wants to bring the past to closure. This desire becomes particularly clear in the last leg of the journey, which leads back to the coast, to the slave forts. One of them, James Fort, which until recently has been used as a state prison, is currently redesigned to host an exhibition of the 'African Excellence Experience'. The museum will be dedicated to 'those Africans in all walks of life . . . who triumphed and continue to triumph over those who sought to enchain them . . . a monument to the true Josephs' (Programme 2005). The reinterpretation of the slave forts from a place of terror to a site of glorification exemplifies the interplay of memory and forgetting that is at work in the pilgrimage. The slave sites are being transformed into shrines where affective rituals are performed in order to draw the visitors into a homogeneously conceived commemorative community. In my conclusion, I pay closer attention to the dynamics behind this kind of historical representation.

Conclusion: Giving Meaning to the Past

The UNESCO Slave Route Project and the Joseph Project have different outlooks. Whereas the former focuses on humanity in general, the latter's focus is on the 'Black family'. UNESCO's approach is more academic, involving archaeological, historical, and anthropological research alongside cultural tourism; the Joseph Project is above all a tourism venture. When I spoke with a member of the advisory board to the Joseph Project who is at the same time involved in the Slave Route Project as an archaeological expert, he denied that the former was of any scientific value – in contrast to the UNESCO endeavour.[44]

Nevertheless, both projects share a heritage-conception in which the past is principally renarrated with the intention of eventually leaving it behind – to achieve 'lasting peace' (UNESCO) or 'healing' (Joseph Project). In the course of creating one dominant narrative that leads straight from cause to effect and further to a 'lesson' for generations to come, other streams of memory that do not immediately fit into the storyline are relegated to the side.

For example, whereas his military operations are remembered as disastrous in those parts of northern Ghana where his troupes engaged in slave raiding and trading, Samori Touré also fought vigorously against the French colonial troupes and could therefore, by the very logic of pan-African ideology, be incorporated into the ancestral gallery of those who resisted European or white control. This ambiguity also applies to the way in which Europeans are remembered in northern Ghana – on the one hand, as shown above, they are known to have assisted local populations in their fight against the slave raiders; on the other hand, they are remembered for the introduction of a system of forced labour and forced military recruitment that was experienced as a continuation of slavery by other means.[45]

The transatlantic framework, as it appears within the Joseph Project, leaves no room for such differentiations. Instead, it reproduces a specific Afrocentric discourse that is quite popular among the target group of African American pilgrims/tourists. Here, a sense of racial solidarity is maintained through a clear distinction between black and white positions in the historical narrative. Through the representation of Samori and Babatu as henchmen of European slave masters, this racialized logic is upheld. It is confirmed in the performance of the pilgrimage that is oriented toward the creation of highly emotional moments. Just as the reverential garden in Assin Manso is secluded from its surroundings, the sense of catharsis that is hoped and planned for in the pilgrimage is limited to a particular event and place.

A similar effect is produced in the UNESCO approach, where the musealization and connected objectification of the slave trade also leads to a situation in which the past appears as a 'foreign country' (L. P. Hartley, referred to in Lowenthal 1985), the relics of which can be retrieved, collected, and put on display for public consumption. The UNESCO project claims to consider the slave trade in an all-encompassing way – by looking at every party involved and by paying attention not only to its painful aspects but also to the creative contributions of African slaves to the cultures (and economies) of the Americas and Europe. However, there are also interpretative filters at work: First, the emphasis on creativity fits in very well with the general cultural policy of UNESCO (cf De Cuéllar 1998); second, the nonreconciliatory stance of groups of slave-descendants is not even acknowledged.

Both projects create narratives of communal identity around the notion of catharsis, only with a different scope in mind. As I have demonstrated, these narrative strategies tend to ignore other discourses that do not fit into the dominant interpretative framework of either the promotion of a culture of peace in the name of humanity as a whole or the constitution of black commonality in a pan-African perspective. Yet far from being completely obscured, those other discourses shine through the closely knit fabric of official historical representation(s).

Finally, I argue that this entire system of representation is fluid and dynamic – dominant and marginal discourses not only intersect but sometimes also intermingle. If, for example, one considers how the public debate on slavery has developed in the United States, one can see a transformation having taken place since the 1960s. From being confined to the exclusive space of a black counter-public,[46] which was formed outside (and against) the dominant white bourgeois social structure that had forcefully excluded black people from the *polis* – first through slavery and later by means of segregation and the Jim Crow laws – the centrality of this subject is now recognized in wider circles.

Not only have issues surrounding Africa and the slave trade found an even broader resonance among black Americans, but they have also entered the sphere of mainstream media and political debate. A formerly subaltern discourse has now become part of the dominant public sphere – even though this does not mean that it would have reached full recognition in its midst. The debate over reparations is a case in point. Even though reparations have not been granted to African Americans, there is a growing public awareness of the fact that reparations do indeed constitute *an issue* to be dealt with. As bills have been brought before parliament/congress and lawsuits have been filed against companies that profited from the slave trade, one can no more speak of a mere counter-discourse.

Now that this debate is transferred to Ghana via the homecoming movement, yet another dimension begins to unfold. As the Ghanaian state takes up the rhetoric of pilgrimage, it pushes African American interpretations of history to the fore. At the same time, there is hardly any discussion on a national level over the significance of that history *for Ghanaian society*.[47] Thus, in the process of its publicization, the memory of slavery and the slave trade becomes completely externalized. Strikingly, this official strategy is applied not only to Diasporan visitors (whose emotions are readily being tapped but are rarely shared) but also to the perception of local memory as an authenticating resource through which the expectations of the tourists/pilgrims can be met. It is presented as a story that is best listened to 'from the horse's own mouth',[48] but only within the carefully structured framework of a guided tour. Such tours, however, are not completely controlled by tourism officials. They rather constitute a forum in which different actors constantly negotiate and remould their position toward the past as well as toward one another. In the process of the incorporation of local memories into the distinct heritage approaches followed by UNESCO or the Ghanaian Ministry of Tourism – and, not to be forgotten, those by Diasporan pilgrims/tourists – these memories and the oral traditions in which they are expressed do not remain the same but are also transformed.

The slave routes form a network with many nodal points where different discursive streams criss-cross and feed into one another. Alongside the dominant narrative, other stories continue to exist, and new ones are being created. Even though the commemorative evocation of the past, as it is done in the ritual staging of the pilgrimage or in the museum approach followed by UNESCO, can be seen as an attempt to eventually close this chapter of history, I have shown that such closure remains an illusion.

Notes

1. This does not apply only to open racist violence but also to ongoing white privilege (cf Lipsitz 1998).
2. This public attention is mainly directed at chattel slavery and the transatlantic slave trade. For a critique of this preferential treatment of the transatlantic framework in academic studies on the African Diaspora, see Zeleza (2005).
3. This marketing effort is mainly directed at African Americans and involves West African states such as Ghana, Senegal, Gambia, and Nigeria. Strikingly, Angola, from where most slaves were transported to Brazil, has not (yet) engaged in this type of heritage tourism.
4. *The Independent*, 20/07/2001; available online: www.ghanaweb.com/GhanaHomePage/NewsArchive/printnews.php?ID=16833 (download 25/06/2006).
5. Since 1972, *all* the European forts and castles along the Ghanaian coast are listed as World Heritage Sites by UNESCO. In the wake of recent tourism developments, three of them (Cape Coast and Elmina Castles, as well as Fort St. Jago) have been renovated. Owing to their prominence, it often happens that only these structures are mentioned in connection with the UNESCO list (cf Gizo 1999).
6. On Cape Coast Castle and Dungeons as heterotopic space, see Schramm (2004b).
7. Cf Ministry of Tourism (1996). Between 1992 and 1998 alone, the number of hotels in Ghana rose from 509 to 730. In the same period, tourist revenues increased from 166.90 million to 283.96 million U.S. dollars (Tourism Statistical Fact Sheet on Ghana). Even though there are no separate statistics for African American or other Diasporan arrivals available, it can be assumed that their numbers have also risen proportionally.
8. On pilgrimage tourism and the complexities of diasporic identity formations; see Schramm (2004a) and Ebron (1999), who focuses on the incorporation of homecoming into the dynamics of global capitalism.
9. For example, in 1998, a slave march was staged on the streets of Accra as part of the Emancipation Day celebrations. 'Musu: Saga of the Slaves' by the Ghana National Dance Company is another performance that employs the imagery of marching slaves (cf Schramm 2004a).
10. This marks only a general trend and does not say anything about individual journeys (cf Okofo [1999]). Moreover, educational programmes outside the tourism framework, such as the SIT 'History and Culture of the African Diaspora' programme, have for a longer time incorporated northern slave sites into their curriculum.
11. In their statistical analysis of the DuBois Institute database on the transatlantic slave trade, Eltis and Richardson (1997) show that the number of slave ships that left the Gold Coast was highest between 1787 and 1811. There is a steep decline afterward, with only little activity going on up to 1836 (around the time when slavery was abolished in the British Caribbean). By 1866, no trade in human beings can be detected for the Gold Coast in the records available. A similar trend is visible in the data on Benin and Biafra. After 1836, however, the Bight of Benin, which was

a major supply area for Portuguese slave exports, experienced a slight rise in slave voyages until around 1870, when the trade finally came to an end there as well.
12. For this project, I spent three months of fieldwork in Ghana (between January and April 2006), mainly in the Upper East Region. The research was facilitated by the Graduate School Asia and Africa in World Reference Systems at the Martin-Luther-Universität Halle-Wittenberg. My previous work on the homecoming of the African Diaspora to Ghana, for which I did fieldwork between 1995 and 2004 (see, especially, Schramm 2004d), provides additional background to my interpretation of this rather preliminary data.
13. Cf Fieldnotes 01/02/2006:7–8.
14. Cf www.unesco.org/culture/dialogue/slave/ (download 12/09/2006). On the UNESCO website on the Slave Route Project, 'the slave trade' is referred to in general terms. Nevertheless, from the content it is clear that it is the triangular trade between Europe, Africa, and America that occupies the centre stage. In addition, there are three subsections, one of which explicitly refers to 'The transatlantic slave trade', while the other two refer to 'The slave trade in the Indian Ocean' and 'Modern forms of slavery'.
15. The most spectacular result of this preservation effort so far has probably been the discovery and rescuing of the slave ship *Fredensborg* off the Norwegian coast, where it had sunk on its return from a slaving expedition to the Gold Coast and the Virgin Islands (cf Svalensen 2000).
16. Cf http://portal.unesco.org/culture; download 20/07/2006.
17. The UNESCO conception of what is considered worthy of preservation treats cultural and biological diversity as two sides of the same coin. In both cases, questions of tolerance and balance are prioritized, whereas conflictive issues that are often entailed in heritage concepts are pushed to the background. For a critical discussion of this policy with regard to controversies around the preservation of sacred groves in Benin, cf Siebert (2004).
18. Quoted after *The Revised English Bible*, Oxford University Press 1989.
19. Such strategic appropriation of pan-Africanist discourse is characteristic for Ghanaian cultural politics over the past twenty years; see Schramm 2004c.
20. In the year 2000, the ruling National Democratic Congress (NDC), a spinoff of the former military government of the Provisional National Defense Council (PNDC), was defeated by the oppositional National Patriotic Party (NPP) with John A. Kufuor as presidential candidate. Flt.-Lt. Jerry John Rawlings, the leader of the (P)NDC had ruled the country for over twenty years, at first as a military ruler and later as elected president. It was under his aegis that Ghana's connection to the African Diaspora had been revived (cf Hasty 2002).
21. Quoted after *The Revised English Bible*, Oxford University Press 1989.
22. Jake O. Obetsebi-Lamptey, www.ghanatourism.gov.gh (download 15/05/2006).
23. Whether or not this promise will be fulfilled is a matter of speculation. There have already been several attempts to ease visa restrictions and to facilitate dual citizenship, none of which has so far been put in place.
24. Interview Jake Obetsebi-Lamptey, Minister of Tourism, 08/08/2005.
25. Although Assin Manso undoubtedly was an important market, slaves who passed through here were mostly taken to the European forts at Anomabu and Kormantin (Lovejoy 2000:100), principal trading posts that do not feature as prominently

in the tourism marketing scheme and popular imagination as do the impressive structures of Elmina and Cape Coast Castles. The present prominence of Assin Manso as a slave route station is partly due to the vigorous promotion work that has been conducted by the town's Traditional Council under the leadership of Paramount Chief Barima Kwame Nkyi XII.

26. Bruner (1996:297) describes similar processes of exclusion for the case of Elmina Castle, where local people were forced to abandon their market stalls around the castle so that they would not disturb the tourists. In addition, signboards were erected announcing that entrance to the castle was prohibited to all persons except tourists. Although those have been removed by now, the general policy of exclusion still remains.
27. Interview; 11/04/2006.
28. On the social distance between pilgrims and local populations at religious shrines, see MacKevitt (1991).
29. Interview Jake Obetsebi-Lamptey, Minister of Tourism, 06/04/2006.
30. Interview Mrs. Dangana, 23/03/2006.
31. Guided tour through Salaga, 23/03/2006.
32. See: http://zitibiantoko.blogspot.com (download 30/06/2006).
33. On a different website, a discussion forum of supporters of Black Panther Activist Assata Shakur, Kwadwo Fodwoɔ Gyase has posted the announcement for the Joseph Project, as it is published on the homepage of the Ghanaian Ministry of Tourism. Cf www.assatashakur.org/forum/showthread.php?t=8123.
34. Fieldnotes 01/03/2006; 05/03/2006.
35. Fieldnotes 14/02/2006.
36. See: www.ghanatourism.gov.gh (download 15/05/2006) (my emphasis). Ward (1966:143) mentions Salaga once in connection with the transatlantic trade. As I indicated before, his book is one of the elementary texts on which current representations of the slave route within the Joseph Project are founded.
37. In fact, this pan-African sentiment is not applicable to the time in which the slave trade took place. On the contemporary construction of the 'African family', see Schramm 2004c.
38. Interview Sulley Kupah, 28/02/2006.
39. Interview Moru Kuala, Gwollu, 28/02/2006.
40. There is an internal discourse among Ghanaian Christians and Muslims alike, who classify people who adhere to traditional religion as 'locals'. This designation is at the same time denigrating and elevating – on the one hand, it indicates lower social status (lack of education and access to Western commodities); on the other hand, it specifies traditional believers as the true custodians of 'authentic culture', which is also viewed as an attractive feature in tourism marketing (see Coe 2005).
41. Interview elders at *fisa*-shrine, Sandema; 19/03/2006.
42. Note that owing to the limited time of my stay, I was also perceived as a tourist in most cases.
43. See GNA, 29/07/2004, www.ghanaweb.com/GhanaHomePage/NewsArchive/article.php?ID=62887 (download 20/07/2006).
44. Interview at Legon University of Ghana; 03/02/2006.
45. Cf Akurang-Parry (2001: 40), who demonstrates that (former) slaves were sometimes directly recruited into the colonial forces.

46. Cf Fraser (1989). For a critical discussion of the notion of counterpublics, see Squires (2002).
47. For an analysis of this situation, see Akyeampong (2001).
48. Tour of Gwollu; 28/02/2006.

Bibliography

Accra Declaration. 1995. *Accra Declaration on the WTO-UNESCO Cultural Tourism Programme 'The Slave Route,' 4 April 1995, Accra, Ghana*. Adopted on 29 April, 1995, in Durban, South Africa, by the 27th meeting of the Regional Commission for Africa of the World Tourism Organization. Paris: UNESCO.

Akpabli, K. 2001. 'A Pilgrimage to Paga', *The Tourist* Nov. 2001:n.p.

Akurang-Parry, K. O. 2001. 'Rethinking the "Slaves of Salaga": Post-Proclamation Slavery in the Gold Coast (Colonial Southern Ghana), 1874–1899', *Left History* 8(1):33–60.

Akyeampong, E. 2001. 'History, Memory, Slave-Trade and Alavery in Anlo (Ghana)', *Slavery and Abolition* 22(3):1–24.

Boahen, A. A. 1992. 'The States and Cultures of the Lower Guinean Coast'. In *UNESCO General History of Africa: Africa from the Sixteenth to the Eighteenth Century*, B. A. Ogot (ed.), pp. 399–433. Paris: UNESCO.

Bodnar, J. 1994. 'Public Memory in an American City: Commemoration in Cleveland'. In *Commemoration: The Politics of National Identity*, J. R. Gillis (ed.), pp. 74–89. Princeton, NJ: Princeton University Press.

Bruner, E. M. 1996. 'Tourism in Ghana: The Representation of Slavery and the Return of the Black Diaspora', *American Anthropologist* 98(2):290–304.

Coe, C. 2005. *Dilemmas of Culture in African Schools: Youth, Nationalism, and the Transformation of Knowledge*. Chicago: Chicago University Press.

Cole, J. 2001. *Forget Colonialism? Sacrifice and the Art of Memory in Madagascar*. Berkeley and Los Angeles: University of California Press.

De Cuéllar, J. P. (ed.). 1998. *Our Creative Diversity: Report of the World Commission on Culture and Development*. Paris: UNESCO.

Der, B. G. 1998. *The Slave Trade in Northern Ghana*. Accra: Woeli.

De Witte, M.. 2004. 'Afrikania's Dilemma: Reframing African Authenticity in a Christian Public Sphere', *Etnofoor* XVII (1,2):133–55.

Diène, D.. 1998. 'The Slave Route: A Memory Unchained', *Unesco Sources* 99 (March):1.

Ebron, P. A. 1999. 'Tourists as Pilgrims: Commercial Fashioning of Transatlantic Politics', *American Ethnologist* 26(4):910–32.

Eltis, D., and D. Richardson. 1997. 'West Africa and the Transatlantic Slave Trade: New Evidence and Long-Run Trends'. In *Routes to Slavery: Direction, Ethnicity and Mortality in the Transatlantic Slave Trade*, D. Eltis and D. Richardson (eds.), pp. 16–35. London: Frank Cass.

Fraser, N. 1989. 'Rethinking the Public Sphere: A Contribution to the Critique of Actually Existing Democracy'. In *Habermas and the Public Sphere*, C. J. Calhoun (ed.), pp. 109–42. Cambridge, MA: MIT Press.

Gilroy, P. 1993. *The Black Atlantic: Modernity and Double Consciousness*. London: Verso.

Gizo, M. A. 1999. Address delivered by the Hon. Minister of Tourism, Hon. Mike Afedi Gizo, at the formal opening of the exhibition on the finds of the slave ship Fredensborg at the National Museum, Accra, on Tuesday, 16th February, 1999. Photocopied speech, Accra.
Hasty, J. 2002. 'Rites of Passage, Routes of Redemption: Emancipation Tourism and the Wealth of Culture', *Africa Today* 49(3):47–78.
Herzfeld, M. 1991. *A Place in History: Social and Monumental Time in a Cretan Town*. Princeton, NJ: Princeton University Press.
Holiday, A. 1998. 'Forgiving and Forgetting: The Truth and Reconciliation Commission'. In *Negotiating the Past: The Making of Memory in South Africa*, S. Nuttall and C. Coetzee (eds.), pp. 43–56. Cape Town: Oxford University Press.
Johnson, M. 1986. 'The Slaves of Salaga', *Journal of African History* 27(2):341–62.
Lipsitz, G. 1998. *The Possessive Investment in Whiteness: How White People Profit from Identity Politics*. Philadelphia: Temple University Press.
Lovejoy, P. 2000. *Transformations in Slavery: A History of Slavery in Africa*. Cambridge: Cambridge University Press.
Lowenthal, D. 1985. *The Past Is a Foreign Country*. Cambridge: Cambridge University Press.
MacKevitt, C. 1991. 'San Giovanni Rotondo and the Shrine of Padre Pio'. In *Contesting the Sacred: The Anthropology of Christian Pilgrimage*, J. Eade and M. Sallnow (eds.), pp. 77–97. London: Routledge.
Mayor, F. n.d. 'Foreword'. In *The Slave Route*, pp. 3–4. Paris: UNESCO.
Ministry of Tourism. 1996. *National Tourism Development Plan for Ghana, 1996–2010: Final Report*. Accra: Ministry of Tourism.
Okofo, I. N. 1999. *Coming Home Ain't Easy, but It Sure Is a Blessing*. Cape Coast: One Afrika Tours and Speciality Services.
Perbi, A. A. 2004. *A History of Indigenous Slavery in Ghana: From the 15th to the 19th Century*. Accra: Sub-Saharan Publishers.
Programme 2005. *Panafest Emancipation Day 2005: The Re-Emergence of African Civilization: Our Heritage, Our Strength*. Tourist brochure.
Schramm, K. 2004a. 'Coming Home to the Motherland: Pilgrimage Tourism in Ghana'. In *Reframing Pilgrimage: Cultures in Motion*, J. Eade and S. Coleman (eds.), pp. 133–49. London: Routledge.
———. 2004b. 'Das Cape Coast Castle als Heterotopie: Geschichte und Gegenwart eines umstrittenen Ortes'. In *Moderne und Postkoloniale Transformation: Eine Schrift zum 60. Geburtstag von Ute Luig*, H. Dilger et al. (eds.), pp. 227–41. Berlin: Weißensee-Verlag.
———. 2004c. 'Panafricanism As a Resource: The W. E. B. DuBois Centre for Pan-African Culture, Ghana', *African Identities* 2(2):151–71.
———. 2004d. 'Struggling over the Past: The Politics of Heritage and Homecoming in Ghana.' PhD dissertation, Free University, Berlin.
———. 2006. 'The Transatlantic Slave Trade: Contemporary Topographies of Memory in Ghana and the USA', *Transactions of the Ghana Historical Society* N.S. 9:125–40.
Shaw, R. 2002. *Memories of the Slave Trade: Ritual and the Historical Imagination in Sierra Leone*. Chicago: Chicago University Press.
Siebert, U. 2004. *Heilige Wälder und Naturschutz: Empirische Fallbeispiele aus der Region Bassila, Nord-Bénin*. Münster: Lit.

Squires, C. R. 2002. 'Rethinking the Black Public Sphere: An Alternative Vocabulary for Multiple Public Spheres', *Communication Theory* 12(4):446–68.
Svalensen, L. 2000. *The Slave Ship Fredensborg*. Accra: Sub-Saharan Publishers.
Thornton, J. 1998. *Africa and Africans in the Making of the Atlantic World, 1400–1800*. Cambridge: Cambridge University Press.
UNESCO. 1999. Operational Guidelines for the Implementation of the World Heritage Convention. UNESCO. Intergovernmental Committee for the Protection of the World Cultural and Natural Heritage (WHC 99/2). Paris: UNESCO.
Urry, J. 1990. *The Tourist Gaze: Leisure and Travel in Contemporary Societies*. London: Sage.
Ward, W. E. F. 1966. *A History of Ghana*. London: George Allen and Unwin.
Werbner, R. 1998. 'Introduction. Beyond Oblivion: Confronting Memory Crisis'. In *Memory and the Postcolony: African Anthropology and the Critique of Power*, R. Werbner (ed.), pp. 1–20. London: Zed Books.
Williams, E. V. 1964. *Capitalism and Slavery*. London: Deutsch.
Zeleza, P. T. 2005. 'Rewriting the African Diaspora: Beyond the Black Atlantic', *African Affairs* 104(414):35–68.

Picturing the Past: Heritage, Photography, and the Politics of Appearance in a Yoruba City
Peter Probst

Studies on collective memory tend to see the relationship between public and popular memory in a state of permanent tension if not outright crisis (De Jorio 2006; Mbembe 2001; Werbner 1998); the focus is on 'monumental seduction', to employ Andreas Huyssen's (1999) apt phrase.[1] Displayed in oversized monuments and public architectures, the often-noted self-monumentalization of the postcolonial state and the lavish celebration of its façade are said to conceal the state's inherent weaknesses. In line with that perspective, postcolonial studies show how the state is instrumentalizing, manipulating, suppressing, and at times even abusing local memories in order to overcome its fragile and fragmented nature (Debray 1999; Hall 2000; Roberts and Nooter Roberts 2002). As a result, not only is heritage often portrayed as a simplistic, sentimentalising, and sanitized version of the past freed of major internal conflicts and contradictions in favour of a common, unifying, public heritage, but the postcolonial successors of the 'temples of empire' (Coombes 1994), which have emerged in the process of heritagization, also stand under the suspicion of being staged, fabricated, and dead (Lowenthal 1998).

Though much of this chapter can be read as a confirmation of this argument, my interest here is not in the historical sanitization of heritage but in the dynamics that have led to its formation. In other words, my starting point is not the function of heritage but its origins. Seen in this light, heritage is defined in relation to history and memory for which it acts as a substitute. It appears as a conscious arrest and framing of the presence of a past, from which modernity constantly seeks to break away (Crary 1999; Habermas 1985; Huyssen 1995). Urban life in late-nineteenth- and early-twentieth-century Europe and the United States provided the prime context for this specific experience leading not only to a proliferation of monuments but also to a series of texts commenting on this development. The respective spectrum is broad ranging, from Alois Riegl's classic study on *The Modern Cult of Monuments* (Riegl 1903), Georg Simmel's (1919) reflection on the aesthetics of ruins, and Robert Musil's (1978) ironic notes on monuments as billboards to more recent works by David Lowenthal (1996) and Pierre Nora (1989). In view of this tradition, Francois Hartog has reminded us to think of heritage

> ... less (as) a question of an obvious, assertive identity but (more as) a question of an uneasy identity that risks disappearing or is already forgotten, obliterated, or repressed: an identity in search of itself, to be exhumed, assembled, or even invented. In this way, heritage comes to define less that which one possesses, what one *has*, than circumscribing what one *is*, without having known, or even be capable of knowing. Heritage thus becomes an invitation for collective anamnesis. The 'ardent obligation' of heritage, with its requirement for conservation, renovation, and commemoration is added to the 'duty' of memory, with its recent public translation of repentance. (Hartog 2005:12)

Hartog's analysis can be read as an invitation to study the 'ardent obligation' of heritage from the perspective of the specific heritage practices aiming to secure this obligation. The particular heritage practice I focus on in this chapter is the practice of photography. As part of the same discourse on loss and absence, photography has functioned to 'substitute' or 'refill' the absence of the past by producing or, in the sense of Roland Barthes, by 'certifying' presence (Barthes 1981:87).[2] Photography therefore has not only been part of heritage; as 'objects of melancholy', as Susan Sontag (1977) put it, photographs helped to create it. In 1853, for example, the French government began to document its patrimony by making photographs of its architectures (Boyer 2005). In 1897, the National Photographic Record Society was founded in England with the purpose of documenting the quickly disappearing English customs (Jäger 2005). Along the same line, photographic societies in North America started to make portraits of the vanishing cultures of American Indians (Dippie 1992; Fleming and Luskey 1986).

In view of these circumstances it can be argued that photography quite literally played a constitutive role in the imagination of national identities discussed so prominently by Benedict Anderson (1991). In fact, given the attention Anderson devoted to Walter Benjamin's ideas about technological reproducibility on the one side and the very title of Anderson's seminal work on the other, one could expect to see an interest in the role of photography. As we know, however, he focused on the role of printing instead. Except for a small footnote on the 'museumizing of the Borobodur' (Anderson 1991:179), photography has remained curiously absent from his analysis. In a way, the same holds true for the subsequently evolving studies focusing on the role of photography in the 'imperial imaginary' (Shohat and Stam 1994). Since the early 1990s, numerous works have shown how the colonial state used photography to imagine itself (cf Landau and Kaspin 2002).[3] As we have learned, issues of surveillance reflected issues of orientalism and vice versa. The value of these insights stands without question. Yet, with few exceptions (for example, Pinney 1997), the interest has been to understand only the colonial state as such. The perspective was thus to look rather from the outside. Hardly any research has been devoted to the photographic imagination of communities *within* the colonial (and postcolonial) state.

Arguing that the increasing globalization of heritage through institutions such as UNESCO provides a powerful framework for the visual production of local and/or national identities, the present chapter aims to help to understand this process.[4] Based on field research in the Yoruba town of Osogbo in Southwest Nigeria, my analysis focuses on two issues: First, I want to know how photography has managed to play a role in the formation of heritage in Osogbo. Second, I am interested how this role has led to a heritagization of memory in the local context. As I show, both questions are closely linked. Both point to questions of appearance and style, issues to which I turn at the end of the chapter.

New Images

Central to my argument are the photographs in the publications of the Osogbo Heritage Council. Next to important persons they show sculptures and architectures that form part of the sacred grove of the local guardian deity, the Yoruba river goddess Osun. As evidence for the presence of the various Yoruba deities residing in the grove, the style of these shrines and sculptures contrasts sharply with the serenity and controlled expression of what has become known as traditional Yoruba art as depicted in African art books and exhibition catalogues. Instead of wood and mud, the primary media in Yoruba art and architecture, most structures in the Osun grove are made of cement. Whereas Yoruba art has a clear sense of symmetry, the sculptures in the Osun grove are ecstatic, and monumental, seemingly showing no regard for formal order.

Figure 4.1 Palace sculptures associated with local deities in Osogbo (photograph: Adigun Ajani, 2003)

Figure 4.2 Cement sculpture by Susanne Wenger and Adebisi Akanji in the Osun grove representing Obaluaye, late 1970s (photograph: Peter Probst)

The story that led to these works constitutes one of the most disputed chapters in modern African art.[5] The story began in the year 1958, when a delegation of Osun officials visited the Austrian artist Susanne Wenger in the nearby town of Ilobu and persuaded her to move to Osogbo. By that time, Wenger's work as an artist devoted to Yoruba religion was already well known. In Ede as well as in Ilobu, she had started to build shrines for Yoruba deities. Having heard about her activities, the Osun officials in Osogbo asked her for help in repairing the shrines in Osogbo and stopping local farmers and businessmen from encroaching into the grove and thereby threatening the sanctity of the place. The expectations of the ritual officials seemed to have been mixed. Issues of prestige certainly played a role. Because of her status and connections, officials hoped that Wenger could help to recusitate the cult of the river goddess Osun in the rapidly changing environment. In fact, as Wenger herself noted, her work had been foreseen by one of her spiritual mentors, who had told her that she would be the one to build a 'storey house' shrine for the deities, meaning that the deities would be rescued from the past and elevated into the realm of the modern (Wenger and Chesi 1983:89).[6]

Wenger knew about Osogbo and its guardian deity. Back in 1950, only a few months after she had arrived in Nigeria, she and her husband, Ulli Beier, had attended the Osun festival. Meanwhile, Wenger had become initiated into the cult of Obatala, one of the main Yoruba deities. As a devotee, she accepted the offer, and repair began with the Idi Baba shrine at the outskirts of Osogbo on the way to Ibokun. After completing this work, she went on to work on the main Osun temple in the grove. However, what was initially intended to be just a kind of minor facelift ended up as nothing but an iconic riot. The grove became flooded with new image works ranging from small and modest statues to huge and imposing shrines. Conceptually, by lending the various Yoruba deities believed to reside in the grove a new material presence, art and culture were to be reunited in order to compensate for the absences that colonialism and capitalism had caused in Yoruba society. Put differently and phrased in Weberian terms, what happened was a shift from the colonial process of disenchantment to a postcolonial project of re-enchantment.

Seen from this perspective, the artistic departure from the conventions of Yoruba aesthetics was a deliberate move. With the world of tradition regarded as doomed and the world of the modern as constituting the root of all problems, the only appropriate solution was the creation of new art forms, or rather 'new images' as the official language said, expressing the fluid, open, and still undetermined phase that society was believed to go through. And, indeed, the 'new images' worked. The artistic production of presence had a public impact. Thus, in 1965, five years after Nigeria's independence, the

Nigerian state declared the Osun grove a national monument.[7] In the 1970s, a festival committee was established. A decade later, a heritage council was introduced. Over the years, the festival became not only one of the biggest cultural festivals in Nigeria but also a prominent site within the memory and heritage-scapes of the Yoruba Diaspora. The last episode in this development has been the inscription of the grove as both a 'site' and a 'cultural landscape' in the UNESCO world heritage list in July 2005.

Unforeseen Exchanges

As the official UNESCO document states, 'the development of the movement of New Sacred Artists and the absorption of Suzanne Wenger, an Austrian artist, into the Yoruba community have proved to be a fertile exchange of ideas that revived the sacred Osun Grove [. . .] as a tangible expression of Yoruba divinatory and cosmological systems; its annual festival is a living, thriving, and evolving response to Yoruba beliefs in the bond between people, their ruler, and the Osun goddess (UNESCO 2005:36).

Indeed, witnessing the Osun festival is an impressive document of this 're-vitalization of the sacred'. Whereas prominent Yoruba deities such as Shango, Ogun, and Sonponna are associated with heat and fire, Osun is linked with water and coolness. The water of her river is said to have healing qualities, especially for children and for barren women. Thus, at the grand finale of the

Figure 4.3 Road clearers with Osun devotee at Osun Festival, 2002 (photograph: Adigun Ajani, 2002)

annual festival, after the Osun priests have offered the sacrifice to the deity at the bank of the Osun river, hundreds of people, many of them women, come down to the river to fetch water, which is then rinsed over the faces and the bodies of small children brought along especially for this occasion. Those who can not make it are eager to obtain at least one of the thousands of plastic containers filled on that day.

Ironically, the interpretation given by the Osogbo Heritage Council differs from the UNESCO justification, which focuses explicitly on the religious dimension of the grove and the festival. Officials of the Osogbo palace downplay this element and stress instead the historical and memorial importance of the festival. Thus, in July 2005, shortly after the announcement in the Nigeria press of the UNESCO decision, Chief Adejare Agboola, Chairman of the 2005 Osun Osogbo Festival, explained that the festival is not 'to worship idols, nor some lesser gods, but to remember our forefathers, celebrate our tradition, and promote tourism'.[8] Thus Agboola followed the official (that is, palace) line of reasoning, which over the years has repeatedly stated that the Osun festival is first and foremost a 'remembrance festival' and *not* a religious event per se.

To understand the stance of the Osogbo palace vis à vis the Osun festival, one needs to know that the 'fertile exchange' referred to in the UNESCO declaration has not been without conflict. Indeed, rather than instigating support, Wenger's activities in the grove initially elicited resistance. At the time Wenger arrived in Osogbo, the city was a booming commercial centre with lots of immigrants (Adepegba 1995). Chronically short of land, people had moved into the grove to generate income from land, fish, and timber. Except for the few members of the Osun cult, the status of the grove as a sacred site that forbids any secular activities such as farming, hunting, and fishing, was hardly observed anymore. When Wenger started her project, the public reaction was therefore anything but welcoming. Realizing that Wenger was posing a threat to their economic transactions, people sought to stop her. The means to do so varied, ranging from straightforward physical threats to sending *egungun* ancestor masks into the grove to frighten the workers. But protests were also articulated along religious lines.

By 1965, Osogbo's ruler, *ataoja* Adenle, had become Minister without portfolio in the new independent Nigeria. In an attempt to stop the conflicts in the grove and to firmly inscribe Osogbo into the history of the young postcolonial state, Adenle ensured that the Osun grove had been declared a national monument. As a result, the land of the grove was officially measured, and signs were put up in the forest forbidding farming, building, hunting of animals, and tree felling. The decision prompted a counter strike in Osogbo; a prominent member of a Muslim group purchased seventeen acres of land in the southern end of the grove from a member of the royal family and began to construct a Qu'ran school. In 1968, the construction was completed and the school opened up. Built as a stronghold of religious righteousness in the middle of idolatry, pagan practices, and cultural decay, the school soon became the centre for a series of attacks on Wenger's image works.

The conflict became prolonged over years.[9] While the Muslim school owner and his teachers were able to receive religious and monetary support from abroad (via institutional links with Islamic institutions in Lebanon and Egypt), Wenger was able to recruit support from Europe, North America, and the elite in Nigeria. In the last group, the attitude toward traditional culture had begun to shift. Increasingly, institutions such as the Osun grove and the festival were to become objects of a national policy that aimed in particular to stress the dignity and the strength of Nigerian culture in particular and African culture in general.

Against Religion

It was right at the beginning of this shift, in 1976, that the modern architect of Osogbo's heritagization of memory, Osogbo's present ruler, Oba Iyiola Matanmi III, ascended the throne. Born and raised in a Muslim compound – Matanmi I (1854–1864) had been the first Osogbo monarch to convert to Islam – Matanmi III witnessed the transformation of the Osun grove and festival from the perspective of the palace.[10] In his youth, he experienced the introduction of marches and bands performing during the festival as well as an increasing number of members of the Christian colonial public coming to attend the grand finale as a demonstration of the power and splendour of the palace. As a personal assistant to his predecessor *ataoja* Adenle, he learned about the close connection between the palace and the colonial world, lessons that led him first to Ibadan and Ife, where he obtained diplomas in education, and then, from 1968 onward, to Lagos, where he worked as an accountant at the University of Lagos.

At the death of Adenle in 1976, Matanmi III was enthroned as the new *ataoja* of Osogbo, and his experiences outside Osogbo turned out to be handy. In view of the upcoming FESTAC – the second pan-African festival of Arts and Culture – the Nigerian government had urged the Osogbo palace to set up a Festival Committee to guarantee a proper organization of the festival.[11] Matanmi III reacted promptly. The idea of a committee suited his experience with bureaucracy and allowed him to exercise control over a new and important realm of monarchical power. At stake was the new kind of ethnic and religious tourism sparked by FESTAC. From 1977 onward, more and more people of African ancestry came to Nigeria to seek and revitalize their ethnic and cultural roots. In Osogbo itself, the development led to the formation of the Osogbo Cultural Heritage Council in 1986. The official tasks of the Council were 'to identify, fully revive, and develop the historical monuments and activities into tourist attractions'. High economic expectations led to the planning of 'kiosks', 'restaurants', 'parking spaces', and even an 'amusement park' in and around the grove.

It would be tempting to understand these plans as a result of the global forces of commercialization and secularization. The truth, however, is that both forces seemed to have bypassed Osogbo. Tourism, the great hope of the future, turned out to be an illusion. The fame of Osogbo as a city of arts had begun to dwindle already in the 1970s, leaving the grove and the festival as the main attractions. Certainly, the festival had become a global event. But lasting for only a couple of days a year, the festival did not create a viable tourist industry. Equally false is the secularization thesis. Rather than a decline of religion, Osogbo has seen an enormous increase of Christian churches and Islamic sects that have turned out to be a serious threat to the religious pluralism and syncretism that has characterized Yoruba society. Indeed, a religious polarization has set in with ardent Christians and Muslims rejecting the festival as an expression of paganism and a rather diffuse majority of the population embracing and supporting it as a symbol of belonging and local identity.

Caught between these two factions, Matanmi III found himself in a precarious situation. Whereas representatives of the Islamic movements reminded him of his Muslim identity and urged him to close down the grove and forbid the festival, the king-makers and ritual officials of the Osun cult made it clear that the history of his office demanded his active participation in the performance of the rituals devoted to the goddess. To counter the Muslim criticism, Matanmi III and his personal consultants opted for a policy of enchantment and desacralization by which they tried to reduce the religious content of the festival and to represent it as a social event and a festival of commemoration and remembrance.

An indication of this approach can be found in the publications of the Heritage Centre. In the course of the last twenty years, they have shifted the frame of reference in their public advertisement of the festival. Whereas in the 1980s the publications referred to religious centres such as 'Mecca' and 'Jersusalem', from the 1990s onward references were made instead to global entertainment centres such as 'Las Vegas' and 'Hollywood'.[12] The policy was made quite explicit in 1993. The official festival brochure declared: 'Osun Osogbo Festival is a festival. That is all. It is the celebration of the birth of

Osogbo and the remembrance of the events that led to the founding of the town. The occasion is an attempt on our part to look back into the life of our forefathers, which we can still appreciate and hope to hand over to generations after us. It is not religion per se but a remembrance festival'.[13]

When this statement was first released, its bluntness caused an outcry of protest in Osogbo. Members of the various religious cults were furious and insisted that the Osun festival did indeed express core religious values and beliefs. For them, the festival was not a matter of remembrance but one of homage to the goddess. They insisted that the reality of the powers of Osun was beyond doubt and that any attempt to deny it would provoke the anger of the goddess and distract her protection of the town. The fear proved to be groundless though. Nothing serious happened. Yet, still now one can hear many disgruntled comments about the way the king is instrumentalizing the grove and the festival for his own political ends.

Opening up the Eyes

Much of the protest concerns a brochure of roughly seventy pages entitled *History of Osogbo*, published by the Osogbo Heritage Council in 1994 – just one year after Matanmi III had declared the Osun festival to be primarily a remembrance festival. The brochure is not the only publication of the Heritage Council; others are entitled *Landmarks in the History of Osogbo* (Aofolaju

Figure 4.4 Osogbo Heritage Council, History of Osogbo, 1994

1999) and *Sacred People, Sacred Places* (Osogbo Heritage Council 2000) – they form a special genre of literary products in Yorubaland.

The origin of this particular genre goes back to the 1930s, when members of the new (Christian) literates were allowed to work in the local councils as mediators between the king and the colonial administration. Often organized in so-called progressive unions, members formed a network of like-minded people mostly devoted to individual career advancements. As Toyin Falola (2002) has noted, it was this very experience of change that provided the context not only for the embracing of progress but also for the embracing of the past. Thus, writers of Yoruba town histories understood their work quite explicitly as a 'rescue mission' (Falola 2002:75), a notion articulated already in 1897 in Samuel Johnson's preface to his classic *The History of the Yoruba*: 'What led to the production was not a burning desire of the author to appear in print . . . but a purely patriotic motive, that the history of our fatherland might not be lost in oblivion, especially as our old sires are fast dying out' (Johnson 1921:vii).[14]

The organizing concept for this experience of loss was *olaju*, a Yoruba word that can be rendered as 'enlightenment' or 'modernity'. Stemming from the two Yoruba words *la* ('to open') and *oju* ('eyes'), *olaju* literally means 'to open the eyes'. As such, *olaju* was deeply associated with the experience of the colonial world. Peel (1978) has described it as a specific 'syndrome' or 'ideology' comprising bureaucratic and administrative as well as economic, educational, and religious ideas. Since printing belonged to that 'syndrome', one is not surprised to see a connection between printing and modernity. As Falola noted in his analysis of Yoruba town histories: 'All the texts, without exception, define what "modern" is either directly or implicitly by way of making demands for change' (Falola 2002:81). In other words, more than just associated with changes, *olaju* was the justification for the demand of change expressed in Yoruba town histories. Underlying these conceptions was an adoption of the aesthetic elements of modernity that combined the metaphorical features of light and darkness with a linear, goal-oriented time perspective. Thus the slogan of the *West African Pilot*, the widest-circulating nationalist newspaper, read: 'Show the light, and people will find the way'. Similarly, local newspapers such as the *West African Vanguard* carried articles that celebrated *olaju* with phrases such as 'The veil is removed, and the fetters of darkness and ignorance are broken and must naturally give way to the rays of light and hope, the spirit of understanding, and steady progress for all and sundry' (Peel 1978:154–55).

Given this Judeo-Christian trope, one is hardly surprised to see photography playing a prominent role in the *olaju* complex. In fact, with their mastery of the technology of light, photographers became popular role models for the *olaju* ideology. Waldwin Holmes, for example, born 1865 in Accra and reputedly the first black photographer, was enrolled as a member of the Royal Photographic Society of Great Britain in 1897, the same year Johnson wrote the preface for his book on Yoruba history. In 1910, Holmes went to England to study law. Seven years later he returned to Lagos to practice both as a barrister and as a photographer. Examples of his work can be found in MacMillan's *Red Book of West Africa,* which appeared in 1920 (MacMillan 1968). Another contributor to this book was George Da Costa. Born in 1853 in Lagos, he was educated at the local CMS (Church Missionary Society) Training Institution. In 1895, after having worked as the manager of the CMS Bookshop in Lagos for eighteen years, he resigned and turned to photography, eventually becoming a respected photographer. For the colonial government, he did the photographic recording of the construction of the Nigerian Railways, a project that was followed by the participation in MacMillan's *Red Book of West Africa.* As can be seen from Olu Oguibe's description of the photographs, not only the pictures but also the subjects represented *olaja*.

> Rather than a society of 'cannibals' and 'pagans', Da Costa's photographs of early-twentieth-century Africa led us to a cosmopolitanism steeped in the awareness of other cultures, a world of burgeoning elite and savvy literati, a society of international merchants, high-flying attorneys, widely travelled politicians, newspaper tycoons, and society ladies, the same images we find in contemporary portrait painting of the period. (Oguibe 2004:76)

These representatives of the new elite also formed the foundation of the Osogbo Progressive Union. Established in 1936, its main aims were the 'social, moral, and intellectual improvement of its members' and the 'promotion of the spirit of unity and patriotism'. Like many unions of its kind, membership was organized in local branches with the Ibadan branch being the most influential one (Falade 2000:153ff). As a result, in Osogbo the union remained rather inactive. From the 1950s onward, however, the situation changed. In 1944 *ataoja* Adenle succeeded Latona II, who had ascended the throne in 1933. Both of them saw the past not as a value in itself but rather as a tool to serve the dynamics of *olaja*. These men were the first Christian rulers of Osogbo (the letterhead of Latona II carried the title *deo adjuvante*). Before his enthronement, Latona had been a successful trader, and during World War I he had served as a sergeant major in the British army. Committed to the ideals of *olaju,* he is praised in local history for having popularized the Osun festival by actively inviting the white colonial elite to the festival and thus turning it into a colonial spectacle, similar to the institution of the Northern Nigerian *durbar*. These changes were assisted by the building of the first aerodrome in Osogbo in 1936 and the construction of a suspension bridge over the Osun river to the Osun grove in 1938. He also commissioned the erection of a new council house and demolished the old storey-house palace built back in 1910, substituting a new, more imposing one. On his death in 1943, his successor Adenle, a former school teacher and successful trader in *adire* cloth, continued to 'open up' Osogbo and make it fit for modern times.[15] Thus new schools were established, the road network was improved, and electricity and street naming were introduced. In addition, he ensured that Osogbo would be adequately represented in the new administrative set-up. By 1952, the Osun Division was created and Osogbo had been made the Divisional Headquarters.

Given these developments, one is hardly surprised to see that the publication of the first Osogbo town history by a member of the Osogbo Progressive Union (Olugonna 1959) practically coincided with the beginning of the artistic transformation of the Osun grove by Wenger and her collaborators.[16] From the perspective of the palace that had sanctioned the projects, both were primarily political enterprises deemed to underline the importance of the historical and cultural heritage of Osogbo as a major force in newly independent Nigeria. In the sense used by Toyin Falola, both projects were truly 'rescue missions'; that is, both sought to save and to preserve the past from the perspective of the experiences of change. But whereas the town history project was written in view of a bright future, the grove project was carried out under the impression of a past glory. As I show below, the conflicting approaches to, or *styles* of, as I would prefer to call them, how to construct and represent heritage form the basis of the sense that the palace is instrumentalizing the grove and the festival for its own political ends. A good deal of this unease concerns the history presented in today's publications of the Osogbo Heritage Council, to which I now turn.

Histories of Osogbo

While the documentation of the past as heritage is part of *olaju* in the sense of 'opening up the eyes', the very representation of the past does not follow *olaju's* linear temporality but follows local traditions of narrating the past. The Yoruba word indicating such narrations is *itan*. Though generally translated into English as 'history', *itan* is much broader, entailing a different approach and attitude toward the past than in modern European discourse (Yai 1993). Operating on two different levels, Yoruba town histories represent a clear proximity to these traditions. After a short introductory section explaining the location and the geographical background of the town, what is presented first as 'legendary' or 'mythical history' is then followed by 'traditional history'. Whereas the former deals with issues of creation, the latter focuses on aspects of migration. The reference to Oduduwa constitutes a crucial element in this context. For Yoruba, power is derived from Oduduwa, the Yoruba culture hero who is said to have founded the Yoruba race by descending from heaven and establishing civilization on earth, with Ile Ife as its centre (Adepegba 1986; Law 1973; Ojuade 1992). Accounts vary as to the process of this foundation, but all accounts can be seen as a mythologization of different stages in history in which different waves of immigration led to subjugation of earlier populations with a subsequent deification of the prime figures involved. While such a differentiation between 'myth' and 'history' makes sense on an analytical level, in everyday life, myth and history are constantly blurred. In actual political practice, deities function as role models for secular political allegiances, just as political allegiances function as models for the understanding of deities.

Accordingly, the 'official' history of Osogbo as narrated in the publications of the Osogbo Heritage Council usually begins with the life and deeds of Osun. The actual time is not specified, except that it was 'as early as the Oduduwa period' (Osogbo Heritage Council 1994:12). Depicted as a queen and endowed with magical powers, she is said to have lived along the Osun river in a palace of her own assisted by her own 'cabinet'. Everybody had his or her task. People were engaged in dyeing and fishing, protecting the grove from attacks, or maintaining internal security. As time passed, the queen and her people gradually 'disappeared into the spirit world' (Aofolaju 1999:7). The question of how this happened is seen as irrelevant, just as is this question:

> ... whether these spirits and fairies were aborigines (real human beings with supernatural powers) or whether they were only imaginary beings is (considered to be) not important. What is important is that their period provided the basis of our history. This period should not be seen just as a myth of the origin of Osogbo but rather as an end of one era (the mythical Oso-igbo) and the beginning of another period (of traditional history of Osogbo). (Osogbo Heritage Council 1994:13)

The 'traditional history' usually starts off, then, with the narration of the migration from Ile Ife to Ipole, an Ijesha settlement a few miles from Osogbo. In Ipole, the forefathers of the Osogbo people experienced a water shortage. As a result, a delegation was sent to find a new settlement. After experiencing a number of obstacles, they eventually discovered the Osun river, where Laroye, the leader of the delegation, made a pact of mutual protection with the deity residing in the river. Just as Osun promised to provide peace and prosperity, Laroye promised to respect and honour the goddess by making annual offerings to her at the river bank. At first, Laroye and his people enjoyed the new environment. But the activities of the immigrants disturbed the deity, and her people and the settlers had to move to the upper terrace of the plain. The new place turned out to be a good one. Soon a flourishing market developed. As the population increased, however, the need to move arose once more. The Ifa oracle was consulted again, and its advice resulted in the third palace, opposite today's market place. It was here that Laroye finally passed way.

Photography and the Narrative of the Nation

The history texts I have summarized above are profusely illustrated with photographs. The latest production is called *Osun in Colors: a Pictorial History of the River Goddess Osun* (Kayode 2006). In fact, the use of photographs can be considered a prime feature of the pamphlets and brochures published by the Osogbo Heritage Council. The use of visual material in the festival brochures goes back to the 1980s. Subsequently, photography was incorporated in the

Figure 4.5 Afolabi Kayode, Osun in Colours, 2006

Figure 4.6 Oba Atanda Olugbena Matanmi II, early twentieth century

historical brochures as well. Falling into two categories, people and places, they represent a kind of royal family album and allude to the Yoruba word for heritage, *oguntihi*, which literally means, 'something we possess or inherit'. In other words, the photographs represent elements of a collective memory that in turn is represented by the figure of the monarch and his subjects.

In the *History of Osogbo*, the oldest photograph depicts Matanmi II. A date is missing, but given the time of his reign (from 1903 to 1917), the picture obviously stems from the early twentieth century. In the brochures and local praise songs (*oriki*), Matanmi II is praised as having witnessed the transformation of Osogbo 'into a modern town'. In practice, this meant the establishment of a district office and a customary court, the building of schools, the foundation of colonial business enterprises, the construction of roads, the arrival of the railway, the introduction of motor vehicles, *and*, although it is not explicitly mentioned, the coming of photography.[17] The establishment of photography implied both the adoption of the cultural conventions toward the new medium as well as its local appropriation.[18]

In the case of the black-and-white photograph of Matanmi II, its mise en scène coupled with the label 'Oba Atanda Olugbena Matanmi II' clearly indicates its representational function or style.[19] Just as Matanmi II used the new colonial architecture to change the old palace into Osogbo's first 'storey' building, he used the new technology of photography to magnify his status. Wearing a plain cap and dressed in what looks like a white embroidered robe, Matanmi II sits on a chair, slightly bent forward, his hands in his lap, his eyes looking straight into the eyes of the beholder. His face has a serene, withdrawn expression of composure conforming to the aesthetic conventions of Yoruba sculpture (Sprague 1978; Thompson 1974). The photograph conveys a double perspective, giving an impression of not only spatial but also temporal depth, as if the portrayed is looking at the beholder from a distant past. In other words, the image may be construed as a kind of revelation, an appearance from the dark past into the light of the present.

The same characteristics hold true for the photographs of the successors of Matanmi II. Sitting before a plain white backdrop or a mountain scene, as Latona I and Latona II do, they allude to the relationship of presence and absence characteristic of photography. Its hidden cipher or code is of course the moment of death as the primal scene of memory and the very birthplace of signs and images. Following Debray (1992), Wendl (1999) has reminded us that the root of the word 'sign' is the Greek word for tomb, *sema*. Similarly, the Latin word *imago*, from which the English 'image' is derived, originally meant 'death mask', the wax print of the face of a deceased person, which was carried during the burial ceremony and later stored in the Atrium. In the same vein, the word 'portrait' has its origin in the process of taking the facial traits of the deceased (*portrahere*) to create a death mask. Surely, Margaret Drewal is right when she writes about Yoruba portraiture: 'The power of portraits is the ability to construct a reality' (Drewal 1990:49). But, in this context, 'reality' is a somewhat misleading concept; 'presence' is probably a better word. After all, representation necessarily implies the substitution of an absence by a presence.[20] Along this line then, it makes sense that the heritage brochures not only present photographs of the deceased rulers but also photographs of the tombs of Ajobogon and Adebuyisoro, the ancestors of Laroye, the founder of Osogbo, in the town of Ibokun. The reproduction is poor. Hardly anything can be seen. But the bad quality of the picture only enhances the idea that the photograph can be seen and understood as a medium that is able to produce presence by visualizing absence (cf Chéroux 2005).

Just as the technical quality of the photographs of the former monarchs gradually improves, the photographs of the historically important places change as well. The events that happened in the grove are depicted by photographs of Wenger's shrines and architectures. The visual narration follows a series of architectures said to be palaces built by Laroye and his successors from the very foundation of Osogbo up to the present. All together, seven palaces are represented. Photographs of the shrines reshaped and newly built by Wenger

Figure 4.7 Part of the Ohuntoto Ogboni Shrine Complex, erected by Wenger, Gbadamosi, Saka, and Akangbe in the mid-1970s (photograph: Peter Probst, 2002)

document the first three. The first one shows the Osun temple at the river side; the second depicts a structure known as *iledi ohuntoto*; the third one represents the Osun temple at the market shrine. The remaining four show the changes of the palace architecture from Oba Kolawola up to Matanmi III in what is now the present palace compound. The last pages depict the prime icon of rulership in Osogbo, the fish as Osun's messenger or medium, *iko*. It is shown either as a fountain in the shape of a large fish or as part of a sculpture showing Laroye holding the fish that jumped out the river as a sign of acceptance of the sacrifice to Osun.

Styles of Imagination

We should note that the photographs published by the Heritage Council are not mere 'illustrations'. Rather they express a particular 'style' of imagination that in itself is part of a wider 'national' narrative about the emergence of Osogbo and its trajectory from the past into the future. The emptiness of the cenotaph, stressed by Anderson (1991:9ff) as one of the primary emblems of the emergence of nationalism in eighteenth- and nineteenth-century Europe, correlates with the play of presence and absence in the photograph of the tombs of Osogbo's ancestors in Ibokun. Framed in this way, not only is photography an element in the local process of nation-building, but it has also remained an element of *olaju* in the sense of 'opening up' Osogbo for change, progress, and modernization. The use of English for the heritage publications indicates the nature of the public addressed. The target group is not primarily the local population but the people inhabiting the 'modern world', the world of *olaju*. The palace interests thus meet with those of the Ministry of Culture and Tourism, which is eager to 'develop' the Osun grove and the Osun Osogbo festival by turning them into profitable assets of a growing heritage industry. The same goes for UNESCO, which is selling its world heritage programme on the premise that it is possible to convert cultural into economic capital. As a technique to visualize absence (either the past or the future), photography quite literally creates dreamworlds. It is no coincidence then that the Heritage Council likens the Osun grove with 'Hollywood' as a dream (and money) factory. However, the photographs published and circulated by the palace-based Heritage Council stand in a double conflict with Wenger's image works erected in the Osun grove. That is to say, in contrast to the future-oriented photographs, the image-works in the grove not only point to the past; their past is also different.

As mentioned above, Wenger began her project to lend a new visible presence to the withering influence of Yoruba deities.[21] For this, she collected information on the history of Osogbo and the various deities believed to reside in the grove. Other than the narrative presented in the heritage brochures, however, the traditions that instructed Wenger's work do not focus on Laroye but on Timehin, a courageous hunter, devotee of Ogun and 'brother' of Laroye. According to these versions, the different places referred to in the brochure as Laroye's palaces are not traces of Laroye's deeds but rather signs that mark the events that happened in the course of Timehin's exploration of the area. Laroye is said to have come after Timehin had prepared the ground, hence much later. Thus the numerous sculptures and architectures standing in the grove act as visual references, or as I would prefer to say, as visual *gestures* of the enduring importance of these events.

A good example of the difference between the two styles in the visual representation of the past is *iledi ohuntoto*, an architectural ensemble Wenger and her collaborators erected in the late 1970s. The heritage brochures refer to the site as the 'second palace'. However, according to members of Wenger's circle, *iledi ohuntoto* has never been a palace. Rather, the place where the architecture stands is said to be the ancient sanctuary of *ohuntoto*, the guardian deity of the autochthonous population, otherwise known as *oro* or prehumans. It is believed that Timehin was the first to encounter the prehumans and their deity. For a while they lived together. After the arrival of Laroye, however, the prehumans disappeared, and *ohuntoto*, their deity, was incorporated into *ogboni*, the earth cult the immigrants brought with them from their former residence in Ipole.

The story resonates with the brass emblems of *ogboni*. Art-historical research has interpreted the *ogboni* brass figures as a possible reference to subjugation and the subsequent introduction of a gendered system of ritual dualism in early Yoruba history (Blier 1985; Lawal 1995). In fact, the gendered pair that features prominently in *ogboni* imagery correlates with a group of four small cement figures that stand unobtrusively in the bush along the way to the main Osun shrine. The group is said to represent both Timehin and Laroye, and Ogidan and Ohuntoto. But the issue of their meaning and representation is delicate. In contrast to Timehin and Laroye, knowledge about Ogidan and Ohuntoto is shrouded in mystery and secrecy. As a group, the figures are depicted as belonging together. In ritual practice, however, an avoidance relationship based on notions of space and gender sets them apart. Thus, whereas Timehin and Laroye are considered to be male figures, Ogidan and Ohuntoto are explained to be the 'mothers' of Laroye and Timehin. While the former have an established place in the public, the latter are worshipped only by the Alare, the head of *ogboni's* executive arm and most secret part of the cult.

Translated into the history of Osogbo, the relationship between Laroye and Timehin versus Ohuntoto and Ogidan can be viewed as functioning as a

Figure 4.8 Group of four cement figures by Adebisi Akanji in the Osun grove (photograph: Peter Probst, 2002)

variation of the well-known ritual system whereby institutions such as *ogboni* stand for the (aboriginal) power of the land, whereas the king – representing the 'strangers' – embodies public power. Indeed, a correlation also exists on the level of the relationship between Osun and Ogun. Thus, the superhuman beings inhabiting the area under the leadership of Osun complement the human invaders arriving under Ogun's devotee Timehin. Whereas Osun is female and associated with brass, Ogun is male and associated with iron.

Surely, a straightforward translation of the classical dualism case of the northern Ghanaian Tallensi (Fortes 1945) into the context of southern Nigerian Yoruba does not work. Owing to the multitude of migration waves and the constant interplay between prehumans (*oro*), humans (*eniyan*), and superhumans (*irunmole*), a clear distinction between immigrants and an autochthonous population does not exist. Yet, resentments have remained. Thus, one of Wenger's closest collaborators, Kasali Akangbe, stems from the Gbonmi compound whose history clearly predates the arrival of the Ipole immigrants. Others, such as Adebisi Akanji, the sculpture of the cement quadriga, are high-ranking members of *ogboni* or stem from the lineages that go back to Timehin. For all of them, the reshaped ritual landscape of the grove represents a kind of Foucauldian heterotopia. As such, it conflicts with the way how the palace has captured the message of the sculptures and architectures by putting them in a photographic frame more suitable to his interests. Murmurs of a counter memory then can still be heard, but public criticism is not only dangerous but also pointless, for among her many characters and appearances Osun is known and praised as 'the one who dances to take the crown without asking' (Verger 1959:426).

Style and the Politics of Appearance

As mentioned at the beginning of this chapter, it was not my intention to repeat the critique of heritage in terms of its often-scolded function as a sanitization of history. My interest was not to validate or to falsify. Given that heritage is part and parcel of a general politics of imagination, we are wise to invoke Benedict Anderson's early insistence on the futility to distinguish between false and genuine, real and imagined. As he noted: 'Communities are to be distinguished not by their falsity/genuineness but by the *style* in which they are imagined' (Anderson 1991:6, emphasis mine).

The importance of style rests then in the effectiveness by which certain styles link and revive shared sentiments and instigate strong feelings of togetherness.[22] Seen in this way, style is not something given. To be recognized and unfold its effects, style has to appear, and in order to appear it has to be appropriated, animated, and embodied by people who identify with it. Framed in such a triangular constellation, style is always a public style. It is tied to the public domain, outside which it cannot exist.[23] As such, style is necessarily both framed and contested.

The material I have presented in this chapter both confirms and differentiates this argument. Thus, the style of Wenger's 'new images', explicitly created by the desire to reenchant Yoruba society, did indeed give rise to new social forms that produced ever more images. That is to say, the image works in the Osun grove did lead to a heritage industry whose characteristic feature is the production of images representing heritage. The use of photography in the publications of the Osogbo Heritage Council illustrates this feature. However, as we have also seen, just as Wenger's 'new images' were able to revitalize religion by shifting old religious practices into the new context of international roots tourism, these new social forms have also helped to foster a process of desacralization or, as the agents of this process themselves say, a 'culturalization' that prompted a series of conflicts between Wenger and the palace. Both groups operate under the banner of heritage. Thus, while the former sees the shrines and the architectures as an effort to enhance or at least to sustain the religious aura of the grove, the latter is using the works to boost its own political hegemony by substituting religion through remembrance.

Notes

1. Funding for the research has come from the German Research Foundation (SFB 560-B4 & B7) and a 2006 FRAC research grant from Tufts University. For help and assistance in Osogbo I would like to thank Adigun Ajani, Jimoh Buraimoh, Olasupo Aremu, and the late Pa Osuntoogun. Special thanks also go to Birgit Meyer for having drawn my attention to the question of style and to Ferdinand de Jong for a thoughtful reading of an earlier draft. Previous versions of the paper were presented at Boston University and the University of Amsterdam.
2. Barthes himself was quite aware of the relationship between photography and heritage. 'By making the (mortal) Photograph into the general and somehow natural witness of "what has been", modern society has renounced the Monument. A paradox: The same century invented History and Photography. Contemporary with the withdrawal of rites, photography may correspond to the intrusion, in our modern society, of an asymbolic Death, outside of religion, outside of ritual, a kind of abrupt dive into the literal Death' (Barthes 1981:93).
3. If we focus mainly on issues of formal aesthetics, the same applies to works devoted to single African photographers as the other main strand of research on photography in Africa.

4. In doing so, I am following Küchler's suggestion. Referring to Riegl's seminal study *The Modern Cult of Monuments,* Susanne Küchler (1999:62) has remarked that what Riegl had identified as the new 'age value' of monuments may by now well have become superseded by a new 'viewing value'.
5. See Beier (1975), Lawal (1977), Cosentino (1991), Kennedy (1992), Kasfir (1999), Okeke (2001). For my own work on Osogbo, see Probst (2001, 2002, 2004a, 2004b, forthcoming).
6. It should be mentioned that Wenger was not the only expatriate working in the realm of Yoruba art. In Ekitiland, Father Kevin Caroll had started Christian workshops for Yoruba carvers (see Caroll [1967]).
7. It was a decision that many observers in the West interpreted as a sign for the capacity of African art and culture to regenerate itself despite the evils of colonialism. Accordingly, a German newspaper article from 1966 reported: 'The ancient kingdom of Osogbo has known to preserve its rank and esteem. From the ruins of a great but lost past, new life is blossoming again. In Osogbo the arts reign. Charmingly painted walls, breathtaking carvings, great cement sculptures dominate the picture of the inner city' (Cube 1966:7).
8. See Anonymous (2005).
9. For an account of the conflicts, see Ogungbile (1999).
10. The incorporation of the Osun festival into the colonial world had already begun in the 1930s. Latona II was the first Christian to become *ataoja*. In contrast to his Muslim predecessors, Latona II refashioned the festival after Empire Day.
11. For a subtle analysis of FESTAC in terms of its role in the Nigerian public sphere, see Apter (2005).
12. See, for example, the Festival Brochures of 1986 and 1998.
13. It should be noted that 'remembrance' is actually the literal translation of what Sufi Muslims do when they recite their litanies of prayers (Arabic *dhikr*, literally 'remembrance of memory'). Since Sufi orders are part of the Muslim world in Osogbo, we cannot rule out that such practice played a role in the shift from religion to memory as discussed above. I am grateful to Benjamin Soares for making me aware of this point.
14. Applying Anderson's printing thesis to the Yoruba context, Peel (1989) has argued that writers such as Johnson and missionary institutions such as CMS helped to bring about the ethnic category of Yoruba into existence.
15. On Adenle as a writer and an inventor, see the recent article by Barber (2006).
16. An account of the history of Osogbo was published already in 1911. It was, however, part of the history of Ibadan written by Oba I. B. Akinyele, then the ruler of Ibadan.
17. As the Yoruba word for photograph, *aworan yiya*, literally 'circulating image', points to, the linkage between the arrival of the railway and that of photography was no coincidence. Photography and railways were both prime agents of social spatialization and in this way deeply embedded in the projects of modern governance and nation-building. As mentioned above, the construction of the Nigerian railway was accompanied by its photographic recording, a job given to George Da Costa as one of the first Nigerian photographers in the country. For the connection between railway and photography in England and Germany, see Jäger (2005); for the situation in South Africa, see Foster (2005).

18. Unfortunately, it was not possible to identify the exact time when the first photo studio opened up in Osogbo.
19. See also Westermann's (1934:102) observation from Ibadan: 'The Oba was constrained to relax his patronage of the artists' works: very much like other African chiefs he thought he could hand on his image to posterity more beautifully by means of an enlarged photograph than by a wooden statue'.
20. See also Plumpe (2001), who conceives nineteenth-century photography as a *Präsenzmedium*.
21. In a series of publications, Wenger explained her work in some detail (see Wenger [1977, 1990] and Wenger and Chesi [1983]).
22. Religious imagery is especially effective in that respect. Not surprisingly, the etymology of the word 'religion' is often explained as coming from the Latin *religio*, meaning to reconnect or to bind together. Yoruba language does acknowledge this relationship between style and religion as *religio*. Thus, the semantic spectrum of the Yoruba word for 'religion' (*isin*) ranges from worship, 'service' to that of bondage. On the anthropological relevance of image, style, and identity, see Maffesoli (1996) and Meyer (2006).
23. See Niklas Luhmann's (1986) illuminating interpretation of style from the perspective of system theory.

Bibliography

Adepegba, C. 1986. 'The Descent from Oduduwa: Claims of Superiority among Some Yoruba Traditional Rulers and the Arts of Ancient Ife', *International Journal of African Historical Studies*, 19(1):77–92

Adepegba, C. (ed.). 1995. *Osogbo: Model of a Growing African Town*. Ibadan: Institute of African Studies.

Anderson, B. 1991 [1983]. *Imagined Communities*. London: Verso

Anonymous. 2005. Osogbo Agog As the People Celebrate Yet Another Osun Festival, *The Vanguard*, August 12 (www.vanguardngr.com/articles/2002/features/tourism/tt112082005.html).

Aofolaju, B. 1999. *Landmarks in the History of Osogbo*. Ibadan: Landmark Communications.

Apter, A. 2005. *The Pan-African Nation*. Chicago: Chicago University Press

Barber, K. 2006. 'Writing, Genre and a Schoolmaster's Invention in the Yoruba Provinces'. In *African Hidden Histories. Everyday Literacy and Making the Self*, K. Barber (ed.), pp. 385–415. Bloomington: Indiana University Press.

Barthes, R. 1981. *Camera Lucida. Reflections on Photography*. New York: Hill and Wang.

Beier, U. 1975. *The Return of the Gods: The Sacred Art of Susanne Wenger*. Cambridge: Cambridge University Press.

Blier, S. 1985. 'Kings, Crowns and Rights of Succession. Obalufon Arts and Ile-Ife and Other Yoruba Centers', *Arts Bulletin*, 68(3):383–401.

Boyer, C. 2005. 'La Mission Héliographique: Architectural Photography, Collective Memory and the Patrimony of France, 1851'. In *Picturing Place: Photography and the Geographical Imagination*, J. Schwartz & J. Ryan (eds.), pp. 21–54. London: Tauris.

Caroll, K. 1967. *Yoruba Religious Carving*. London: Chapman.

Chéroux, C. (ed.). 2005. *The Perfect Medium: Photography and the Occult*. New Haven, CT: Yale University Press.
Coombes, A. 1994. *Reinventing Africa*. New Haven, CT: Yale University Press.
Cosentino, D. 1991. 'Afrokitsch'. In *Africa Explores: 20th Century African Art*, S. Vogel (ed.), pp. 240–55. New York: Prestel.
Crary, J. 1999. *Suspensions of Perception: Attention, Spectacle and Modern Culture*. Cambridge, MA: MIT Press.
Cube, A. von. 1966. Die Götter Bauen Nachts, *V-Illustrierte*, September, pp. 6–8.
Debray, R. (ed.), 1992. *Vie et mort de l'image: une histoire du regard en Occident*. Paris: Gallimard.
———. 1999. *L'Abuse monumental*. Paris: Fayard.
De Jorio, R. 2006. 'Introduction to Special Issue: Memory and the Formation of Political Identities in West Africa', *Africa Today*, 52(4):v–ix.
Dippie, B. 1992. 'Representing the Other: The North American Indian'. In *Anthropology and Photography*, E. Edwards (ed.), pp. 132–36. New Haven, CT: Yale University Press.
Drewal, M. 1990. 'Portraiture and the Construction of Reality in Yorubaland and Beyond', *African Arts*, 23(3):40–49.
Falade, S. A. 2000. *A Comprehensive History of Osogbo*. Ibadan: Tunji Owolabi Printers.
Falola, T. 2002. 'Yoruba Town Histories'. In *A Place in the World: New Local Historiographies from African and South Asia*, A. Harneit-Sievers (ed.), pp. 65–86. Leiden: Brill.
Fleming, P., and J. Luskey. 1986. *The North American Indians in Early Photographs*. New York: Harper and Row.
Fortes, M. 1945. *The Dynamics of Clanship among the Tallensi*. Oxford: Oxford University Press.
Foster, J. 2005. 'Capturing and Losing the "Lie of the Land": Railway Photography and Colonial Nationalism in Early Twentieth-Century South Africa'. In *Picturing Place: Photography and the Geographical Imagination*, J. M. Schwartz and J. R. (eds.), pp. 141–61. London: I. B. Tauris.
Habermas, J. 1985. *Der Philosophische Diskurs der Moderne*. Frankfurt: Suhrkamp.
Hall, S. 2000. 'Whose Heritage?', *Third Text*, 49:1–12.
Hartog, F. 2005. 'Time and Heritage', *Museum International*, 227(57, 3):7–18.
Huyssen, A. 1995. *Twilight Memories: Marking Time in a Culture of Amnesia*. New York: Routledge.
———. 1999. 'Monumental Seduction'. In *Acts of Memory: Cultural Recall in the Present*, M. Bal, J. Crew, and L. Spitzer (eds.), pp. 191–208. Hannover, NH: UP of New England.
Jäger, J. 2005. 'Picturing Nations: Landscape Photography and National Identity in Britain and Germany in the Mid-Nineteenth Century'. In *Picturing Place: Photography and the Geographical Imagination*, J. M. Schwartz and J. Ryan (eds.), pp. 117–40. London: I. B. Tauris.
Johnson, S. 1921. *The History of the Yorubas*. Lagos: CSS.
Kasfir, S. 1999. *Contemporary African Art*. London. Thames & Hudson.
Kayode, A. 2006. *Osun in Colors: Pictorial History of the River Goddess Osun*. North Charleston, NC: BookSurge.
Kennedy, J. 1992. *New Currents, Ancient Rivers: Contemporary African Artists in a Generation of Change*. Washington, D.C.: Smithsonian Institution Press.

Küchler, S. 1999. 'The Place of Memory'. In *The Art of Forgetting*, A. Forty and S. Küchler (eds.), pp. 53–72. Berg: London.

Landau, P., and D. Kaspin (eds.). 2002. *Images and Empires: Visuality and Colonial and Postcolonial Africa*. Berkeley and Los Angeles: University of California Press.

Law, R. 1973. 'The Heritage of Oduduwa Traditions: History and Political Propaganda', *Journal of African History*, 14(2):207–22.

Lawal, B. 1977. 'The Search for Identity in Contemporary Nigerian Art', *Studio International*, March-April:145–50.

———. 1995. 'A Ya Gbo, A Ya To. New Perspectives on Edan Ogboni', *African Arts*, Vol. 28 (4):37–49.

Lowenthal, D. 1996. *Possessed by the Past: The Heritage Crusade and the Spoils of History*. New York: Free Press.

———. 1998. 'Fabricating Heritage', *Memory and History*, 10(1):5–24.

Luhmann, N. 1986. 'Das Kunstwerk und die Selbstreproduktion der Kunst'. In *Stil. Geschichten und Funktionen eines gesellschaftswissenscaftlichen Disbursements*, H. U. Gumbrecht und L. Pfeiffer (eds.), pp. 620–72. Frankfurt: Suhrkamp.

MacMillan, A. 1968. [1920] *The Red Book of West Africa*. London: F. Cass.

Maffesoli, M. 1996. *The Contemplation of the World: Figures of Community Style*. Minneapolis: University of Minnesota Press.

Mbembe, A. 2001. *On the Postcolony*. Berkeley and Los Angeles: University of California Press.

Meyer, B. 2006. Modern Mass Media, Religion, and the Dynamics of Distraction and Concentration. Lecture given at the conference on Modern Mass Media, Religion and the Question of Community, University of Amsterdam, June 30.

Musil, R. 1978. 'Denkmale', *Gesammelte Schriften*, Bd. 7, pp. 506–09. Frankfurt: Fischer Verlag.

Nora, P. 1989. 'Between Memory and History: Les lieux de mémoire', *Representations*, 26:7–25.

Oguibe, O. 2004. *The Culture Game*. Minneapolis: University of Minnesota Press.

Ogungbile, D. 1999. 'Interaction of Islam and Traditional Culture: A Case Study of Osogbo-Yoruba Community in Nigeria', *Africana Marburgensia*, 31:48–61.

Ojuade, J. S. 1992. 'The Issue of "Oduduwa" in Yoruba Genesis: The Myths and Realities', *Transafrican Journal of History*, 21:139–58.

Okeke, C. 2001. 'Modern African Art'. In *The Short Century: Independence and Liberation Movements in Africa, 1945–1994*, O. Enwezor (ed.), pp. 20–36. Munich: Prestel.

Olugonna, D. 1959. *Osogbo: The Origin, Growth and Problems*. Ibadan: Fads Printing Works.

Osogbo Heritage Council. 1986. *Osun Osogbo Festival Brochure*. Osogbo: Local Government.

———. 1993. *Osun Osogbo Festival Brochure*. Osogbo: Local Government.

———. 1994. *The History of Osogbo*. Osogbo: Local Government.

———. 1998. *Osun Osogbo Festival Brochure*. Osogbo: Local Government.

———. 2000. *Sacred Sites and Sacred People*. Osogbo: Local Government.

Peel, J. 1978. 'Olaju: A Yoruba Concept of Development', *Journal of Development Studies*, 14 (2):139–65.

———. 1989. 'The Cultural Work of Ethnogenesis' In *History and Ethnicity*, E. Tonkin, M. McDonald, and M. Chapman (eds.), pp. 198–216. London: Routledge.

Pinney, C. 1997. 'The Nation (Un)Pictured? Chromolithography and "Popular" Politics in India 1887–1995', *Critical Inquiry*, 23(4):834–67.

Plumpe, G. 2001. 'Tote Blicke: Fotografie als Präsenzmedium'. In *Medien der Präsenz: Museum, Bildung und Wissenschaft im 19. Jahrhundert*, J. Fohrmann et al. (eds.), pp. 70–86. Köln: Dumont.

Probst, P. 2001. 'Traumwerk, Bildwerk, Kunstwerk: Visualität und ästhetische Praxis in Osogbo, Nigeria'. In *100 Jahre Traumforschung: Kulturwissenschaftliche Perspektiven*, B. Schnepel (Hg.), pp. 187–97. Köln: Köppe Verlag.

———. 2002. 'Osogbo oder das Wunder der Wandlung: Eine Nigerianische Geschichte'. In *Afrikanische Reklamekunst*, T. Wendl (ed.), pp. 137–46. Wuppertal: Hammer.

———. 2004a. 'Keeping the Goddess Alive: Performing Culture and Remembering the Past', *Social Analysis*, 48(1):33–54.

———. 2004b. 'Vital Politics: History and Heritage in Osogbo'. In *Beyond Expansion and Resistance: Explorations of Local Vitality in Africa*, P. Probst and G. Spittler (eds.), pp. 331–58. Münster and Rochester: Lit.

———. forthcoming. *Producing Presence. The Art of Heritage in a Yoruba City*.

Riegl, A. 1903. *Der Moderne Denkmalkultus: Sein Wesen und seine Entstehung*. Wien and Leipzig: W. Braunmüller.

Roberts, A., and M. Nooter Roberts. 2002. 'Visual Tactics of Contemporary Senegal'. In *African Cultures, Visual Arts and the Museum*, T. Döring (ed.), pp. 191–228. Amsterdam: Rodopi.

Simmel, G. 1919 [1907]. 'Die Ruine: Ein Ästhetischer Versuch'. In *Philosophische Kultur*. Stuttgart: Kröner.

Shohat, E., and R. Stam. 1994. *Unthinking Eurocentrism*. London: Routledge.

Sontag, S. 1977. *On Photography*. New York: Penguin.

Sprague, S. 1978. 'How Yoruba See Themselves', *African Arts*, 12(1):52–69, 110.

Thompson, F. 1974. *African Art in Motion*. Berkeley and Los Angeles: University of California Press.

UNESCO. 2005. *Osun Grove of Osogbo*. World Heritage Documents No. 1118.

Verger, P. 1959. *Notes sur le Culte de Orisa et Vodun*. Dakar: L'Institut Francais d'Afrique Noire.

Wendl, T. 1999. 'Tod und Erinnerung'. In *Snap Me One: Studiophotographen in Afrika*, T. Wendl and H. Behrend (eds.), pp. 40–49. München: Prestel.

Wenger, S. 1977. *The Timeless Mind of the Sacred: Its Manifestation in the Osun Grove*. Ibadan: Institute of African Studies.

———. 1990. *The Sacred Groves of Osogbo*. Wien: Kontrapunkt.

Wenger, S., and G. Chesi. 1983. *A Life with the Gods in their Yoruba Homeland*. Wörgl: Perlinger.

Werbner, R. (ed.). 1998. *Memory and the Postcolony: African Anthropology and the Critique of Power*. London: Zed Books.

Westerman, D. 1934. *The African Today and Tomorrow*. London: Oxford University Press.

Yai, O. 1993. 'In Praise of Metonomy: The Concepts of "Tradition" and "Creativity" in the Translation of Yoruba Artistry over Time and Space', *Research in African Literature*, 24(4):29–37.

Entangled Memories and Parallel Heritages in Mali
Michael Rowlands

In the recent postcolonial history of Mali, cultural heritage has been viewed by the State as a fundamental part of its development strategy. The President of the Third Republic of Mali, Alpha Oumar Konaré, and several Ministers of Culture argued that to develop a nation, economic change had to be preceded by cultural development. In the words of Aminata Traoré, a former minister of culture and tourism and now a fierce opponent of World Bank-funded policies in Mali: 'Valorizing cultural heritage must be the foundation and the engine of social and human development in Mali' (Traoré 2002:194). It was along these lines that during the 1990s various efforts were made to promote national cultural activities such as revitalizing the Biennale des Arts et de la Culture in Bamako and creating the Festival of Segou and the Festival of Music in the desert outside Timbuktu. It is no accident, therefore, that, in recent years, Mali has become celebrated for its world music, for the photography of Seydou Keita and Malick Sidibé, and for heritage tourism. Aspects of the use of cultural heritage to build a national identity in the 1990s echo those of an earlier period of rediscovered authenticity in the 1970s, when artists and musicians, subsidised by the Malian state, were urged to return to their African roots. If authenticity is a key value in African political development, its rediscovery returns us to pan-Africanist ideals of the immediate post-indepence period in the 1960s. It also becomes a contested category that has revealed deep antipathy in its expression both by the Malian state and by religious orthodoxy.

Alpha Oumar Konaré argued that architecture was one, if not the, enduring feature of the cultural heritage and national identity of Mali. Government investment in monumental art was presented to the populace as a way of promoting a 'democratic form of citizenship' as well as a means to 'replace an elitist and cliquish form of culture with a popular and egalitarian culture' (cf De Jorio 2003:827). The building of a new National Museum, which has opened recently in the capital Bamako, strives to promote the museum experience as an enduring educational process – particularly among the young. In the last few years of Konaré's presidency, over twenty monuments were built in various quarters of Bamako, and others were planned for other Malian cities (Arnoldi 2003). They were built to celebrate historical events, such as national Independence; to represent key national values, such as homage to the martyrs of the 1991 civil war and national heroes such as Modibo Keita (the first President of Mali); and to celebrate peaceful coexistence between ethnic groups through the construction of an obelisk in central Bamako. This programme of monumental art and museum building was designed to promote the formation of a new public memory that would take attention away from the monopoly on state memory by *jeliw* (praise singers) and in particular, the Mande creation myth of Sunjata Keita, the founder of the Medieval Empire of Mali. This epic cycle had been celebrated after Independence by Modibo Keita to legitimate an autonomous history of Mali that would reveal the true nature of its national culture after the period of French colonial rule (cf Schulz, this volume). By the 1990s this celebration of national identity had become publicly associated with a particular Mande ethnic political hegemony, and Konaré's concern was to find alternative ways of representing the unity-in-diversity of Malian national culture. At the same time, various attempts were made to harmonise local cultures with national development goals, by stressing the essential unity they held in possessing particular cultural values. As Rosa De Jorio describes, these included frequent references to key values in the national culture of Mali, such as the value of hospitality and the Mande notion of the human being (*Maaya*), values subsequently made famous by the songs of Habib Koita and others (De Jorio 2003). More recently, the materializing of heritage has shifted from architecture to performance, with that of the music festivals deliberately emphasizing the rich diversity of traditions in Mali (Arnoldi 2003; Schulz, this volume).

All of these activities suggest a scarcely concealed attempt to materialize the cultural heritage of Mali as the product of a coherent collective memory. To follow this line of thought in an uncritical manner promises the inevitable tendency in heritage studies to be a description of the freezing of commemoration into permanent forms (cf Todorov 2001). But if cultural heritage in Mali is to be identified with the strengthening of collective memory, it can do so, it seems, only by reducing the latter to various generic aspects of national identity formation. What Anthony Smith once called the 'governing myth' of the nation has at its core a commemorative event, frozen in time (Smith 1999). But this eliminates collective memory from having any role in challenging 'national myths' as shared understandings or representations of past events (cf Bell 2003). I argue, against the collective memory thesis, that notions of heritage and memory are entangled together in more complex and contested forms of everyday practice in contemporary Mali. Collective forms of remembrance rely both on performed discursive elements and on more diverse and unexpected images and material forms that help make sense of experience and relate pasts to futures through the linkage of expectations to anticipations. At the same time, I argue for an intersubjective notion of memory that attracts different technologies of heritage to create more turbulent worlds in which group identities become materialized and motivated. These, I argue, form memory and heritage constituents that underlie national hegemonic mythologies and form a discursive realm in which control over people's memories and formation of national myths are debated and contested (cf Bell 2003:66; Shelton 2006). In Mali, we shall see that the creation of world heritage sites, the building of monumental architecture, and the organization of cultural festivals create heritage technologies as a central focus for such contestations.

National Identity and Cultural Heritage in Mali

UNESCO has created three World heritage sites in Mali: the great mosque and mud architecture of Djenné, the mosques and library of Timbuktu in 1988, and the Bandiagara cliff with its Dogon architecture in 1989. Because Mali is one of the poorest countries in the world, such an imposition may not have been seen as welcome by some, but since 1991 the Malian state has consistently promoted the legal status of these sites and the sensitization of local populations to their enduring value as a major goal of national cultural policy.

The UNESCO committee defines a world heritage site by considering the contribution it makes to 'universal cultural value' (Cleere 2001). In practice, choosing what enters a World Heritage list turns out to be a highly subjective matter resting on claims about the objectification of 'human value' in monumental art. Moreover, the concept of culture used by UNESCO has been criticized by anthropologists (for example, Eriksen 2001), although the critiques often miss the point that culture as property can be a privileged mode of identity.

A particular quality injected into these debates involves the relationship among monuments, collective memory and national identity, and the impact of colonial history (cf Rowlands and Tilley 2006). Architecture was not 'discovered' in Mali by UNESCO experts. A shared colonial history with France beginning in 1894 with the conquest of the Western Sudan and an almost immediate perception of the creativity of indigenous mud architecture suggest that French and Malian collective colonial memory are deeply entwined in these heritage deliberations. Richard Terdiman has spoken of a time of 'memory crisis' in late-nineteenth-century France, when people struggled to deal with a new relationship to the past (Terdiman 1993). This was not post-French revolutionary nostalgia but a product of coming to terms with urbanization, industrialization, and demographic expansion. As memory became envisaged as a representation of the past, not its repetition, it became amenable to nostalgic desires provoked by sociohistorical change. Post-1850 nostalgia, as a yearning for an ideal past, became re-attached in France to a more patriotic sense of home figured in literature, monuments, and national ceremonies (Terdiman 1993). At the same time, a series of sociological theories reveal a deep nostalgic base haunted by a sense of loss. Terdiman argues that Ferdinand Tönnies, in formulating his well-known distinction between *Gemeinschaft* and *Gesellschaft*, was actually making a case for a historical division between two forms of memory. Tönnies, he maintains, was pleading for a reorientation of modern social life to the rural as an antidote to the ephemerality of the Baudelairan urban flaneur. Memory was thus envisaged as something belonging to the rural or the colonized periphery – to the people without history as opposed to the 'too much' history of the metropolis.

The projection of nostalgia into a colonized periphery has led many to treat it as a 'social disease', as a fear of change saturating left-wing visions of preindustrial utopias and as an opiate justifying the position of elites. Boym (2001) tries to save the situation by distinguishing between restorative and reflective nostalgia, the former being the problematic longing for a past and the latter having a more positive connotation of engaging the past to promote authenticity in the present. Significantly, Pierre Nora's sentimental attachment to *milieux de mémoire* in the French idea of nation (that period when the past was authentic rather than reinvented as *lieux de mémoire*) is taken by Boym as an example of restorative nostalgia, a lost object of desire epitomized in peasant culture and the quintessential repository of collective memory. But she also argues that such times of authentic memory are not just believed to be before modernity but also *outside it*. Real memory, as that place of repetitive everyday experience, was preserved not only in the remnants of 'peasant societies' in Europe (*Volkerkunde*) but also in the peripheries of colonial empires (as *Volkskunde*). Only in colonial societies had real memory been preserved in the homes of 'primitive or archaic societies'.

The creation of Soudanic architecture and the reconstruction of the thirteenth-century mosque in Djenné in 1907 can be reinterpreted as part of this search for authentic *milieux de mémoires* in the French colonial periphery. The military doctor Rousseau, attending the wounded at the conquest of the town in 1893, took the first photos of Djenné. Dubois' book, *Tombouctou, la mystérieuse*, first published in 1896, immediately touches the romantic imagination of a large public in France and goes through several editions and translations. Photos of Djenné, taken by Dubois, Fortier, and others, are used to produce thousands of *cartes de visites* and form the models for the construction of several pavilions in several universal exhibitions. The building of a model of the Djenné mosque at the 1931 colonial exposition in Paris, less than thirty years after the thirteenth-century original had been rebuilt, under French auspices, to take the place of the austere mosque built by Chekiou Ahmadou, is restorative nostalgia in action. By 1931, truncated by the First World War, the restorative appeal of the collective memory of the nation may not have been as it was in France, but still the reorganizing of the nation-space around a sense of authentic *milieux de mémoire* being rediscovered in Africa retained its power to bring coherent meaning to identity transition. It was a project still in line with the nationalist thought of Ernest Renan, who placed the soul of the French nation in memory rather than territory after the loss of Alsace and Lorraine in 1870. Djenné and its mosque, or images of its inhabitants standing in front of the traditional Toucouleur house, appealed to the French nation as a site of authenticity, indeed as a *milieu de mémoire*.

Ironically, the restorative nostalgia that created 'Soudanic' architecture for French metropolitan consumption became a site of postcolonial resistance and then subsequently a mode of reincorporation of a distinctive Malian modernity. After Independence in 1960, Malian leaders were faced with the problem of how to distance the new state from a French colonial image of it as an archaic state suitable for metropolitan nostalgic image-making. Once formed out of the colonial ruins of the French Western Sudan, Mali had to be transformed into a modern state with a bright future. There were two basic problems in doing this, First, for many the idea of a Malian nation was not a deeply rooted principle. Moreover, at Independence, Malian national identity was already associated with a dominant Mande idealization that provided the elite with feelings of primordial ties and an imaginary timeless antiquity. Second, at Independence, aspirations of the Malian elite were focused on the creation of a pan-African socialist federated union. But when this union failed abruptly in 1960, they found they had to rapidly create a sense of a new nation-state for the former French Sudan. Both these problems could be resolved by identifying the modern state with the ancient medieval empire of Mali and its successors, which had produced some of the oldest towns in West Africa: Djenné, Timbuktu, and Gao. The first president, Modibo Keita, a descendant and namesake of the founder of the Medieval Empire of Mali (Sounjata Keita), could lay claim to having bypassed colonialism as a short and disturbing interlude and reengaged with the natural process of Malian history. Yet, he could also claim to have retained some positive elements from colonialism, such as education and technical expertise, but now harnessed to a Malian future. Being shaped by a rich history also included the idea that all the principal ethnic groups in Mali had at one stage or other experienced state rule both as rulers and as being ruled, and so would recognize the value of national unity. Ironically, therefore, all the sentiments of nostalgia for a former unified past that characterized the history of France and its relationship to its colonies up until 1960 were reproduced in the establishment of Mali as an independent state – including the frequent criticism of the time, that any popular awareness of ethnic diversity was repressed for fear of damaging a tenuous national unity based on shared language and culture.

This doesn't mean that the idea of the nation in Mali was not a contested category, but rather the form this took was couched in the opposition between history and memory. In his description of *lieux de mémoire*, Pierre Nora describes these places as 'ulitimate embodiments of a memorial consciousness that has *barely survived* in a historical age that calls out for memory because it has abandoned it'. History, in this case, is undeniably dominant, but certain minorities are said to jealously guard their privileged memory that has retreated to protected enclaves. 'True memory', he says, 'resides in gestures, habits, skills, unspoken traditions, the body's self-knowledge, unstudied reflexes, and ingrained memories' (Nora 1989:5). Memory as habitual resistance, therefore, becomes the unspoken, and in the same way it retreated from Metropolitan France to colonial enclaves in the face of the dominance of national history, in post-Independence Mali it retreated to more ethnically defined places of refuge, that is, what Nora calls 'sanctuaries of devotion and silent pilgrimage, where one finds the living heart of memory' (ibid.:6). In particular, the contrast between a history of oral poetry, crafts, and music and a heritage of landscape and architecture is used to orchestrate a distinction between a former elite idea of a single unified national culture and the recognition of multiethnic aspirations through material culture.

But these aspirations were not so easily satisfied. De Jorio has recently reported that, in building a monument to the memory of the first president of Mali, Modibo Keita, former President Alpha Oumar Konaré decribed it as part of a narrative that 'would erase past divisions and ideological differences and constitute the basis for widening the imagined community of citizens'

(De Jorio 2003:847). In such pursuit of new forms of civic engagement, the building of monuments would encourage a more detached, critical approach to the past – more intellectual and less embedded in the actions of a particular president. It is significant that this visual re-presentation of the modern history of Mali takes place at the same time as the initiative by the Malian state, supported by UNESCO, to create three world heritage sites. The latter action forms the basis for the narrative to be shifted once again from history to memory, but this time memory sites as *lieux* rather than *milieux de mémoire* – that is, those places that are marked by the ways in which history has appropriated the space and function of memory. For these concepts to be in physical space, they should occupy sites outside those of modern, urban industrial, bureaucratic functioning and instead be sought in those peripheral places in which everyday material practices can survive. It is to one of these sites of survival, the restoration of architecture in Djenné, that I now turn, as an exemplar of the modern memory project by which the State in Mali attempts to create a sense of shared memory. Ironically, the claimed purpose of the project was not just to restore the architecture of Djenné but more importantly to plan, document, and restore it as a living archive and therefore open it to more than one claim of authenticity.

Djenné and the Restoration of Architectural Memory

The Dutch Ministry of Foreign Affairs, the Dutch National Museum of Ethnology, and the Ministry of Culture and Communication of Mali signed a contract for phases 1 and 2 of a project for the restoration and conservation of the architecture of Djenné in 1996. A scientific committee was established to oversee the project, which in turn established an office in Djenné to plan and oversee the individual projects. The responsibility for supervising the office was put in the hands of the Mission Culturelle de Djenné, under its Director, Dr Boubacar Diabey, which had been established in 1994 by the Malian state to protect Djenné as a world heritage site.

The purpose of the project was not restoration alone. Following the Charter of Venice, the authors of the Djenné project insisted on respect for the authenticity of the buildings and the need to provide a precise documentation of their intervention and to allow for and yet critically examine architectural modifications that had taken place over time. Within this context, the aim of the project was to restore the town as a monument. This is reminiscent of Alois Riegl's famous essay *Modern Cult of Monuments,* wherein the values of age/authenticity, measured in patina, damage, and everyday wear and tear, are laced with anxiety over change. The conflict between whether to conserve or restore, resolved according to Riegl by showing respect for historical existence as such, was exported to the special circumstances of Mali. Following Article 11 in the Nara document on Authenticity, this meant that 'the respect due to all cultures requires that heritage properties must be considered and judged within the cultural contexts to which they belong'. It meant that a choice had to be made as to which buildings to preserve, what period of construction to aim for in restoration, and what not to allow – for example, the introduction of modern doors or windows or the use of fired tiles. In other words, strategic choices were made within a definition of what constituted the authentic architectural form of the town. The historical period of 1890–1910 was chosen as a benchmark for authentic restoration, since documentation, both photos and drawings, of the houses of Djenné existed for this period, linking the buildings to public spaces and pathways, that is, to their wider physical context. Restoration often critically involves deciding why one date should be defined as more authentic than another. The issue is usually not why a particular date is chosen, which in this case has much to do with documentation, as why a date has to be chosen at all. The aim of the Djenné project was also not to restore the whole town but to make a choice of important buildings that represented an ideal while allowing the rest of the town to evolve (95 percent of the buildings in the town were not catalogued as a priority in this sense). So, it is a trace of a memory from 1890–1910 – about 100 houses – that was restored as an indicator of an original authentic architectural state for the town.

Moreover, what is being restored is not just buildings. The aims of the project were grouped into completing an inventory of the houses/groups of houses; reinforcing cultural identity by sensibilizing local people to the importance of preservation and cultural promotion of their architecture; and restoring the association of masons – the *barey-ton* – who built and restored the houses and, by conserving their technical knowledge, giving the masons long-term regular employment. Also, the project would later introduce a means of managing and dispersing water from the houses with the idea that this would convince local people of the value of preserving the architecture, that is, show that culture brings development benefits. But an important concern was how to include people in the programme, to make it more participatory, producing a more adaptive programme shared by all the actors involved and reinforcing the local administrative means to achieve these aims. The ambition was to promote pride in the town among its inhabitants and a desire in householders to participate in the project, both of which, it was argued, were best assured by promoting the cultural and tourist importance of Djenné and by demonstrating the economic value of the restoration programme. The ideal outcome would be the promotion of Djenné as part of the unity of the Malian nation – to achieve the material restoration of an invaluable architectural knowledge and to provide for the economic well-being of its inhabitants.

At the core of the project was the restoration of 150 houses (of which about a hundred were finally restored) as part of a state-led modernization programme. What did this mean in practice? There existed clear examples of 'bad restoration' whereby inappropriate materials or modern doors and windows had already been inserted into structures. The aim was to replace these with suitable replicas or 'traditional' forms using authentic materials. But there were technical features that could not be replaced. For example, the houses were made originally with a special type of mud brick (called *djenné ferey*) made in a cyclindrical, hand-made shape. To produce these required a special composition of clay, straw, and urine, and for forty years or more, the stronger, moulded rectangular mud brick, introduced by the French, had replaced them. Since it was deemed impossible to go back to building in the *djenné ferey* brick (although there is a view that this should have been done), retaining the houses' authentic shape depended on restoring the layers of mud (*crepissage*) that protects the houses from the wet-season rains and floods. This is what gave a curved surface texture and shape to the houses, which had appealed immediately to the French colonial gaze in 1896 and was widely copied in Europe as a vernacular style of architecture (cf Prussin 1994).

Authenticity in Djenné, in other words, relies on the public appearance of houses. But if authenticity is a matter of appearance, then the practicalities of what constitutes the interior of houses, it was argued by the householders, could be open to negotiation. However, the aims of restoration could not be satisfied by a focus on the external façades of the houses alone. Treating the house as a unified heritage object meant that the interior plan of the house and the façade were indissolubly linked to each other. And it is this interface, interestingly enough, between external image and inner function of the houses that reveals the tension between the need for nationalism in Mali to have a sense of its historicity and the modernity projects of local householders.

Aspirations and Heritage Healing

Strong aspirations exist to modernize houses in Djenné both in terms of use of 'modern 'materials such as cement, moulded columns and paint; the installation of electricity, telephones, and water; and in the reorganization of the use of space. Bassoumaila Maiga, the owner of house 37, said the restoration team came to his house with an old photograph, and they restored the outside exactly like it was in the photo. He did not mind that the front façade, the windows, and the doors were restored using traditional materials, but, after much discussion, he had been allowed to change part of the interior and use cement and paint where it was not obvious to people coming in to visit him. However, for him the real issue was the reorganization of space. As a *chef de famille* he had responsibility for seven houses in Djenné occupied by his offspring, and he needed enough rooms in his house for sons to stay if they were working outside Djenné. Whether to have a cement floor or to have electricity was therefore not really a problem. What was important was to be allowed to reorganize the interior space of the house and related houses to accommodate a constantly changing household. He estimated that as *chef de famille* he should be prepared to provide all his family with food once a day and a room to sleep in if they came to stay from outside Djenné. In his case, this could mean as many as seventy-eight people needing to be seated, fed, and have somewhere to sleep. It would be impossible to do this in the house as currently organized, and he was planning to build another 'modern' house on a nearby plot where he could have a large courtyard for people to come and eat and talk with him. In the meantime, he was still hoping to add another room to the courtyard of the house where he could meet people and relax.

For the male house owner, expanding the courtyard area and the shaded patio area around it was essential for a social life and in particular for demonstrating his capacity to entertain and fulfil the obligations of a *chef de famille*. Sekou Touré and his younger brother and their four wives live in their father's house (no. 168). They cook every two days in the expectation that up to thirty-two members of the family could require feeding. Neither of the brothers liked the way the wives cooked out in the courtyard and thought they should have a more closed kitchen area. Also they did not like the small rooms that remained after the façade of the house had been restored. They were considering a solution to the need for space by converting the corridor on one side of the courtyard into a big living area. Even this was going to be too small. The ideal solution, for which they did not have the money, would be to build a larger house on another site where they could use 'modern' materials and introduce new ideas in use of space.

Restoration has created rather different problems for Tata Soucko, a woman who lives in her father's house (no. 104) and whose brother is an absentee *chef de famille* living in Bamako. The aim of restoration had been to rebuild the house to the form prior to the previous rebuilding in 1950, that is, to something like it was in about 1910. This meant raising the walls and restoring the wooden doors and windows, none of which she minded, having gained permission to do this from her brother living in Bamako. If she had a choice, she would have liked to add another floor to the house, because her children were now grown up, and she needed more rooms for them. In the past, women had their own bedroom for themselves and their children. But now they prefer to have a larger room, called a *salon*, opening out on to a veranda on one side of the courtyard and joined on to a smaller attached bedroom. By secluding wives from the gaze of husbands and other men, the *salon* allows a woman to sit together with other wives and women friends and their children, to watch satellite television and to speak on their mobile phones. The walls of Tata's salon are covered in brightly coloured woven textiles and carpets, placed overlapping one another and jostling for space to show off those that had been bought in Bamako or abroad. Against the walls are several chairs and sofas for special visitors, and the central area is covered in carpets, cushions, and a low table. Piles of enamel pots, glass ornaments, and china plates, given to her at marriage by her husband's family, are stored and displayed in formica cupboards. In other words, the *salon* has become the social core of the house where much socialising and gossip goes on by the married women. By contrast, older men have rooms upstairs, from which they can overlook the entrance to the house and can see what is going on in the street below. The house owner comes down to meet visitors either in the entranceway to the house or to sit in the courtyard, if he knows them well. It is a feature of the migration of the younger men in search of work that they leave young wives and children behind in their father's house. Apparently, 'it is not good to be married and see your mother still in the kitchen'.

Men think they need larger public spaces like the courtyard and the vestibule area both to entertain visitors and to provide for members of the household residing outside Djenné. Women want larger rooms as salons where they can eat, entertain, and conduct business. The overall shift in aspiration, therefore, is from the tall Djenné house with a small courtyard and many small rooms to a lower and more extensive dwelling of larger rooms around a large, central courtyard. In fact, the solution is a compromise that maintains the tall house with a more extensive courtyard area to the rear. On the one hand, this maintains the distinctive Djenné style of architecture as a façade, which all the house owners interviewed recognize as important to preserve, for tourism and the development of the town, and, on the other hand, it provides for the aspirations to be modern while accommodating the pragmatics of daily living. The migration of young men from Djenné over a long period is a particularly important factor in local changes in architecture. Men who, in their forties, return to live in the house bring with them aspirations to continue living the modern 'lifestyle' to which they have become accustomed. The walls of the house and the courtyard will be covered in glazed tiles, cement balustrades block the gaps between the mud columns to create a balcony, a satellite dish will appear on the roof. Such innovations, which are not in themselves particularly serious, suggest to the visitor that there are men in the house who have lived and worked abroad, know about modern consumption, and have some influence.

Architecture therefore contributes in contradictory ways to building a national culture in Mali. While the householders' view of modernity may be a source of visual contradictions for the conservator, the inhabitants do not seem to experience it as such. On the contrary, the hybrid object of a Djenné house can articulate a coherent message to their inhabitants about social status and their future. It is also quite likely that there is nothing new in this, and the Djenné style, originating perhaps in some amalgam of external North African style of building with local social forms, is itself of hybrid origin. In contrast to state-led modernity, whereby restorative memory works to preserve a past and accommodate the exigencies of change, Djenné householders operate with a more contested notion of memory. None professes to wanting to abandon the distinctive architectural styles of Djenné, and some are shocked by examples whereby an old house has been replaced by a modern cement-block house with glazed tiles – usually adopted by someone returning to live in Djenné after many years in Ghana or Cote d'Ivoire and anxious to show off his access to modernity.

The Cultural Mission in Djenné, established by the Ministry of Culture to ensure the future world heritage status of Djenné, and its director, Boubacar Diabey, have the difficult job of mediating between the constraints of preservation and the demands for change. Diabey claims to be attentive to the needs of the houseowners and to recognize that demands for modernizing the houses can be accommodated within the constraints of the restoration programme. Although his position on the *comité pilotage*, which includes the mayor, a representative of the prefect, and the Imam, means that he has significant power to prevent certain developments, he seems to rarely impose his will and instead negotiates a compromise usually in rather ambiguous circumstances (cf Joy, this volume). In a sense, therefore, he is already stepping outside the ethos established by the Djenné restoration project.

This evokes an ideal of Djenné architecture as it existed at French contact in 1894, of an era when the masons maintained an organic relationship to the houses that their ancestors had built, protected with family amulets buried in the foundations, and whose living descendants still reserved the right to refurbish and rebuild. The householders, however, actively use 'tradition' to dwell on the present. They parody the essentialism of the architecture and of a recycled past in order to attract tourism and development projects, get their houses rebuilt, and provide employment in the town. Heritage in this sense is a resource, actively engaged in a manner that heals past disputes and losses.

The promise of heritage for householders lies in its economic possibilities and the wealth brought into Djenné through the restoration programmes. Interestingly, what it doesn't do is challenge the collective memory in play. There are no counter-memories or works of individual recollection that would oppose the unifying plot of a nationalist narrative. Rather, it breaks it up into various individualistic versions that can be claimed to provide a unique 'sense of place' for all the actors involved, without challenging the basic integrity of the whole Djenné restoration project.

Islam and the Refusal of Nostalgia

A challenge to this nation-building project came instead from the most obvious fact, so far ignored, which is that Djenné is probably one of the most conservative centres of Islamic Koranic learning and belief in West Africa. Tensions over the form of Islamic architecture, in particular the mosque, have recently drawn religious authorities in Djenné into conflict with the State. The present mosque was built in 1907, on the ruins of the first mosque, said to have been built in the thirteenth century, in part to legitimize the form of Islamic rule that the French wished to support. The first and the third mosque were very different in style from the one the inhabitants knew when the French conquered Djenné in 1894. At this time, the inhabitants had been worshipping for half a century in a much simpler mosque built without towers or decoration by the jihadic reformist Cheikou Ahmadou in 1834. He left the first mosque to decay, and it still survived in ruins when Dubois visited Djenné in 1894. The ruins were finally demolished in 1907, on the site where the present mosque is built. Historical layering of buildings in Djenné is therefore characteristic of the right to rule as each group rewrites history expressed in space by selectively shaping and transforming an urban visual memory.

Political decentralization in Mali in the 1990s encouraged significant changes in the balance of power between state and religion. The Mayor of Djenné, as an elected representative, is now able to independently raise taxes and negotiate with the provincial deputy over both the use of taxes and the distribution of state funds. Together they are also responsible for security and various development projects. The authority of the *chef de village*, a 'traditional' inherited office, had been greater under French rule but has been diminished and effectively undermined by that of the mayor. Whereas previously the *chef de village* would have supported the deputy, now he is more likely to side with the Imam, the religious leader of Djenné, in restoring traditional authority to the town. The Director of the Cultural Mission, when he first came to Djenné, perceptively recognized this new cleavage in local power and promptly acted to restore several sacred sites as a sign of support for Islamic tradition by the State. This was used by the Director to confirm the role of the Cultural Mission as a mediator between secular and religious power in Djenné, and certainly the large-scale archaeological excavations at Jenne-Jeno and since 1996 the house restoration project have provided it with exceptional means to influence local inhabitants and their interest in cultural heritage.

The growth of 'neotradition' in Djenné has also been influenced by the government policy of decentralization, which gave more power to the mayor to manage local affairs. But the dominant trading class in Djenné, with important commercial links to Saudi Arabia and the Gulf States, has been influential in bringing offers of external, principally Saudi, financial support to rebuild the mosque and to pursue other developments in Djenné. The Imam is now the recipient of large amounts of Saudi money, which he proposes to use to rebuild the mosque along more Middle Eastern architectural lines. As Soares has pointed out, the idea of a separate 'Islam noir' in West Africa that was localized and distinct from 'Islam blanc' is a colonial myth propagated by the French in an attempt to keep West Africans beyond the influence of other centres of Islam (Soares 2000:279). The idea of a separate Islam in Africa was also supported by pointing to the development of a distinctive mud architecture for mosques that was unique to the region. The problem with this idea of a separate African Islam is that it could expose Djenné to reformist/activist tendencies in Islam, which aim to 'purify' it of local or indigenous African ideas. 'Spirit possession', for example, perhaps the most widespread of these practices and defined by some as un-Islamic, is a source of tension in Mali. According to reported 'traditions' of the Prophet Mohammad, idolatry or polytheism (in particular, the giving of a blood sacrifice to a spirit rather than to God) is the greatest of sins (Soares 2000:232). It is well known, for example, that the masons who built the houses in Djenné protected them with special foundation deposits and sacrifices, which also means that only they or their descendants can safely return to restore or to rebuild them. Probably much the same belief exists for the mosque, although it would not be explicitly stated. A loose group of reformers have existed in Mali since the 1940s to bring the practice of Islam in Mali closer to 'correct' practices modelled on the Arabic Middle East. A tendency exists for the Imam and others in Djenné to adopt these ideas in their conflict with the State in Mali and use Saudi (*wahhabi*) money to purify the mosque and other buildings of un-Islamic practices. In the last two years, the Imam has made various proposals to change the doors of the mosque, to build a wooden fence around it, to restore the outside with green glazed tiles, and to place gold minarets on the upper towers. The doors of the mosque have since been changed, but the Minister of Culture refused the erection of black painted iron gates for the four entrances to the mosque area as inappropriate to the conventions governing the preservation of the mosque as a world heritage site. At present, many of the concerns about what is the 'pure' form of Djenné mosque architecture may be held in abeyance or at least not used to bring the issue of the purity of Islam to a head.

There is nothing new in claiming that architecture should be a contested category. As mentioned, historical layering in the preservation of buildings is widely cited as a feature of Islamic preservation in contrast to the Western conception of a pure original state to which a building should be returned (for example, Bierman 1995). This acceptance that 'layering' should be the inevitable outcome of power also constitutes the urban memory of Djenné. Hence, for the Imam there is no necessary fixed form that the mosque should take. As witnessed by the austere style introduced by Cheikou Ahmadou, an old mosque can be left to decay while a new one is built by its side. Marilyn Waldman, in her discussion of Islamic tradition, describes three modes of dealing with change (Waldman 1986). I am using her suggestions here rather tentatively, to contrast with the restorative nostalgic form of memory characteristic of both the colonial and postcolonial state in Mali. She defines Islam as an organic model in which the religious and the political should ideally remain fused. She characterizes an Islamic religious tradition as incorporating a renewal, a maintainance, or a reformist stance. For example, an old content can be invested with a new form as when prohibitions of usury in Islam allow for modern forms of interest to be defined as profit indexed to inflation, or the emergence of women's banking in the Middle East may be fostered by maintained traditions – for example, sex segregation, the public veiling of women, and the Shari'a law that guarantees independent control of property to women. Waldman argues that 'tradition' in Islam is not fixed or done away with but open to how well it manages change without violating religious prescription.

Islamic preservation is therefore not a matter of returning to some point of origin as a pure state but rather fosters, following this understanding of basic Qur'anic values, a mode of 'rethinking'. The Imam is able to 'rethink' the relation of religion to the state in Mali through an architectural exegesis on whether to adopt *wahabi*-inspired elements as part of a historical layering of the mosque to create a composite urban memory. In contrast to the Venice charter version of authenticity, which requires attention to the 'age value' of the monument, Islamic renewal in Djenné produces a composite layered architecture in which glazed tiles and minarets can be added to the mosque and individual houses modernized. The radicalization of authenticity is materialized through acts of building and renewal, and attention is consequently drawn to the difference in trajectory from the one espoused by the colonial and postcolonial state in Mali.

Conclusion

My argument returns to how the materialization of heritage makes certain memories realisable and authentic and capable of imagining a future. Djenné is one of the few examples in sub-Saharan Africa of monumental architecture that fits the criteria for entrance to the UNESCO tangible World Heritage list. The nostalgic memory of the colonial and postcolonial state in Mali relates to the outside in terms of colluding with its demand, currently as heritage tourism, for memory to be 'retained as the secret of so-called primitive or archaic societies' (Nora 1989:8). The fact that Djenné is neither of these types of society does not prevent it playing a role as resistance to history, as the fear that memory recedes in the face of a collapse in space-time distanciation. The fact that the inhabitants of Djenné have their own modernizing projects is not compromised by this but facilitated by it. The public/private dichotomy that opens up the daily negotiation over what to do with a building relates it to the street and the daily experience of encounters in contrast to the aspirations of transforming domestic interiors. However, the restoration programme in Djenné also problematizes the distinction UNESCO makes between tangible and intangible heritage. The prescriptive nature of the restoration programme not only pertains to façades but also encompasses the internal organization of vernacular architecture and thereby has a direct impact on the use of space in Djenné houses. The preservation of tangible heritage has a direct impact on the organization of social life and must be understood as shaping kinship and gender relations. Finally, I argue for the existence of a radically different notion of heritage in Islam and its influence in Djenné. As elsewhere in Mali, the Imam wishes to modernize the mosque and bring it into line with events occurring more widely in the Islamic world. This desire does not necessarily imply reformist denunciation of pre-Islamic or other practices in Djenné, but it is sufficient, it seems, to bring these ideals into conflict with the conserving impulses of nostalgic memory and the postcolonial state.

In September 2006, the concatenation of forces that had organized the last ten years' response to Djenné as a world heritage site was forcibly disturbed by riots. Several thousand, mostly young, inhabitants of Djenné were antagonized by the appearance of an expatriate conservation team sent by the Aga Khan Foundation to repair the roof of the mosque. The team was seen digging a hole in the roof, and a crowd gathered and forced the conservators to flee for their lives. The inhabitants had destroyed the ventilators installed in the mosque a few years previously (as a gift from the U.S., embassy intent on showing that U.S. foreign policy was not hostile to Islam) and went on to attack the offices of the prefect and the mayor and burned the principal building of the Cultural Mission and several vehicles belonging to the Imam. The anger of the crowd was, it appears, directed against all the power holders involved in Djenné as a heritage site. The building of the Talo dam on the Bani River, which diverted water away from the town, had roused considerable resentment against outside interference, and the unannounced appearance of the Aga Khan team seems to have been the last straw. But the indiscriminate attacks on state, religion, and aid agencies together suggest that violence is being directed against what is experienced as a combined external oppression. The technologies of memory instigated by UNESCO and national states that are aimed at restoration, in a material and immaterial sense, inevitably privilege some memories at the expense of others, and the traces of their occupation in Djenné have been particularly singled out for destruction – which brings me to a final point: Heritage technologies can be fairly blunt tools for preserving memories and may be ill-suited at justifying their authenticity.

Acknowledgments

I am very grateful to Rogier Bedaux for his advice about this chapter and to him and members of his team for their support in allowing me to participate in the Djenné restoration project.

Bibliography

Arnoldi, M.-J. 2003. 'Symbolically Inscribing the City: Public Monuments in Mali, 1995–2002', *African Arts*, summer 2003.

Bell, D. 2003. 'Mythscapes: Memory, Mythology and National identity', *British Journal of Sociology* 54:63–81.

Bierman, I. A. 1995. 'Urban Memory and the Preservation of Monuments'. In *Restoration and Conservation of Islamic Monuments in Egypt*, J. L. Bacharach (ed.), pp. 1–12. Cairo: American Univesity Press.

Boym, S. 2001. *The Future of Nostalgia*. New York: Basic Books.

Cleere, H. 2001. 'Uneasy Bedfellows: Universality and Cultural Heritage'. In *Destruction and Conservation of Cultural Property*, R. Layton, P. Stone, and J. Thomas (eds.), pp. 22–29. London : Routledge.

De Jorio, R. 2003. 'Narratives of the Nation and Democracy in Mali: A View from the [sic] Modibo Keita's Memorial', *Cahiers d'Études africaines* 172:827–55.

Eriksen, T. Hylland. 2001. 'Between Universalism and Relativism: A Critique of the UNESCO Concept of Culture'. In *Culture and Rights: Anthropological Perspectives*, J. K. Cowan, M. Dembour, and R. A. Wilson (eds.). Cambridge: Cambridge University Press.

Nora, P. 1989. 'Between Memory and History: *Les lieux de mémoire*', *Representations* 26 (spring):1–10.

Prussin, L. 1994. 'Vérité et imaginaire de l'architecture'. In *Djenné, une ville millénaire au Mali*, R. M. Bedaux and J. D. van der Waals (eds.). Leiden: Rijksmuseum voor Volkenkunde.

Rowlands, M., and C. Tilley. 2006. 'Monuments and Memorials'. In *Handbook of Material Culture*, C. Tilley et al. (eds.). London: Sage.

Shelton, A. 2006. 'Museums and Museum Displays'. In *Handbook of Material Culture*, C. Tilley et al. (eds.). London: Sage.

Smith, A. D. 1999. *Myths and Memories of the Nation*. Oxford: Oxford University Press.

Soares, B. 2000. 'Notes on the Anthropological Study of Islam and Muslim Societies in Africa', *Culture and Religion,* 1(2):277–85.

Terdiman, R. 1993. *Present Past: Modernity and the Memory Crisis*. Ithaca, NY: Cornell University Press.

Todorov, T. 2001. 'The Uses and Abuses of Memory'. In *What Happens in History*, H. Marchitello (ed.), L. Golsan (trans.). London: Routledge.

Traoré, A. 2002. *Le viol de l'imaginaire*. Bamako: Fayard Actes Sud.

Waldman, M. R. 1986. 'Tradition As Modality of Change: Islamic Examples', *History of Religions* 25(4):318–40.

'Enchanting Town of Mud': Djenné, a World Heritage Site in Mali
Charlotte Joy

Over the last few decades there has been considerable growth in the recognition of cultural heritage sites in Africa. In many ways, UNESCO (United Nations Educational, Scientific and Cultural Organization) has provided a highly successful model for developing this new focus on the identification and documentation of national heritage. Initiatives such as Africa 2009 are ensuring the training and funding of heritage professionals in Africa.[1] Many African nation-states now have a permanent body of personnel committed to the recognition of the cultural value of their patrimony, and UNESCO provides the appropriate framework for its promotion. While tourism and material cultural heritage remain the major focus, the growth of concern with Intangible Cultural Heritage (ICH) within UNESCO has given a new impetus to the identification and celebration of cultural performances in Africa. However, all these initiatives are subjects of contestation and involve various actors who relate to significantly different networks of interests and power.

While the ethnography of African 'heritage elites' and their institutional frameworks still remain little understood, so does the impact of heritage programmes on local people. In this chapter, based on ten months fieldwork in Djenné, a World Heritage Site in Mali, and two months in the Intangible Heritage Division of UNESCO in Paris, I explore the historical and present-day conditions under which 'value' is attached and detached from Djenné's cultural heritage. I proceed to consider how the recent rethinking of the term 'value' within UNESCO can lead to insights for its future dealings with World Heritage Sites in the developing world. The picture that emerges is one of a divide, between a universalising and bureaucratic approach to the protection of heritage, on the one hand, and the local reality of living in a poverty stricken town in Mali, on the other. I explore how this divide is negotiated locally and internationally and how UNESCO's recent attempts to grapple with the protection of intangible heritage may provide some insights into future thinking about the protection of tangible heritage.

UNESCO and Cultural Heritage

As stated by Janet Blake, the concepts behind the protection of cultural heritage have a long history, intimately tied to events faced by the West since the turn of the twentieth century:

> It is worth noting that the three Conventions so far adopted by UNESCO reflect the political and/or intellectual concerns of the time at which they were developed: The 1954 Convention expressed the powerful post-World War II desire to reduce potential sources of international conflict; the 1970 Convention embodied an approach to cultural property which might be characterised as 'nationalist' or 'statist' . . . And the 1972 Convention reflected both the growing concern in environmentalist issues in its integration of the cultural with the natural heritage as well as the concept of 'common heritage of mankind', which had been developing at this time in relation to seabed mineral resources. (Blake 2000:62)

An explicit link is therefore drawn between a specific context that reveals the need for heritage legislation and its subsequent implementation. Blake goes on to argue that, for legal purposes, cultural heritage is viewed in terms of ownership and inheritance and by definition as a scarce or nonrenewable resource. Additionally, much of the legislation concerning cultural heritage operates on a communal and not an individual level. Such difficulties in legal definitions, together with the fact that much of the cultural heritage legislation to date has emerged as a response to Western concerns and concepts, inevitably mean that any attempts to apply the legislation to non-Western contexts can lead to difficulties.

Following UNESCO's adoption in 1972 of the Convention concerning the Protection of the World's Cultural and Natural Heritage (widely known as the 'World Heritage Convention'), a 'World Heritage List' was begun in 1978 to identify and protect sites of 'outstanding universal value' throughout the world. To date, there are 830 properties inscribed on the list, of which 644 are cultural, 162 are natural, and 24 are mixed sites.[2] Only 65 of these sites can be found in sub-Saharan Africa,[3] leading to the launch in 2006 of an 'Africa Fund' to help African State Parties prepare national inventories and nomination dossiers (known as Candidature Files).

The eurocentricity of the World Heritage project has often been commented on (see, for example, Cleere 2001; Eriksen 2001). The list has so far favoured monumental buildings and seems to articulate the cultural superiority of Europe through its archaeological and architectural heritage, leaving big parts of the world underrepresented. The criterion of outstanding universal value is the one thing that unites all the World Heritage Sites found on UNESCO's World Heritage List. However, it has long been problematic and subject to different and changing interpretations (Titchen:1996); indeed, its definition cannot be found in the World Heritage Convention itself but in its Operational Guidelines and is thus subject to constant review.

Intangible Cultural Heritage and the Abandonment of 'Outstanding Universal Value'

For the protection of ICH, the criterion of 'Outstanding Universal Value' and an attempt to draw up a World Heritage List of intangible heritage have been abandoned in favour of each country drawing up a 'Representative List'. The 'Proclamation of Masterpieces of the Oral and Intangible Heritage of Humanity' (from hereon, the Proclamation) was launched by UNESCO in 1997 and at first was intended to do for ICH what the World Heritage List does for tangible cultural and natural heritage. Three Proclamations, taking place between 2001 and 2005, saw the inscription of ninety 'Masterpieces' on a new global list drawn up by UNESCO.[4] In each case, the inscription procedure for the Proclamations echoed that of the World Heritage List, with member states submitting Candidature Files to be considered by an international panel of experts.

In 2006, UNESCO decided to discontinue any further proclamations and instead set up a Representative List drawn from member states' own inventories of ICH. Officially, this decision was due to the coming into force of the Convention for the Safeguarding of the Intangible Cultural Heritage in April 2006. UNESCO states that the Proclamations were only ever intended to be an awareness-raising exercise and were never to be an ongoing list like the World Heritage List.

However, it can be argued that behind the decision to abandon the criterion of 'outstanding universal value' in relation to ICH lie a number of practical difficulties confronted by UNESCO. Partly, there was a realisation within UNESCO of the difficulty of assigning a static cultural value to changing expressions of cultural life, such as those expressed through ICH. There was an awareness that the approach chosen to protect ICH had to be different from that used to protect tangible cultural heritage and that exercises of documentation would not suffice. Additionally, the criterion of 'outstanding universal value' proved problematic in relation to ICH because it could be argued that the ICH that lends meaning to people's lives is rarely 'outstanding' or 'universal' and most often is commonplace, such as language or regular cultural performances. This lack of definition led to a huge diversity in the kinds of Candidature Files put forward by member states, ranging from national cuisine to singing, specialised craft, festivals, and minority activities. A concrete measurement of 'value' could therefore not be achieved by UNESCO in relation to ICH because the value that UNECO was trying to protect was that embodied by the human actors themselves and therefore highly personal. Performances, cultural spaces, and endangered languages proved to be moving targets and, as cultural expressions rather than cultural artefacts, much harder for UNESCO to archive. This reassessment in relation to ICH can be used as a lens through which to see the difficulties encountered by UNESCO's original World Heritage Project, especially in cases where the restrictions imposed by World Heritage Status directly affect peoples' everyday lives.

Cultural Heritage in Mali

By African standards, Mali has been very successful in terms of World Heritage presence. It has four World Heritage Sites inscribed on UNESCO's World Heritage List as well as a Masterpiece declared by the Third Proclamation in 2005, before the Proclamations programme was discontinued. All four World Heritage sites have a strong architectural component (Timbuktu inscribed in 1988, Tomb of the Askia inscribed in 2004), whereas the Old Towns of Djenné also has an archaeological component (inscribed in 1988), and the Cliffs of Bandiagara: Land of the Dogon (inscribed in 1989) is a combined natural and cultural site. The Masterpiece is the Cultural Space of the Yaaral and Degal, a series of festivals that mark the annual crossings of the river by herds of cattle and that celebrate Peul culture.

Mali's success in this field is not a coincidence. Through the influence of French colonial interest in the country's vernacular architecture (Caillé 1830; Dubois 1897; Monteil 1903) and the sensitization of the Malian elite to issues of sustainable heritage, such as the protection of archaeological heritage following major discoveries (Brent 1996; Diabey 2000; McIntosh 1998; McIntosh and McIntosh 1986), Mali has for a long time been concerned with its cultural heritage. Mali's ex-President, Alpha-Oumar Konaré, himself holds a doctorate in archaeology and put the promotion of cultural heritage at the heart of his policies throughout the 1990s. The recent explosion in Mali of music and photography festivals, such as the annual Essakane music festival, and the rise in popularity of Malian musicians and artists, such as Salif Keita, the recently deceased Ali Farka Touré, Amadou and Mariam, and Malick Sidibé, to name but a few, mark a new direction for Mali's intangible heritage, which is now equal in prominence to tangible cultural heritage on an international stage.

The impact of these global trends on a town such as Djenné is complex, intimately tied as it is to the need for the success of the UNESCO World Heritage Project in Africa. Unlike Timbuktu, which spent some time on the World Heritage in Danger List from 1990, and the Cliffs of Bandiagara, put on the World Monuments Watch List of the 100 Most Endangered Sites in 2004, Djenné has so far escaped such a fate. It is of great importance to the Malian State to live up to its declared obligations toward its World Heritage Sites, and so there has sprung up what could be termed a 'heritage elite' in Mali, conversant in the language of heritage that best resonates with UNESCO's values and expectations. In Djenné, the heritage elite is in part represented by the Cultural Mission, a body set up by the Malian government to oversee its protection in accordance with the World Heritage Convention.

Djenné

The Old Towns of Djenné, consisting of approximately 2,000 mud brick houses and its mud mosque, together with a 4-km radius of surrounding archaeological sites, were judged as meeting two criteria necessary for inscription on the World Heritage List: '(criteria iii) to bear a unique or at least exceptional testimony to a cultural tradition or to a civilization which is living or has disappeared; and (criteria iv) to be an outstanding example of a type of building, architectural or technological ensemble or landscape which illustrates (a) significant stage(s) in human history'.

UNESCO's World Heritage Project is explicitly not a development project, yet it operates in some of the poorest parts of the world. Today, approximately 12,000 people live in Djenné, out of a total Malian population of 13.1 million. Mali is among the world's poorest countries, GNI per capita being a mere $330 (U.S.) in 2004, and adult literacy is low at only 19 percent. It is estimated that 224 of 1,000 children die before the age of 5.[5] In contrast to these statistics, UNESCO showcases on its website a short film about Djenné entitled 'Enchanting Town of Mud'.[6] Like most of the current literature on the town (Bedaux and Van der Waal 1995; Bedaux et al. 2003; Brunet-Jailly 1999;

Maas and Mommersteeg 1992), the film airbrushes out the lack of sanitation, poverty, deprivation, and cramped living conditions that are most peoples' lived experience. Djenné is a particularly popular World Heritage Site within UNESCO and features on a lot of its promotional literature because it embodies rare characteristics: representing at once Africa, monumental architecture, and uniqueness through being built entirely out of mud.

To explore the lives of a few people in Djenné, however, is to begin to see the distance between UNESCO's Djenné and the life of people in the town. UNESCO's impact on Djenné can be felt in a number of ways. Tourism represents a significant income for the Malian economy, and Djenné, like the other World Heritage Sites in Mali, provides compelling reasons for thousands of tourists to visit each year. The Director of the Malian Tourist Office (OMATHO) recognises 'culture' as Mali's biggest asset, since Mali is a landlocked country with little wildlife to attract visitors.[7] The emphasis on Mali's culture – music, photography, architecture, and archaeology – has long been the country's most compelling selling point to the outside world. UNESCO has helped to raise the profile of Mali's World Heritage Sites, and most tour companies design their itineraries around the three longest-established World Heritage Sites in the country: Djenné, Dogon Country, and Timbuktu. Infrastructure has sprung up to support this trade, benefiting other towns that link the three sites, such as San, Ségou, and Mopti.

Djenné's UNESCO status also attracts Western heritage sponsors to the town, in the form of restoration projects and other financial support, and has to a certain extent helped to protect it against major development projects, such as the Talo Dam (D'Entremont:2001). However, one can argue that UNESCO's biggest impact on the town of Djenné is the restrictions that are imposed on its architecture. In order to retain its World Heritage Status, the whole of the town of Djenné must continue to be built entirely in mud, and no other materials may be used for domestic housing construction. To enforce these restrictions, a Cultural Mission has been established by the Malian Government on the outskirts of the town. The remit of the Mission is to ensure that no material changes are made to the town without previous authorization, to protect the archaeological sites surrounding the town from looters, and to raise the profile of cultural heritage for the local population.

However, the task facing the Cultural Mission is not a simple one. First, the people working at the Cultural Mission are not from Djenné, and there is sometimes a lack of trust between the residents of Djenné and the Cultural Mission. Second, the Cultural Mission comes into regular conflict with other self-declared heritage organizations within the town that in turn have their own agenda when it comes to the protection of cultural heritage. One such organization is 'Djenné Patrimoine', made up of local people and run by a Frenchman who has built a house in the town. The organization's position could be described as conservative, with a hard-line attitude toward what it feels is 'authentic' in Djenné, particularly with reference to the restoration of houses and the work of artisans.[8] Another group has formed around the Imam and his supporters and has a strong Islamic agenda when it comes to envisaging the future of Djenné's cultural heritage. It has come into conflict with the Cultural Mission when attempting to beautify and modernise the Mosque to better fit with an Islamic aesthetic of a place of worship. A third stakeholder is the Malian Tourist Board (OMATHO), which set up a dedicated Tourist Office in Djenné in 2004. The Tourist Office would like to see the town sanitised and bring annual events, such as the re-mudding of the Mosque (which can be done at any time during the months of spring, depending on the river's water level and the annual rainfall, as judged by the elders of the town) into line with a predictable tourist calendar.

Within this context, the protection of Djenné's architecture is not as straightforward as it might at first appear. Added to the political and economic struggles over heritage in Djenné, changes in kinship structures, agricultural practices, and climatic and economic conditions have all had an impact on the viability of the local architecture.

Houses in Djenné

The international reputation of Djenné's architecture is founded on the image of its spectacular mud mosque and the houses that stand as testimony to the skill of their masons (Marchand:2003). Trevor Marchand's (2003) study of becoming a mason in Djenné describes how 'mason' is a profession passed down from one generation of a family to the next, with an ongoing relationship between the masons and the houses they build and maintain. Once a mason retires or dies, the relationship is inherited by the next generation of masons within his family. The relationship between house owner and mason comprises a spiritual as well as a practical dimension.

Despite the continuity in the masons' apprenticeship described by Marchand, the architecture of Djenné has changed over the years and continues to do so. The two major changes have been the style of mud brick used and the materials used to make the bricks. Before colonial times, the masons of Djenné used hand-moulded cylindrical bricks called *djenné ferey*; these incorporated mud (that was plentiful due to the regular flooding of the Bani river), rice husks, 'beurre de Karité', a powder made from the fruit of the Néré tree, and a powder made from the fruit of the Baobab tree. The mud mixture was left to break

Figure 6.1 Traditional Djenné houses (photograph: Charlotte Joy)

down with the use of animal urine and dung until it was ready to be moulded and left to petrify in the sun. These bricks were very hardwearing and lasted far longer than the mud bricks do today. The technology to make the mud bricks used today, called *toubabou ferey,* was brought to Djenné by the French in the region during colonial times. They are square bricks, made using moulds, and, owing to their shape, they are easier to make and faster to build with.

Changes in agriculture and the economy have meant that the mud bricks used today are not only a different shape but comprise fewer and less appropriate ingredients than do those used in the past and are therefore not considered to be of the same quality and durability. One change in agricultural practices that has led to the degradation of the quality of the bricks has been the use of mechanical rice dehuskers, which reduce the rice husks to powder (traditionally, this job was done by hand, thus protecting the husks). Rice husks were used as a crucial ingredient in binding the mud together. Today, masons either import expensive rice husks from other parts of Mali or use the stalks of the rice plant, which are longer and not as effective a binding agent. Animals kept in compounds are also liable to eat the accessible rice stalks, thus destroying the outer layers of mud-protecting houses.

A reduction in rainfall and fish stocks has also meant a degradation in the quality of the mud, since it is the concentration of calcified bones of fish that

Figure 6.2 Masons in Djenné at work applying the yearly layer of mud needed to protect the houses (photograph: Charlotte Joy)

makes the mud resilient. Additionally, pollution in the river and the town has meant that plastic debris and bottle tops are now found in the mud today and simply applied to the facades of the houses during the annual upkeep work, because *banco* (mud brick) houses require a yearly relayering of mud to protect them from the wind and the rain.

Consequently, despite an intuitive feeling that the housing in Djenné, being made from local materials and built by local masons should be cheap and sustainable, the reality is that the costs of the upkeep of houses in Djenné is spiralling beyond the means of many of the town's inhabitants. In 2005, upkeep could cost anything from 100,000 to 300,000 CFA francs (approximately $200 to $600 U.S.), depending on the size of the house. The costs are considerably more than in the past not only because of the difficulty in finding the appropriate building materials but also because traditional kinship structures that ensured cheap labour have disappeared. The disastrous rainfall and failing crops of 2004/2005 in Djenné have meant that many of its residents have not been able to afford the annual upkeep on their houses. After a while, peoples' houses simply collapse, often reducing families to live in cramped conditions in the remaining bottom part of the house. Additionally, peoples' expectations of their houses have changed over time, leading to a conflict between modern aspirations and static architecture (Rowlands 2003).

Against this backdrop, the residents of Djenné are trying to find new solutions. One recent trend has been the rendering of walls with fired clay tiles,

Figure 6.3 Fallen down house in Djenné (photograph: Charlotte Joy)

held in place by cement. Despite the initial high cost, it takes away the need for yearly re-mudding and is becoming increasingly economically viable. The practice is condemned by the authorities and the Cultural Mission, who see it as a desecration of local architecture. Yet, despite their protests, it is gaining in popularity. Critics of the new tiles claim that they are a short-term fix for a long-term problem. They point out that, fundamentally, mud and cement do not mix and that after a few years, cracks in the tiles and cement will allow rain to seep through and undermine the entire *banco* structure beneath. Despite the fact that many of them have reservations, the masons of Djenné are prepared to adopt the new practice because they claim that if they do not do so, other masons will step in, and they will lose money and break their relationship with the house and house owners. There is also the feeling that the tiles, being made locally and having in the past been used to cover the floors of houses, are not a radical departure from traditional architecture. One thing apparent in Djenné today, however, is that the practice is radically changing the appearance of the town as more and more house owners choose to tile their homes as an insurance policy against the uncertainty of future years. Despite condemnation of the practice of tiling houses, the Malian authorities represented in Djenné are also subject to financial constraints and consequently choose to build their public buildings, on the outskirts of the town, in cement. Additionally, other public buildings, such as the hospital and the radio station, are built in cement for similar financial and practical reasons. The attempts at enforcing restrictions on domestic housing are therefore undermined by the pragmatic measures taken by local officials.

Figure 6.4 House covered in tiles in Djenné. Photograph: Charlotte Joy.

Figure 6.5 Cement government building in administrative district of Djenné (photograph: Charlotte Joy)

UNESCO and Djenné Residents (the Djennenkes)

During a visit by UNESCO officials to Djenné at the beginning of 2005, the subject of lifting some of the restrictions imposed on Djenné's 2000 houses and surrounding archaeological sites was raised. Local officials asked whether the outskirts to the east of the town could be set free for development. This partial lifting of restrictions will not, however, alleviate the problems faced by thousands of house owners who can no longer cope with the demands of upkeep on their homes.

Aside from the 'heritage elite' described above, most people in Djenné have either never heard of UNESCO or may have heard of it but do not know who or what UNESCO is. If they have come across UNESCO, it will tend to have been through restrictions: those concerning access to the archaeological sites and restricting architectural practices. In an interview with a Djenné resident in early 2006, Djenné's World Heritage status was described as 'something that has landed on us from the sky'.

The poor living conditions in Djenné are by no means unique and are in many ways far superior to the living conditions of the majority of the population of Mali owing to the presence of clean drinking water, electricity for some, and the beginnings of a sanitation project. What is unique about the case of Djenné is the attention given by the outside world to its built and archaeological heritage, in a large part through UNESCO's attention, and the town's relative ease in raising money for cultural heritage protection projects. Given this attention, it should be a straightforward process to improve peoples' living conditions. This has been achieved in some measure by income from tourism and restoration and sanitation projects that have come to the town. The limitations of heritage projects coming to Djenné lie in the narrow definition of tangible cultural heritage and the inevitable separation of people from their built and material environment. However, this separation does not make sense to people locally. For example, in an interview with an ex-looter of the town's archaeological sites, it was explained to me that collecting terracotta objects from the sites was something he had done as a child, when out hunting with his father and grandfather. These objects were then sold to dealers in the town for as little as 200 CFA francs (approximately $0.40 U.S.). Some of the most impressive objects were kept by people in their homes.[9] However, being pre-Islamic cultural heritage, the majority of the archaeological objects hold little emotional appeal for people in Djenné today. The Cultural Mission's plea to the town to 'protect their heritage' through putting a stop to looting does not have much resonance with most people in Djenné. Instead, the local understanding is that the archaeological sites have been sold to the 'whites' (represented by the Cultural Mission), which is why they are now so well protected and why people go to prison when caught looting. It is believed that the archaeological objects are sold to Western museums or collectors. The sense of alienation is reinforced by the absence of any visible link beteeen the income from tourism and the town's archaeological heritage. Djenné has long been promised a museum, but it has never materialised, so none of the objects from the archaeological excavations is on display or accessible to the people in the town.

Conclusion

A brief sketch of some of the difficulties facing the people of Djenné today brings to light many of the issues facing UNESCO's World Heritage project in the developing world. The distance that exists between the bureaucratic restrictions imposed on a town, their imposition through local agencies, and their impact on local residents illustrates that UNESCO's global decisions often have consequences beyond those originally intended. The insights that can be gleaned from UNESCO's recent dealings with intangible heritage provide new avenues for exploration when applied to tangible heritage. First, in the case of Djenné, what is UNESCO seeking to preserve? As stated above, Djenné was inscribed on the World Heritage List because it was deemed to be 'an outstanding example of a type of building, architectural or technological ensemble, or landscape which illustrates (a) significant stage(s) in human history'. How much of the town needs to be preserved for the criterion to still apply? How can such a criterion be applied to a town that is essentially in constant transformation, without accepting an element of change? UNESCO does recognise that World Heritage cities are a special category and cannot be dealt with in the same way as discrete monuments and landscapes.[10] However, the difficulties encountered in Djenné amount to more than this; they demonstrate the enduring eurocentricity of the World Heritage Project, with its focus on monumental architecture and nostalgic remembrance of the past.

As things stand, the lack of help with the growing crisis facing house owners in Djenné threatens to result in Djenné being put on the World Heritage in Danger list, a measure that at least would provide the town with some direct financial assistance. However, a more constructive approach may be to take the lessons learned from the difficulties of designing legislation to protect ICH and apply them to the case of Djenné. Only through a thorough understanding of the constantly changing context in which World Heritage legislation is operating in Djenné, together with a realistic evaluation of the meaning of tangible cultural heritage to peoples' everyday lives, can UNESCO really claim to be promoting peoples' identity and cultural rights through preserving their cultural heritage.

Notes

1. www.africa2009.net
2. http://whc.unesco.org/en/list
3. http://whc.unesco.org/en/news.253
4. www.unesco.org/culture/intangible-heritage
5. Statistics taken from World Bank 2004, http://web.worldbank.org.
6. http://whc.unesco.org/en/list/116
7. Personal communication, Bamako, 17/08/05
8. See Djenné Patrimoine's website for an archive of its newsletters: www.djenne-patrimoine.asso.fr.
9. Personal communication, 12/09/2005
10. See Organisation des Villes du Patrimoine Mondial (OVPM).

Bibliography

Bedaux, R., & J. D. Van der Waal. 1995. *Djenné: Une ville millénaire au Mali*. Leiden: Rijksmuseum voor Volkenkunde.
Bedaux, R., B. Diabey, and P. Maas (eds.). 2003. *L'Architecture de Djenné, Mali: La pérennité d'un patrimoine mondial*. Gent: Snoeck.
Blake, J. 2000. 'On Defining the Cultural Heritage', *International and Comparative Law Quarterly* 49(1):61–85.
Brent, M. 1996. 'A View Inside the Illicit Trade in African Antiquities'. In *Plundering Africa's Past*, P. R. Schmidt and R. J. McIntosh (eds.), pp. 63–78. Bloomington: Indiana University Press.
Brunet-Jailly, J. 1999. *Djenné d'hier à demain*. Bamaka: Editions Donniya.
Caillé, R. 1830. *Travels through Central Africa to Timbuctoo; and Across the Great Desert to Morocco, Performed in the Years 1824–1828*. London: H. Colburn & R. Bentley.
Cleere, H. 2001. 'The World Heritage Convention in the Third World'. In *Destruction and Conservation of Cultural Property*, R. Layton, P. Stone, and J. Thomas (eds.), pp. 99–105. London: Routledge.
D'Entremont, D. 2001. 'The Djenné Project, Mali: Jean-Louis Bourgeois, Coordinator', *Cultural Survival Quarterly* 25(2).
Diabey, B. 2000. 'Fixed and Moveable Heritage in Djenné: Problems of Conservation and Protection'. In *Museums and History in West Africa*, C. Ardouin and E. Arinze (eds.), pp. 22–28. Washington, D.C.: The Smithsonian Institution.
Dubois, F. 1897. *Tombouctou la mystérieuse*. Paris: Librairie E. Flammarion.
Eriksen, T. H. 2001. 'Between Universalism and Relativism: A Critique of UNESCO's Concept of Culture'. In *Culture and Rights: Anthropological Perspectives*, J. K. Cowan, M.-B. Dembour, and R. A. Wilson (eds.), pp. 127–48. Cambridge: Cambridge University Press.
Maas, P., and G. Mommersteeg. 1992. *Djenné: Chef d'œuvre architectural*. Eindhoven: Université de Technologie.

Marchand, T. 2003. 'Devenir maître-maçon a Djenné, rang professionel laborieusement acquis'. In *L'architecture de Djenné, Mali: La pérennité d'un patrimoine mondial*, R. Bedaux, B. Diabey, and P. Maas (eds.), pp. 29–43. Gent: Snoeck.

McIntosh, R. J. 1998. *The Peoples of the Middle Niger: The Island of Gold*. Malden, MA: Blackwell.

McIntosh, R. J., and S. K. McIntosh. 1986. 'Dilettantism and Plunder: Illicit Traffic in Ancient Malian Art', *UNESCO Series: Museum*, XXXVIII(1):49–57.

Monteil, C. 1903. *Soudan Français: Monographie de Djénné, cercle et ville*. Tulle: Jean Mazeyrie.

Rowlands, M. 2003. 'Patrimoine et modernité a Djenné: Identités nationale et locale'. In *L'architecture de Djenné, Mali: La pérennité d'un patrimoine mondial*, R. Bedaux, B. Diabey, and P. Maas (eds.), pp. 78–84. Gent: Snoeck.

Titchen, S. M. 1996. 'On the Construction of 'Outstanding Universal Value': Some Comments on the Implementation of the 1972 UNESCO World Heritage Convention', *Conservation and Management of Archaeological Sites* 1(4):235–42.

A Masterpiece of Masquerading: Contradictions of Conservation in Intangible Heritage
Ferdinand de Jong

On 25 November 2005, the Director-General of UNESCO, Koïchiro Matsuura, proclaimed forty-three new Masterpieces of the Oral and Intangible Heritage of Humanity. One of these 'Masterpieces' was the Kankurang or Manding initiatory rite, sponsored by Senegal and The Gambia (UNESCOPRESS 2005). The Kankurang masked performance, staged in the context of circumcision and initiation rituals in Senegal and The Gambia, will henceforth benefit from UNESCO institutional support toward its safeguarding and conservation. I was most surprised to hear this news: A performance that I had studied for years as a local practice that was generally seen as 'degenerated' suddenly acquired recognition as 'intangible heritage'. This raises the question of how this practice should now be conserved. Should cultural performances be preserved? Can they be preserved? Will preservation not result in fossilisation? To what extent anthropologists should endorse the UNESCO policy has been a matter of academic debate (Nas et al. 2002).

One of the aims of the UNESCO policy is to identify, classify, and authorise 'intangible heritage' and make a contribution toward its conservation. The conservation of cultural practices inevitably requires their objectification according to some globally recognised bureaucratic format. Restoration brings about a transformation of the original object (cf Bruner 2005; Errington 1998; Handler 1988; Herzfeld 1991). Indeed, it seems strange that UNESCO offers a *global* cultural policy to identify, preserve, and promote *local* cultural practices. UNESCO policy has been analysed as undecidedly universalist *and* particularist (Hylland Eriksen 2001). The conservation of cultural practice seems rife with contradictions.

The objectification of material structures and cultural practices as 'heritage' is part of the making of a global subjectivity that posits the ownership of culture or cultural heritage as a condition for recognition (Brown 2003; Clifford 2004; Kuper 2003; Oakdale 2004; Sylvain 2005). UNESCO's policy indeed contributes to the making of this global subjectivity, which requires cultural visibility and the visualisation of culture. While the UNESCO policy claims to restore the actual cultural artefact in question, it simultaneously brings that artefact under a new regime of value (cf Appadurai 1986). However, the recontextualisation of objects and performances from one regime of value to another is riddled with contradictions (Myers 2002, 2004). In this chapter, I examine how a masked performance is subjected to a variety of regimes of value that impose contradictory conditions on its performance, and I examine how the recontextualisation of ritual as 'heritage' affects its performance.

Conservation strategies of the performance by grassroots initiatives and UNESCO are diametrically opposed in terms of how they envisage to preserve the masked performance. One of the contradictions that pertain to the conservation of the Kankurang is that of its visualisation. Traditionally defined as 'secret', this cultural practice is now increasingly put on stage for all to see. However, although visualisation is an important technology in the objectification of the performance, it does not result in complete objectification of the elusive masked performance. Inverting Benjamin's (1999) argument about the loss of aura in the age of mechanical reproduction, I show that recontextualisation through new regimes of value opens up possibilities for re-enchanted performance.

The Kankurang Masquerade

The Kankurang masquerade is one of the cultural traditions of the Casamance region in Senegal. The mask has an odd physical appearance. The Kankurang does not wear a wooden face mask but a costume of multiple pieces of bark fixed in such a way as to render the identification of the masked individual impossible. The Kankurang carries cutlasses in both hands, adding a terrifying aspect to his mysterious appearance. When the mask is brought out, it announces itself through a distinct cry, which is instantly recognisable and signals the audience to flee and hide. The masked figure is usually accompanied by around ten young men who are fifteen to thirty years old. They carry sticks and threaten to beat the numerous spectators in the audience. These companions are usually more dangerous than the masked figure himself. Their acts are

A Masterpiece of Masquerading: Contradictions of Conservation • 163

Figure 7.1 Kankurang and one of his cross-dressed 'guardians' (photograph: Ferdinand de Jong)

Figure 7.2 Cartoon in national newspaper *Le Soleil*. Kankurang beating up a man who claims: 'This is not a true Kankurang. It's Modou, whose brother I disciplined yesterday' (artist Samba Fall, courtesy *Le Soleil*).

attributed to the mask, but the mask acts with impunity. Thus the companions can display licentious behaviour, which may have far-reaching consequences; the masked performance sometimes results in physical punishments. Historically, the Kankurang mask was used to impose regulations issued by the male secret society. The mask was the disciplinary technique of the secret society, and the mask was entitled to use violence.

The Kankurang masquerade is the ultimate secret of the Mandinko initiation. The knowledge that the mask is a man in disguise is marked as a 'secret' that is revealed to the initiate during his initiation. Every initiate is morally obliged to preserve secrecy with regard to the nature of the mask and is committed to its secret. Confrontations occasionally occur between the community defined by its commitment to the secret of initiation and the agents who defy this secret. These confrontations are a recurrent theme in popular stories about Kankurang performances. Many examples are cited of violent confrontations between the mask and its opponents, who presumably violate the rules set by the mask. Although some of the violations are eventually settled by the payment of a fine, other such clashes result in more serious punishments (de Jong 2007). But whatever the outcome, popular stories always claim a moral victory for the Kankurang.

Male initiation is the contemporary context in which the Kankurang masquerade is performed. Such villagewide initiations are held at five-year intervals in Mandinko villages of southern Senegal and The Gambia. In the city of Ziguinchor (Casamance), however, such initiations are performed every year. Organised by extended families, these ceremonies have the purpose to circumcise boys in order to purify them and make them comply with Muslim standards. In the context of circumcision ceremonies, the Kankurang is meant to protect the circumcised initiates against the nefarious activities of witches. The Kankurang is meant to induce fear and prevent intruders from entering the 'initiation camp'. The protection of the camp is an endeavour in which the 'guardians' of the initiation camp mobilise occult forces against those of the intruders. However, the Kankurang himself also requires protection against the intrusive gaze of ill-intentioned persons, women in particular. One of the oral traditions on the origin story of male initiation relates how a curious woman wanted to find out what was going on in the initiation ceremony. She transformed herself into a bird and subsequently entered the sacred grove in which the initiates were secluded and guarded by the Kankurang. There she was found out. The woman was singled out for her curiosity, beaten by Kankurang, and punished with blindness. The oral tradition tells us that 'seeing' things forbidden to non-initiates may have serious consequences.

Performing the Prohibition

When the mask roams about the city at night, it makes a distinct cry, followed by the answers of his guardians: '*Cior Mama, issabaree!*' (Our Father, forgive us!), '*Asay! Afa!*' (Kill! Cut!). The Kankurang performance construes its audience as potential witches to be persecuted. The only appropriate reaction on the part of the audience is to flee and hide. The prohibition 'to see' the Kankurang is part of the ritual script and is enacted during performances. Women and non-initiates are not to look at the mask and thereby signal their subservience. In the 1930s, the French priest Doutremépuich observed a Kankurang performance and noted: 'He terrorises the initiates. They are not allowed to watch him and sit down, their heads bowed down' (Doutremépuich 1939:490). But some of the initiates clearly could not resist their curiosity: 'Some of them nonetheless take a quick glance at him' (ibid.). Even today the mask pursues bystanders, women in particular. The effect is that no bystander is in a position to watch the performance without fear of being chased and beaten by the masked figure or its followers. The performance allows the audience glimpses of the masked figure that will instill fear and thereby creates the 'aura' typical of the masked performance. The Kankurang's essential distance is deliberately maintained in performance by securing its unapproachability (cf Benjamin 1999:236–37). When men talk about the masked performance, they speak in metaphors that are characteristically ambiguous and open to multiple interpretations. They add to the suspense created by the masked performance. Indeed, the creation of suspense is what the masked performance is all about. Audiences are forced to give up their criticality. And to extend the impossibility of critical reflection in the age of mechanical reproduction, representations of the masked performance are discouraged.

Today, the prohibition to watch the masked performance is extended to technologies of reproduction such as photography. In 1990 I began researching the Kankurang masquerade. However, even after several weeks of research I had not yet witnessed a performance. When I finally had the opportunity, I watched Kankurang dancing on the backs of his guardians, who lay stretched out on the street as a sign of their submission. My assistant encouraged me to take a picture. But one of the guardians suddenly appeared before me, grabbed the camera out of my hands, and left me puzzled. After some patient negotiating by my assistant, I was allowed to buy my camera back. Of course, the act can be interpreted as a seizure triggered by the atmosphere of license that prevails at Kankurang performances, but the guardians legitimised their action by invoking the possibility that I could reproduce the photograph as a postcard. This, they claimed, is what they wanted to prevent. I reassured them that this was not my intention and that I was an anthropologist. I was then allowed to keep the film. The photograph I took, however, did not turn out well.

Time and again I was told that the mask should not be photographed. It is said that photography of the mask will result in the mask losing its power. This assertion is part of a more encompassing discourse prohibiting representations of the secret/sacred, a discourse that simultaneously attributes to the secret/sacred the power to subvert its successful mechanical reproduction in visual representations. Indeed, there is a widespread belief in Casamance that photographs of Kankurang will always fail (cf Spyer 2001:315). Undoubtedly, this discourse sustains the conditions for a successful performance: Kankurang's terror must not be taken lightly, and audiences are to express their fear by fleeing the masked figure. As a contemporary extension of the prohibition for women and other non-initiates 'to see' the masked performance, tourists and anthropologists are nowadays also forbidden to photograph the Kankurang. Spectators should feign fear so as not to subvert the masked figure's claim to occult power. This prohibition sets the conditions for a successful performance and is *performed* as part of the masquerade. While the formal prohibition may be implemented because photography is believed to diminish the sacred/secret, it is the actual *performance* of the prohibition that produces Kankurang's aura. One could therefore argue that the contemporary masked performance is framed by the possibility of its mechanical reproduction; its aura results from the deliberate negation of this possibility (cf Benjamin 1999).

Figure 7.3 Cartoon in national newspaper *Le Soleil* (artist Samba Fall, courtesy *Le Soleil*)

True and False Kankurangs

As a result of the transfer of the circumcision/initiation ritual to Ziguinchor, the Kankurang masquerade has been performed in the city ever since the early twentieth century. In the 1980s, however, some dignitaries in Ziguinchor felt the Kankurang performance was subject to *banalisation*, also referred to as *dégénération*. They claim that in the past Kankurang was capable of performing miracles and combating witches and evil spirits. The performance of Kankurang was dangerous, and those beaten by the mask were thought to experience the mystical consequences afterward. This applied to women in particular.[1] This nostalgic discourse on the occult power of the mask also claims that the public behaved more respectfully to Kankurang in the past. When the mask roamed the streets at night, cooking fires were extinguished, lights were switched off, and women shut themselves in their homes.

However, by the 1980s, none of these rules was observed in Ziguinchor. At that time, an increasing number of city-dwellers had their sons circumcised and initiated in a 'minor initiation' (*kuyandingo*). Novices in *kuyandingo* did not retreat in an initiation camp in the bush but were secluded in a room in their father's compound instead (de Jong 2007). This transformation in the initiation practice is thought to have had serious implications for the Kankurang performance. The Kankurang was now dressed in the novices' rooms, and the

Figure 7.4 Boys playing with their Kankurang (courtesy Royal Tropical Institute, Amsterdam)

secrecy formerly so carefully observed was now ignored. Moreover, where the initiations in the bush had been invigilated by male elders, the day-to-day supervision of the 'minor initiation' was left to teenagers who did not have the authority to make women subservient. The Kankurang performance lost much of its fearsome character and was increasingly appreciated for its playful character. Kankurang performances in Ziguinchor started attracting large crowds of children, who were delighted to participate in the play. During the performances, the children ventured as close to the mask as they dared, and as soon as the mask lunged in their direction, they ran away laughing and joyfully sought refuge around the nearest corner. The Kankurang was no longer feared the same way. Moreover, young maskers boasted about their Kankurang performances to their girlfriends. Instead of chasing witches at night, the mask was increasingly seen chasing girls at daytime.

The transformation of the masked performance also involved changes in the mask's costume. With the bark of the *Fara* tree increasingly hard to find, the mask performers have started using industrially produced material for the costume (de Jong 2007). These masks are considered mystically less dangerous. A new classification of masks has emerged to account for this transformation, whereby a distinction is made between masks of the city and those performed in the countryside. The 'real' Kankurang is supposed to wield powers that his urban counterpart does not possess. For instance, the real Kankurang is believed to be able to fly and jump from one roof to another. He is presumed capable of splitting and being in two places at once. He combats witches and remains invulnerable to their powers. But this real Kankurang is found only in the countryside, not in Ziguinchor. The classification is translated into spatial and temporal categories. Thus, most urban dwellers project the 'real' Kankurang onto the past or to faraway places in the bush. These spatial and temporal dichotomies that project the real Kankurang in the 'there and then' allow the incredulous to maintain their belief in the mystical powers of the mask. The distinction between true and false Kankurangs reinforces the belief in the venerated qualities of the mask in a context in which many mundane Kankurangs defy these beliefs.

Obviously, the Kankurang performance has evolved from a serious ritual into a play (cf Kasfir 1988). However, I presume that a 'false' Kankurang may at any time appear to be a 'true' one. Serious conflicts frequently occur, resulting from a lack of reverence for the masked figure on the part of disrespectful bystanders (de Jong 2007:Chapter 5). But in the 1980s and even today, many men felt the masquerade had lost its terrifying power and potential to instil fear in women and novices. The men attribute this lack of awe to the fact that everyone has become familiar with the secret of the mask. Their nostalgic discourse on the loss of the secret situates the mask in a regime of revelation in which Kankurang should be seen only by initiated men. The transformations in the Kankurang performance that were all too real were metaphorically expressed as the loss of the secret of male initiation.

Restoration of the Regime of Revelation

The view that contemporary mask performers violate the secrecy required for its efficacy motivated a number of Ziguinchor dignitaries to regulate the Kankurang performances in their town. In 1988, some of the elders in Ziguinchor – usually referred to as the city's dignitaries (*notables*) – made a first effort to regulate the masked performance. They went to see the Governor and the Chief Constable and asked them to cooperate in preventing the further *banalisation* of the mask by regulating its performance. The dignitaries proposed making it mandatory for mask performers to apply for a license that was to be distributed by the authorities. The licenses would be given only to the people who organised initiations in the bush of Ziguinchor. With several violent conflicts involving Kankurang still fresh on their minds, the Governor and the Chief Constable were pleased with the proposition. In subsequent years, Kankurang performances were indeed rare. However, a couple of years later Kankurangs were being performed again.

In 1994, Sana Diolo, a spokesman of the Mandinko community in Ziguinchor, made another effort to regulate the Kankurang performances. Diolo was in charge of two programmes on Mandinko culture on the local broadcasting station in which the predicament of traditional values in the modern world were discussed by, usually, elder men. During the circumcision period of 1994, he regularly discussed the virtues and vices of Kankurang performances on his broadcasts.[2] Upon the positive response to his ideas from the public, Diolo decided to resume the work done by his predecessors and introduce a regulation of the masked performance. He invited a number of the city's dignitaries to a meeting, including representatives of four ethnic groups: Mandinko, Jola, Balanta, and Bainunk. In addition, the chiefs of several quarters (*chefs du quartier*) were invited. At the meeting, all the dignitaries expressed their grievances about the 'abuse' of the masked performance and its use as a pretext for theft and the settlement of old scores. One elder informant pointedly described the performers as 'thieves, offenders, minors, and gangsters'. Everyone agreed that interference with the 'degenerate' tradition was necessary. A resolution was adopted prohibiting Kankurang performances in Ziguinchor for a period of five years. It was decided that, after this five-year period, Kankurang performances would be allowed only during the initiations in the bush of Ziguinchor that were to be organised at five-year intervals, 'in correspondance with the customs of the various communities'. The site of the ritual's enactment was to be stipulated by the dignitaries. The resolution was signed by three representatives of each ethnic group (Bainunk, Jola, Mandinko, and Balanta), who requested the administration to implement this decision and see to its observance. The Mayor and the *chefs du quartier* were asked to appoint vigilantes in all the town's districts. The public response to the decisions was favourable, although there were incidental expressions of discontent from the young men. For a few years no Kankurangs were performed in Ziguinchor.

The dignitaries designed the regulation to 'preserve' a 'tradition'. The town's dignitaries wanted the mask to be the terrifying secret that was kept in awe by everyone. Interestingly, the elders decided Kankurang performances would be allowed only in the bush. Their initiative to confine the masked performance to initiations in the bush was designed to exclude women from the ritual space where the mask is dressed. By redefining the appropriate context for the masked performances, the dignitaries also denied young men any authority in the matter. Young men and women did not welcome this but certainly did not publicly contradict the elders. Bringing the masked performance back to the bush meant resituating the mask in the domain that, cosmologically, legitimises male authority over women and youth. The dignitaries tried to restore a gendered gerontocracy, which is obviously obsolete in Senegal's urban life today.

The regulation of the masked performance was also designed to preserve the mask's aura. Surprisingly, the dignitaries and the self-proclaimed spokesmen for the various ethnic communities turned to the administration to impose their decisions. They admitted that they no longer controlled the young men involved in the mask's performance and needed the state to intervene. The dignitaries asked the local authorities to assist in implementing its decisions. In view of the secrecy required regarding the Kankurang, the process was very surprising, indeed. Some young men reproached the dignitaries for discussing the mask's regulation at the town hall and argued that the meeting should have been held in the bush. It is indeed ironic that the elders should have required the assistance of the administration in the management of the secret of initiation. But it also shows that the dignitaries have started to reconceptualise the Kankurang performance as a 'tradition' that should be subservient to the rule of law. The secret was to be restored and subordinated to State control.

But there was more at stake. The Mandinko dignitaries did not publicly say so, but they believed that members of other ethnic groups were not as seriously committed to keeping the mask's secret. In other words, their imposition of a regulation was also a subtle effort to claim Mandinko ownership of the masked performance. In Senegal, cultural practices are increasingly reified as 'traditions' or 'cultural heritage' (*patrimoine culturel*). The regulation of the Kankurang masked performance by the dignitaries was thus designed to increase the respectability of a Mandinko ritual and assert a Mandinko heritage in the national public sphere. In Ziguinchor, the Mandinko cultural entrepreneurs transformed the Kankurang into part of their ethnic 'heritage'. The policy adopted by the dignitaries revolved around an attempt to make its appearance once again awesome. The 'aura' of the Kankurang was to be restored by a regulation that was to limit the exposure of the mask. As we will see, the UNESCO heritage policy to conserve the masked performance as 'heritage' has adopted a very different strategy.

Festival of Mandinko Heritage

The attempts at regulation of the Kankurang performance are to be understood as attempts at conservation of the masked performance. But the strategy to transform Kankurang into heritage by restoring its secret went hand in hand with attempts at its increased visualisation. While the dignitaries of Ziguinchor proposed to limit the number of performances, some cultural entrepreneurs were rather inclined to establish recognition for the masked performance by enhancing its status in other ways. Attempts at restoration of the regime of revelation have recently given way to initiatives to showcase the masked performance as 'heritage'.

The biennial *Festival du diamba-dong* is held in Sédhiou (Casamance) and is officially registered as part of the Senegalese cultural calender.[3] The aim of the festival, I was told by one of its organisers, was to instruct the town's youth in the real significance of the Kankurang. Contemporary Kankurang masked performances, he reminded me, do not conform to the traditional standards for proper performances. At this festival, youth would be shown the *real* Kankurang.[4] One of the most interesting scenes at the festival happened at the opening ceremony. After several words of welcome by Sédhiou's Mayor and other dignitaries, words of gratitude to the Government and the politician who acted as the festival's patron, one of the speakers drew attention to the educational aspects of the *diamba-dong* and the initiation ceremony. He started singing initiation songs to illustrate his argument. Supported by drumming, the audience soon joined in the singing. Even the dignitaries and politicians joined in. The opening of the festival ended in a festive mood, with everyone enjoying the communal spirit of initiation that they had gone through in their youth. Men and women were confounded, and nobody felt it inappropriate for these (secret) songs to be sung in public. The town's population had already got used to the public performance of these songs; popular bands such as *Tourécounda* and *UCAS de Sédhiou* had long since included initiation songs and rhythms in their repertoire. At the opening of the Festival, the singing and dancing of initiation songs and rhythms created a true sense of conviviality between the politicians and the population.

The next day, the programme resumed with a lecture by the regional expert on Kankurang.[5] His lecture warned against the effects of globalisation, which, he felt, could potentially destroy local culture. The speaker established a necessity to 'rescue' Kankurang from its current predicament, but he also argued for the necessity to 'market our cultural resources'. The conference was richly inconclusive and revealed all the tensions accruing to the recontextualisation of Kankurang: restricted revelation versus public recognition; secrecy versus publicity; pride in cultural heritage versus fear of losing it to capitalist commodification.

After the *table-ronde,* all went outside to watch a spectacle involving a Kankurang performance. On the road in front of the Town Hall, chairs had been placed for the participants in the conference.[6] After a while, a Kankurang appeared from afar, chasing the bystanders in all directions. The conference participants, however, remained seated on their chairs and watched the other bystanders flee for the masked figure. Dancing young men subsequently entered the spectacle space in front of the chairs, accompanied by their Kankurang. The masked figure honoured the festival's organiser by crouching in deference to him, and subsequently disappeared. The young men went on to demonstrate their invulnerability by sowing at their limbs with machetes. Indeed, all the performance elements associated with the initiation ceremony were demonstrated. However, the performances were not staged within the context of initiation but within the context of a festival to promote Kankurang as 'cultural heritage'. The performance standards of secrecy and suspense that accrue to the context of circumcision and initiation were clearly redefined in the festival context. In addition to transforming the masked performance into a public spectacle, the festival also inculcated new forms of spectatorship. Within the context of the festival, the mask was not performed to hunt down witches but as a form of entertainment. While the random bystanders were chased by the Kankurang, the seated audience of conference participants was allowed to contemplate the performance without being part of it, undisturbed by the Kankurang. So, the festival produced two different audiences: an audience of commoners chased by the Kankurang and an audience of politicians and conference participants undisturbed by the mask, well placed to look at the masquerade *and* its audience.

Clearly, the recontextualisation of the Kankurang as heritage produces a spectatorship that differentiates the audience along new lines of distinction, transforming some into an audience for others (cf Barber 1997; Mark 1994). While the singing of initiation songs at the opening ceremony had briefly created a sense of conviviality between politicians and the population, the closing ceremony reaffirmed the distinction between them by allowing the politicians to watch the population perform its 'heritage'.

A UNESCO 'Masterpiece of Intangible Heritage'

At the festival, the Mayor of Sédhiou referred to the Kankurang performance as 'a national heritage in a united nation' (*un patrimoine national dans une nation unie*), defining Kankurang as a national heritage. Interestingly, UNESCO presents Kankurang as a transnational, Senegambian heritage. The national governments of Senegal and The Gambia have jointly submitted an application to UNESCO for the recognition of Kankurang and the Mandinko initiation as a Masterpiece of Intangible Heritage. In November 2005, the application was rewarded, and 'Kankurang and the Manding initiatory rite' now figure on the UNESCO list of Masterpieces of the Oral and Intangible Heritage of Humanity.

The Masterpiece is presented as the property of the Mandinko ethnic group. The representation of the contemporary predicament of Kankurang in the report is very much in keeping with the perception of the male elders of the Mandinko community, but the policies suggested to remedy the perceived problems and to preserve the masquerade are entirely different. Whereas the Mandinko dignitaries proposed to restore the masquerade by limiting the frequency of its performances, the UNESCO proposal seeks to restore the masquerade by increasing its visibility.

The UNESCO proposal identifies the Kankurang as a 'ceremony' and describes the masquerade in structural-functionalist terms as a ritual that expresses the moral authority of the elders of the Mandinko community (which, clearly, is no longer recognised by Mandinko youth). The proposal goes on to argue that Kankurang insures the social order and pursues evil spirits. Moreover, the Kankurang fulfils an important social function by disciplining the initiates in the Manding initiatory rite. During their retreat, the initiates are taught the ethics of social life (respect, solidarity, courage, and humility). Although the report does not ignore the contemporary context of its performance, it provides a rather idealised version of the Mandinko initiation rite, privileging the ritual's function to restore order rather than its capacity to inspire rebellion, as it sometimes does (de Jong 2007).

One of the threats to Kankurang's salvation is its *banalisation,* which the report suggests is a consequence of the multiethnic composition of the population of the cities in which Kankurang is performed. It is indeed suggested that non-Mandinko do not respect the rules pertaining to Kankurang performances. Urbanisation is thus identified as one of the threats to the continued performance of the masquerade. In other words, unlike the Mandinko elders, who identified unruly youth as the culprit, this report identifies forces beyond local society – urbanisation, modernisation, and globalisation – as the causes for the alleged *banalisation* of the Kankurang. Instead of blaming the youth involved in masquerading, as the elders do, the report prefers to identify an abstract 'modernity' as the reason for Kankurang's *banalisation*. In its modernist discourse, the report suggests that local traditions are disappearing in the onslaught of modernity and are giving way to a uniform, global culture.

Ironically, while modernity is considered one of the root causes for Kankurang's *banalisation*, the masquerade is also called on to establish an equilibrium between 'tradition' and 'modernity'. In fact, Kankurang is thought to symbolise Mandinko identity and preserve Mandinko cultural values.[7] Kankurang is presented as a bulwark against the ravages wrought by modernity. To counter modernity, Kankurang's restoration is required. To restore Kankurang and the Manding initiatory rite, a range of activities is planned that revolve around the regulation of the grassroots initiatives discussed above. To that effect, new legislation is said to be required. The report claims that such local level initiatives are in need of help and coordination by heritage professionals. We witness that the conservation of Kankurang involves a measure of formalisation and indeed, bureaucratisation. For example, one of the aims to be pursued is the formal transmission of knowledge related to the Kankurang through the establishment of museum programmes, summer camps, and the publication of initiation songs. A variety of media are suggested to promote this exercise in salvage ethnography, including the making of videos, catalogues, postcards, theatrical performances, an annual festival, and a website on the Kankurang. Even miniatures are to be produced as part of the programme (while the report remains committed to the sacred aspect of the ritual and the prevention of further *banalisation* . . .).

The report identifies modernity as an experience of loss to be remedied through restoration. Ironically, while the Kankurang and Manding initiatory rite are presented as ravaged by modernity, they are simultaneously presented as the remaining repositories of Mandinko values. But the report selects only those values that UNESCO supports (respect, solidarity, and so on), passing over the values that would not be endorsed by an international jury. Nothing is said about the aspects of masquerading that are incompatible with the modern state. For instance, we learn that Kankurang is implicated in 'exorcism', but we do not learn about the violence perpetrated by the Kankurang when it attacks witches. To salvage the ritual, its dark sides that are incommensurable with bureaucratic conservation are silenced.

In short, UNESCO presents the Kankurang and Manding initiatory rite as the precolonial heritage of the Mandinko civilisation. This heritage is thought to have survived in spite of colonisation and is here presented as a potential *pharmakon* to heal the wounds of postcolonial modernity. The operation is not forward-looking but focused on the restoration of selected values associated with an imaginary precolonial past. Essentially nostalgic, the restoration of Kankurang is part of the salvage paradigm that denies the coevalness of the 'other' (Fabian 1983). While UNESCO's discursive framing of the ritual performance as 'heritage' denies its current performance practices, its proposed strategies to 'conserve' the masked performance all amount to objectification and increased visualisation.

Visualisation of the Masked Performance

The visualisation and the objectification of Kankurang have a longer history than is recognised in the UNESCO documentation. In The Gambia, the transformation of Kankurang into 'heritage' has been pursued for even longer than in Senegal. The National Museum in Banjul presents Mandinko traditions as part of the national cultural heritage. The ethnographic department of this small museum displays a Kankurang miniature and drawings of various Kankurang types. By displaying the mask at the National Museum, the Gambian State has incorporated it in the national cultural heritage in order to further its nationalist project. The Gambian Kankurang is made into a national symbol and used by the State to create a national culture (cf Ebron 2002), but the recontextualisation of the masquerade goes beyond 'nationalisation'. The Gambia is a popular destination for African American pilgrims on homeland tours. Kankurangs are often performed for them, for instance in the context of the annual International Roots Festival in Banjul. The masked performance is thus presented as a pan-African heritage. Clearly, the interpretation of the masked performance offered to the tourists is not necessarily congruous with local understandings. One pilgrim who had witnessed a Kankurang performance when visiting The Gambia sent me an email congratulating me with my important research on African 'martial arts'.

The reframing of Kankurang as 'heritage' is likely to contribute to its increased commodification for foreign audiences.[8] Obviously, when Kankurang is performed for an audience of tourists or African American pilgrims, their submission to the mask cannot be enforced. When the participants of the Third International Mande Studies Association convened in The Gambia in 1998, the evening programme included a visit to a compound where local cultural traditions were performed. After a performance of 'Jola dances', in which some scholars vigorously demonstrated their skills acquired during fieldwork, a Kankurang was to perform next. Needless to say, the masked figure did not pursue the audience, as such would be considered highly inappropriate by the conference participants. The audience was not supposed to flee and hide but was instead allowed to watch the Kankurang and to photograph and film its performance. The regime of revelation in which Kankurang is to be seen only in glimpses is giving way to a regime of visualisation that requires its exposure.

Such visualisation can now increasingly be witnessed in Senegalese newspapers, too. Especially during the summer vacation, Senegalese newspapers dedicate holiday sections of the paper to issues ranging from popular music to history and heritage. Usually such sections dedicate one page to 'tradition'. The coverage of 'traditions' is usually of a rather nostalgic mode; immersion in tradition is invariably held to have a healing effect on the alienating effects of modern life. Ever since Léopold Senghor invoked tradition as the basis of African identity, a *retour aux sources* is advocated to strengthen one's African identity. Invariably, the papers invoke the occult as an aspect of tradition. The occult is never explicitly dwelled on but always referred to in passing as a way of authenticating the African tradition. Kankurang is often covered as one of Senegal's traditions, and the newspaper articles often feature photographs of the mask.

The masked figure is thus increasingly represented through photographs that mechanically reproduce the performance into an object to be looked at. But representation of the masquerade is not restricted to photography. At least one Senegalese painter, Omar Camara, has depicted Kankurang in a number of his paintings. One painting depicts the Kankurang removing the bark cloth that covers its head, using one of its machetes. However, instead of uncovering the masker's face, the painting reveals a darkness that gives little away about what's inside the mask. The painting conveys a sense of mystery. Playing with secrecy and revelation, Omar Camara has represented Kankurang as a mystery. In his painting, the mystery of the mask is not violated, but enhanced. In this painting the mask nonetheless becomes an object of contemplation, as even the most mysterious representation of the mask cannot instil the fear that a performance can. Kankurang, once upon a time not to be seen by non-initiates, is now transformed into an object of contemplation.

A Masterpiece of Masquerading: Contradictions of Conservation • 177

Figure 7.5 *Detail* by Omar Camara, oil on canvas

Figure 7.6 Kankurang as statuette (photograph: Ferdinand de Jong)

Kankurang is objectified in other ways, too. Miniatures are offered for sale in tourist shops in Ziguinchor. Their pavement advertising consists of Kankurang models, frozen in movement and meant to promote the sale of baskets, figurines, and tourist art. In other words, Kankurang is increasingly commodified in performances and objects. While such commodification can easily be seen as yet another aspect of the masquerade's *banalisation*, it is also part of the proposed policy of its conservation. The UNESCO application for Masterpiece status for the Kankurang and Manding initiatory rite clearly negotiates between conservation and commodification, sacralisation and visualisation. The production of tourist performances and miniatures is part of a process of objectification whereby audiences are increasingly allowed and encouraged to gaze at the mask. The masked performance is indeed increasingly objectified and literally materialised in objects. Paradoxically, the promotion of the intangible heritage of Mandinko cultural values relies on its materialisation in tangible commodities.

Masquerading As Intangible Heritage

The recontextualisation of the masked performance from a religious ritual into 'heritage' involves a shift from the register of ritual secrecy to that of public performance. One observes a shift from religious awe for a 'spirit' (*djinn*) to a secular, 'ethnographic' reading of the masked performance. The reception of the performance involves a change from embodied participation ('suspense') to discursive 'nostalgia'. Whereas the mask formerly subjected its audience to surveillance in an occult pursuit of witches, it is now itself subjected to the inspecting gaze of tourists, anthropologists, and heritage pilgrims. Yet, the new regime of recognition that the masked performance is subjected to – which requires its visibility – does not necessarily amount to objectification. The performers incorporate the shifts in meaning into their performance, which takes a 'reflexive' turn. To demonstrate this point, I provide a vignette.

In 2004, I lived in the part of town near the river where the initiates were 'bathed' before they were taken home, accompanied by a Kankurang. On every Saturday in September, scores of Kankurangs made their way through this neighbourhood. When I watched some of them pass by, keeping my camera ready, one of the passers-by told me: 'It is formally forbidden to photograph the Kankurang!' The choice of words clearly mimed the bureaucratic language of the State. But the official language is but one part of the incorporation of the new contexts of performance within the performance itself. One of the 'guardians' of the masked figure shouted at me: 'This is our tradition! This is all that is left of our tradition!' Clearly, the idea that 'tradition' is vanishing in the onslaught of modernity echoes the 'salvage paradigm' that also informs the UNESCO classification of Kankurang as intangible heritage. My vignette suggests that the assumptions and the procedures that inform the recontextualisation of Kankurang as 'intangible heritage' are incorporated into the performance itself. The performers contribute as much as the cultural brokers do to the definition of Kankurang as heritage. But the difference between the youthful performers and the cultural brokers is that the young men enjoy performing the Kankurang in a playful and improvised manner, while the cultural brokers insist on a ritual script that is based on an outdated, village-based model. Their discourse on the Kankurang performance is nostalgic and restorative.

Ziguinchor's youth do not seek to make the performance compatible with the respectable modes of performance required for national and international recognition. They are happy to transform the masked performance from an awe-inspiring ritual into a burlesque performance involving the inversion of gender roles. Their performance even 'reflects' on the current predicament of Kankurang as a highly appreciated cultural heritage. In 2004, I noticed that a few performers had fashioned wooden makeshift cameras, using plastic tubes and waste, while they themselves were dressed up as transvestites. The performers played with their makeshift cameras and pretended filming the entire performance. They were proud of their performance and allowed me to take a photograph, demanding a donation in return. The irony of the situation was not lost on me: I needed to pay in order to photograph my mimed self. Questions were not allowed. After I had given my donation, they then swiftly moved on to the rhythm of the *diambadong*.

Figure 7.7 Performers with makeshift cameras (photograph: Ferdinand de Jong)

Figure 7.8 Performers performing as journalists (photograph: Ferdinand de Jong)

This case suggests that the performers were very much aware of the interest others have in photographing the mask. Miming the photographers, they acknowledged the interest in mechanical reproductions of the mask and simultaneously drew attention to their own photogenic qualities. Obviously, the performers knew that the contemporary interest in filming, taping, and photographing the masquerade is but a logical consequence of the recognition for the Kankurang as a Senegambian heritage. Their performance celebrated that recognition by embodying it. Yet mimesis involves a critical difference. If mimesis implies that the copy assumes the power of the original (Taussig 1993), then the performers' mimicry involved an appropriation of the gaze. Indeed, they allowed me to photograph, but not to ask questions (*they* held the microphone; see illustration). My ethnographic project was subverted, my gaze returned.

Conclusion

This chapter has examined two different regimes of performance for the Kankurang masquerade. The regime of revelation requires that Kankurang cannot be seen by non-initiates; its invisibility is a prerequisite for its auratic appearance. In contrast, the regime of recognition requires the visibility of cultural heritage. The recontextualisation of sacred ritual as intangible heritage necessarily diminishes its original aura, as Benjamin (1999) predicted.

However, the coexistence of various regimes opens up the possibility for playful resistance against the regimes in place and the objectifications that they establish. In some performances, the object of visualisation resists and escapes its objectification. Through mimesis of the gaze, reflexivity is embodied in performance. Although the original aura of the masked performance is lost, the performers have re-enchanted their performance by mimicking the gaze and incorporating the objectification of the performance. While Mandinko elders, the State, and UNESCO propose to *restore* the masquerade, the young performers *reinvent* through embodiment. Their performance embodies beyond the politics of restoration.

The contradictions of conservation seem to revolve around two contradictory tenets: Kankurang and the initiation ritual are threatened by the process of modernisation and so are the values transmitted within these cultural practices. To ensure that these values are preserved for 'humanity', the cultural practices of Kankurang and the initiation ritual need to be salvaged through restoration (and replacement in other media). This chapter has examined various attempts at conservation. First, we looked at how Mandinko elders have tried to restore the mask's aura through interventions in the process of performance. Their project of 'conservation' consisted of restoring the secret by hiding the performance from the 'gaze'. In contrast, the policy pursued by the national states in collaboration with UNESCO seems to promote an increased visibility of the masquerade in modern media. Whereas mediation of secretive practices has been conducted with sensitivity among Australian Aborigines (cf Ginsburg 2006), the visualisation discussed here seems bound to objectify the sacred. The State-led restoration of Kankurang subjects the masquerade to the transnational gaze of the tourist spectacle (cf Bruner 2005; Mitchell 1989). It seems that restoration is a self-defeating project and that recognition can be obtained only through commodification.

However, the youth implicated in the performances of Kankurang do not seem to deplore the loss of Kankurang's awesome nature. They incorporate the modern in a new visual performance in which the gaze of the spectators is deliberately returned, both reflecting and reflecting on the visibility of Kankurang. Their playfulness neither is nostalgic nor does it give in to the project to turn Kankurang into an object for visual contemplation. This suggests that, in spite of the objectification of a performance into an object for the archive, its performativity will continue to escape the curators of tradition. The performers 'restore' the ritual through embodied improvisation (cf Bryant 2005), negating the mechanical reproduction of masquerading by incorporating it into the performance. They masquerade *as* intangible heritage.

Acknowledgments

Research for this paper was funded by The British Academy (grant SG-36720) and the Economic and Social Research Council (grant RES-000-22-0735). I would like to thank the Senegalese Ministry of Scientific Research for allowing me to conduct research in Senegal, and Dr Hamady Bocoum for his assistance. A preliminary version of this article was presented at the Art and Archaeology of Africa and the Americas seminar at the School of Oriental and African Studies.

Notes

1. Even today, women consider it a liability to be beaten by the Kankurang, because this is thought to turn them barren. But the mystical dangers associated with the masked figure apply to the masquerader, too. He may be hurt while performing the masquerade.
2. I accidentally found myself involved in these broadcasts, which demonstrates that this discussion about the Kankurang was not only about the conservation of a Mandinko practice but, through the involvement of scholars, also about the assertion of a Mandinko heritage in the world at large.
3. The festival was organised by a native of Sédhiou (referred to as *'homme de culture'*), who had invited several folklore dance troupes to perform at the festival. The festival was announced in the national and local media. Three young French apprentice-journalists had come all the way from Dakar to cover the event. Apart from these journalists and the local participants, the festival attracted very few visitors.
4. The second aim of the festival was to promote peace. The *diamba-dong* dance is performed at the end of the circumcision/initiation ceremony and is known by members of all ethnic groups in Casamance. Its performance creates a sense of communion that, it was argued, contributes to the making of peace in this region that has been plagued by an insurgency for more than twenty years. It should be noted that many grassroots initiatives have developed using 'tradition' in the peace process. 'Tradition' is thought to be an effective device in the establishment of peace, as opposed to the 'modern' political process, which is often thought to be corrupt. The Kankurang, like other traditions, is thus conceived of as a medicine against the malcontents of modernity. Such 'grassroots' peace initiatives are often supported by the political class and involve a reification of a tradition (de Jong 2005).
5. The Director of Ziguinchor's Lycée Djignabo, Nouha Cissé.
6. Meanwhile, on a two-storey building in the vicinity, a Kankurang was demonstrating its capacity to withstand the natural law of gravity. In other words, even the supernatural capacities of the masked figure are performed and exemplified through visualisation.

7. These values are transmitted in the context of initiation, in which the most senior generations teach the initiates myths, law, song, dance, and local knowledge (of the hunt, agriculture, climate, meteorology, and medicine).
8. The Kankurang masquerade is also increasingly commodified for local audiences in The Gambia (see Weil and Saho 2005).

Bibliography

Appadurai, A. (ed.). 1986. *The Social Life of Things: Commodities in Cultural Perspective*. Cambridge: Cambridge University Press.

Barber, K. 1997. 'Preliminary Notes on Audiences in Africa', *Africa* 67(3):347–62.

Benjamin, W. 1999. 'The Work of Art in the Age of Mechanical Reproduction'. In *Illuminations*, introduction by H. Arendt (ed.), H. Zorn (trans.), pp. 211–44. London: Pimlico.

Brown, M. F. 2003. *Who Owns Native Culture?* Cambridge, MA: Harvard University Press.

Bruner, E. 2005. *Culture on Tour: Ethnographies of Travel*. Chicago: Chicago University Press.

Bryant, R. 2005. 'The Soul Danced into the Body: Nation and Improvisation in Istanbul', *American Ethnologist* 32(2):222–38.

Clifford, J. 2004. 'Looking Several Ways: Anthropology and Native Heritage in Alaska', *Current Anthropology* 45(1):5–30.

de Jong, F. 2005. 'A Joking Nation: Conflict Resolution in Senegal', *Canadian Journal of African Studies* 39(2):389–413.

———. 2007. *Masquerades of Modernity: Power and Secrecy in Casamance, Senegal*. Edinburgh: Edinburgh University Press for the International African Institute.

Doutremépuich, E. 1939. 'Visite à un 'camp' de circoncis en Casamance', *Les missions catholiques* 72:474–77, 486–92.

Ebron, P. 2002. *Performing Africa*. Princeton, NJ: Princeton University Press.

Errington, S. 1998. *The Death of Authentic Primitive Art and Other Tales of Progress*. Berkeley and Los Angeles: University of California Press.

Fabian, J. 1983. *Time and the Other: How Anthropology Makes its Object*. New York: Columbia University Press.

Ginsburg, F. 2006. 'Rethinking the "Voice of God" in Indigenous Australia: Secrecy, Exposure, and the Efficacy of Media'. In *Religion, Media, and the Public Sphere*, B. Meyer and A. Moors (eds.), pp. 188–204. Bloomington: Indiana University Press.

Handler, R. 1988. *Nationalism and the Politics of Culture*. Madison: University of Wisconsin Press.

Herzfeld, M. 1991. *A Place in History: Social and Monumental Time in a Cretan Town*. Princeton, NJ: Princeton University Press.

Hylland Eriksen, T. 2001. 'Between Universalism and Relativism: A Critique of the UNESCO Concept of Culture'. In *Culture and Rights: Anthropological Perspectives*, J. K. Cowan et al. (eds.), pp. 127–48. Cambridge: Cambridge University Press.

Kasfir, S. 1988. 'Masquerading As a Cultural System'. In *West African Masks and Cultural Systems*, S. L. Kasfir (ed.), pp. 1–16. Tervuren: Musée Royal de l'Afrique Centrale.

Kuper, A. 2003. 'The Return of the Native', *Current Anthropology* 44(3):389–402.
Mark, P. 1994. 'Art, Ritual, and Folklore: Dance and Cultural Identity among the Peoples of the Casamance', *Cahiers d'études africaines* 136, XXXIV-4:563–84.
Mitchell, T. 1989. 'The World As Exhibition', *Comparative Studies in Society and History* 31:217–36.
Myers, F. R. 2002. *Painting Culture: The Making of an Aboriginal High Art*. Durham, NC: Duke University Press.
———. 2004. 'Ontologies of the Image and Economies of Exchange', *American Ethnologist* 31(1):5–20.
Nas, P. J. M., et al. 2002. 'Masterpieces of Oral and Intangible Culture: Reflections on the UNESCO World Heritage List', *Current Anthropology* 43(1):139–48.
Oakdale, S. 2004. 'The Culture-Conscious Brazilian Indian: Representing and Reworking Indianness in Kayabi Political Discourse', *American Ethnologist* 31(1):60–75.
Spyer, P. 2001. 'The Cassowary Will (Not) Be Photographed: The 'Primitive,' the 'Japanese,' and the Elusive 'Sacred' (Aru, Southeast Moluccas)'. In *Religion and Media*, H. de Vries and S. Weber (eds.), pp. 304–19. Palo Alto, CA: Stanford University Press.
Sylvain, R. 2005. 'Disorderly Development: Globalization and the Idea of "Culture" in the Kalahari', *American Ethnologist* 32(3):354–70.
Taussig, M. 1993. *Mimesis and Alterity: A Particular History of the Senses*. London: Routledge.
UNESCOPRESS. 2005. 'The Samba of Roda and the Ramilia Proclaimed Masterpieces of the Oral and Intangible Heritage of Humanity.' Press release no. 2005-144.
Weil, P., and B. Saho. 2005. 'Masking for Money: The Commodification of Kankurang and Simba Mask Performances in Urban Gambia'. In *Wari Matters: Ethnographic Explorations of Money in the Mande world*, S. Wooten (ed.), pp. 162–77. Münster: Lit Verlag.

From a Glorious Past to the Lands of Origin: Media Consumption and Changing Narratives of Cultural Belonging in Mali
Dorothea E. Schulz

For many telespectators in urban Mali, Tuesday night is a *jour fixe* to be spent in front of the television screen, either at home or at a friend's house – because at about 9:30 at night, the television programme *Terroir* ('From the Earth') starts, featuring the music and 'cultural traditions' of Mali's diverse regional cultures.[1] It is usually introduced 'live' by its producer, a journalist whose renown even in the most remote urban areas of the north is largely a result of this programme and who gives a short explanatory note about the particular 'traditions' to be shown that night. At about 11:00 p.m., when the programme comes to a close, the producer, sitting outside the studio, is bombarded with phone calls from spectators who, as they put it, want to express their 'gratitude' to him.[2] Wherever he shows up in the days to follow, people from all walks of life will approach him and express their appreciation of his programme in ways that bear a remarkably moralising undertone: 'We shall be grateful for your work until the end of our days'. 'You really show us what our traditions, what our roots are'. 'You render us our [sense of] dignity'. 'You have enhanced our name in the eyes of the nation'. 'No, really, you know us better than we do it ourselves'.

How can we understand the strong emotions this programme evokes among numerous television consumers? Why do spectators attribute such an eminent importance to the fact that their local traditions are broadcast on national television? And what processes of subjective identification come to the fore in their assertion that watching their or other people's 'authentic traditions' being performed to a national public increases their 'dignity'?

Patently, that 'authentic traditions' broadcast on national television resonate with, and in turn foster, feelings of communal belonging is not a peculiarity of Mali or postcolonial Africa. After all, in the European-American West, too, certain segments of the television audience crave their favorite weekly rural folklore show and tend to associate it with similar sentiments. Yet, one could argue, the formation of collective identities in the postcolonial world contrasts sharply with the emergence of a sense of national belonging in the West and therefore deserves closer understanding in its historically determinate manifestations. It seems imperative to make sense of the attractiveness of 'authentic traditions' among Malian spectators by relating it to the specifics of the contemporary moment, including the repercussions of democratisation politics. Among these repercussion are various idioms of belonging, such as the one of 'autochthony', that have gained a remarkable currency over recent years (for example, Ceuppens and Geschiere 2005; Geschiere and Nyamnjoh 2001). These idioms are closely associated with a search for 'authentic' origins, thereby ironically reproducing the insecurities they appear to resolve. They thrive in and reinforce the atmosphere of generalised and often violent competition for shrinking resources that characterises African multiparty democracies in the era of postneoliberal economic reform. In other words, the 'politics of recognition' (Taylor 1994) that have become a dominant modality through which politics are apprehended around the globe take on a characteristically (though not exclusively) African shape in discourses on belonging and 'authentic roots'.

Meyer and Geschiere (1999) submit that the great attraction of ideas of local particularity should be seen as part and parcel of cultural globalisation and as a manifestation of interlocking processes of flow *and* closure. Not only are new flows of people, images, ideas, and capital countered by new modalities of 'closure', such as assertions of local identity and of authentic traditions (Bayart 1996), but the stress on local particularity, as Ceuppens and Geschiere (2005) following Mbembe (2001) and Simone (2001) point out, often appears as a defense of the local, yet is frequently tied to trajectories of transnational capital and institutions. What these authors emphasise, then, is that the global circulation of certain institutions and ideals fundamentally resets the terms under which politics are conducted in the era of post-authoritarian governance in Africa (also see Comaroff and Comaroff 2000; Englund and Nyamnjoh 2004; Werbner 2004).

I agree with the authors' observation that African state politics cannot be understood without taking account of their insertion into a global political economy. Nevertheless, the analytical perspective I apply in the following discussion is decidedly national. My intention is to understand how Mali's insertion in a global order affects politics at the national and the local levels and creates new dilemmas for political elites and their efforts to impose 'law and order' on constituencies with highly diverse aspirations and concerns. I explore the new challenges to Malian state power in the era of multiparty democracy where calls for the realisation of citizenship rights are often couched in the idiom of cultural belonging or rights.

Drawing on the pioneering work by authors such as Derek Sayer (Corrigan and Sayer 1985) and Steinmetz (1999), who emphasise that state making always constitutes a cultural process, I understand 'culture', and the making of national culture, as a focal arena in which the state displays its capacity to ensure the commonwealth by overcoming the centrifugal tendencies of current politics of difference (Comaroff and Comaroff 2004). I examine the specific forms that the making of national belonging takes in the contemporary era of (at least nominal) post-authoritarian politics, yet I do so by situating the resulting paradoxes in the longer history of official attempts to imagine and project national community.

I argue that telespectators' enthusiastic responses to the programme, particularly their tendency to define their 'identity' via references to 'authentic tradition', should be understood as the result of a long-standing narrative on national culture in which official, mass-mediated invocations of a common 'glorious past' interacted with media consumers' various assertions of locally specific historical experiences. Although the claims by particular segments of Mali's television audience continue to be at variance with the ones articulated in official discourse, they should all be seen as elements of a common narrative and of a shared modality of constructing belonging via '(authentic) culture'.

Rather than assuming that 'authenticity' refers to clearly defined and unchanging cultural forms, I emphasise that what is taken as 'authentic tradition' has always been subject to change and is, by necessity, of a composite nature. Notions of 'the authentic' and of 'genuine' tradition should therefore be analysed as figures of speech that operate to the point of regression by never pinpointing the unaltered and immutable version of tradition that they claim exists. In a historical situation in which membership in a particular locality gains both in material and symbolic importance, references to authenticity form part of an expressive repertoire that allows people to frame their claims to membership in a discourse of cultural belonging.

By exploring the effects of contemporary politics of belonging on changing registers of the 'authentic', my analysis complements earlier explorations of the relationship between 'authentic tradition' and the making of national culture (for example, Dominguez 1989; Handler 1988; Hobsbawm and Ranger 1983;). I am particularly interested in the subjective process through which notions of the authentic are formed. That is to say, I focus on authenticity as the result of a process of spontaneous appreciation of something as 'genuine' and 'unaltered'. I view this subjective process of identification as an act of 'authentification' and emphasise that, without assessing how this particular sensually and aesthetically mediated process works, it is impossible to fully understand how national (or local) identity, as a sense of belonging, is created. With my emphasis on the emotional and aesthetic dimensions of 'authentification', I differ from studies of national or ethnic identities that, in my view, sometimes risk overemphasising the role of cognition and 'construction' at the expense of sensually mediated identification processes (but see Askew 2004; Danielson 1997; Turino 2000).

This brings me to the last objective of this chapter: to understand the role that mass media, as technologies of mediation and as institutions, play in the process of authentification and how they complicate official invocations of national community by furthering spectators' subjective experience of local particularity. Until recently, there has been a tendency in academic publications as well as in the popular press to oppose notions of the 'authentic' and 'cultural traditions' to modern media technologies and mass culture and to see them as mutually exclusive. Perhaps the most powerful critique of modern mass media and their destructive effects for 'tradition' was mounted by thinkers of the Frankfurt School. In the countermodern critique of Horkheimer and Adorno (1972) and of Benjamin (1963), for instance, genuine or authentic artistic production, once it is produced for mass consumption, loses its 'aura' that is, its original and unique essence. The masses who consume this art are, as it were, culturally malnourished and are driven by the endless desire to satisfy the appetites projected onto the screen as an ever more commodified, ever more 'spectacular' universe.

Clearly, there is a striking contrast between this view of the corrupting power of mass culture and the assertion by many Malian telespectators that broadcasting their 'authentic traditions' on national television 'renders them their dignity'. This emphatic statement suggests that, rather than conceiving of 'authentic culture' and mass-mediated entertainment culture as mutually exclusive phenomena, one should explore the complex interplay between the two. The statement also intimates that the present sociopolitical significance of 'authentic tradition' develops its full potential only with its dissemination to a nationwide audience and within a national public.[3] Yet, it also hints at the centrifugal forces and thus paradoxical dynamics that the mass-mediated display of local difference generates in contemporary politics. It is to the historical roots of these paradoxical dynamics that I now turn.

Making a National Community through 'History' in Early Post-Independent Mali

What material and symbolic means did the first regimes of post-independent Mali employ to 'imagine the nation', in other words, to invoke a political community grounded in a long-standing historical continuity? In what ways did the new political elites strive to instill in its subjects a sense of belonging to this community? And how did people, particularly listeners of national radio, evaluate the state-orchestrated efforts to create a sense of national unity and identity by virtue of particular musical and oral traditions? To respond to these questions, I retrace the dialectic production (and contestation) of the image of a national culture during the first three decades after Mali's independence. This period was brought to an abrupt end by the 1991 military coup under Colonel Amadou Toumani Touré, whose *regime de transition* granted the country's first democratic elections, thereby fundamentally resetting the parameters for the making of political community and national belonging.[4]

After Mali's independence in 1960, *Radio Soudan*, created in 1957, was instrumental in the implementation of the highly centralised, socialist agenda of President Keita and his party US-RDA.[5] In a situation in which national unity constituted a 'work in progress', radio broadcasting was designed to promote the appearance of national consensus. From the outset, chief party ideologues selected the making of national culture as a prime modality to infuse the nation-state with a nimbus of legitimacy. However, this project, and its attendant attempts to instill in people feelings of pride in their traditions, had paradoxical results. Official creations of national culture revolved around the claim to give 'the people' an active role in 'revalorising tradition', but this claim was contravened by the autocratic attitude implied by their *mission civilisatrice*. Ironically, in order to become full-grown and dignified 'citizens' of the independent nation, people had to be 'formed' and to be told what they should be proud of. In other words, most Malians continued to be subject to, rather than subjects of, the nation-state. In this sense, the policy of 'promoting national culture' under US-RDA authoritarian rule illustrates how state politics, in spite of the party's anticolonialist agenda, were haunted by the repressive legacy of colonial administration (for example, Crawford Young 1988).

To draw on 'culture' as a source of national consciousness and of the nation-state's legitimacy, state officials first had to create it, along with 'tradition'. In this process, 'culture', based on a conglomerate of oral genres and associated with particular musical performance conventions and a specific category of performers, became objectified. Because its constitutive musical and oral traditions were regionally and ethnically specific, the link established between 'culture' and 'the past' was a very particular and exclusive one. Party officials' tendency to identify these particular expressive genres as the centrepiece of national culture perpetuated an understanding of 'culture' that had been articulated by the leaders of the independence movement since the 1940s. US-RDA militants singled out theatre as a means to recruit young party members and to disseminate the political goals of the US-RDA. By staging historical genres on the occasion of national holidays and on national radio, they insinuated a close connection between particular historical traditions and the culture of the independent nation they fought for.[6]

Even if 'tradition', in its objectified form, emerged as a result of the state-directed administering of cultural performances, one should keep in mind that it was constructed in a dialectical process that involved some segments of the Malian population more than others. One example for this dialectical process were the annual youth festivals in which adolescents from the different regions of Mali were invited to perform their 'local traditions'. Notions of 'authenticity' and 'originality' played a central role in evaluating their performances and in identifying the group that staged the 'most undistorted' version of local music. Performing (in the double sense of the term) culture was closely associated with the project of celebrating a national community.[7] Participants in the festival were told that, by representing the authentic culture of their home region, they played a role as *bâtisseurs de la nation*.[8] These adolescents were thus implicated in a process by which the imaginary making of a nation-state (or imagination) was legitimated in the idiom of 'modernisation' and effected through the creation of 'tradition'. The latter simultaneously served as a backdrop against which 'development' should be achieved and as a repository of values that could inspire experiences of belonging and community. However, because logistical reasons made it often difficult for youth groups from the northern regions to attend the national festival, the regional traditions of Mali's southern triangle tended to be more broadly represented. Also, paradoxically, the act of performing local culture in the capital and on national radio altered the very genres the 'originality' of which was to be staged and celebrated. In this sense, the youth festivals illustrate the link between the historical processes of institutionalising national culture and nation making as an everyday cultural production in which, notably, some members of the national community participate more than others do.

State administration of culture under Modibo Keita was effected partly through the creation of structures of state patronage that facilitated the incorporation of various cultural producers, among them *jeli* musicians and oral traditionists, into the nationalist project. Musical and artistic production, closely monitored by the Ministry of Culture, became central elements of an officially promoted national culture. Considerably less broadcasting time and attention during official celebrations were devoted to the oral arts of the peoples from the northern triangle of Mali.[9] The marginalisation of these peoples on national media, and the denial of the existence of difference and inequalities within the nation, was in line with the persistent exclusion of northern people from positions of political influence and economic advantage, an exclusion effected primarily through the structures of single-party rule that concentrated power in the capital and left inhabitants of the northern regions very little leverage in accessing the resources of the state through patronage relations. The resulting major divide between Mali's northern and southern triangles translated into repeated secessionist movements in the north that were on several occasions bloodily repressed.

The Ministry of Communication reserved from the outset a major share of broadcasting time to cultural programmes that featured extensively songs and oral traditions recounted by specialists of the spoken word, the *jeliw*[10] (*griots* in French).[11] In the nineteenth century and until late colonial rule, *jeliw* had worked as professional speakers and praise singers on behalf of wealthy individuals and powerful families, and they accomplished various tasks of social mediation and reputation management for their patron families. *Jeli* women conventionally specialised in songs in which they publicly praised and exhorted their patrons. *Jeli* men played most of the instruments and recited the local political history and their patrons' genealogies. The historical knowledge and recitations invested *jeli* men with great prestige and generated generous gifts in recompense. Even if in their recitations the line between remembering facts and fabricating fictions was sometimes difficult to tell, the long-term affiliation between *jeli* families and their patrons helped listeners to keep a 'check' on *jeli* performers and the claims they articulated. Also, the truthful reporting of past events was not the only or even primary criterion for a successful performance. Of similar importance was a traditionist's or singer's effectiveness in increasing a patron's reputation through an aesthetically compelling performance. This rationale of performative success, as well as its social recognition and generation of material favors, changed gradually in the colonial period. The transformations were reinforced by Malian national radio in 1957 and even more radically by national television, created in 1983 (Schulz 1998, 1999, 2001b).

Because *jeliw* were generally associated with 'the past', they were in a privileged position to become potent symbols of the new nation's history. National history, and *jeli* singers who articulated it, were represented as emblems of

Mali's contemporary status in an international community of nation-states. Not mentioned in this representation of *jeliw* as guardians of truthful memory was, of course, that the political elites' motivation to constantly invoke historical continuity differed from the rationale of *jeliw's* recitation of a patron family's historical accomplishments. Nevertheless, countless radio broadcasts of *jeli* performances constituted Mali's 'authentic traditions' in a complex interplay between state-orchestrated celebrations of 'national culture' and its subjective resonance among particular radio audiences, that is, those who lived in the heartland of the Mande world from which most of the oral traditions were taken and who therefore recognised these pieces as part of their 'authentic' cultural heritage. Thus, radio broadcasting did not serve to celebrate the new political order in any simple way but shaped the particular image of the nation it invoked.[12]

The emotional appeal that these broadcasts held for listeners from the Mande-speaking areas of southern Mali derived essentially from the combination of its 'word music' (Coplan 1994) with familiar lyrics and speech style.[13] Listeners' appreciation of individual songs derived from their recognition of this music as referring to locally specific social and political relations.[14] There are also indications that early radio broadcasting furthered experiences of personal attachment and emotional identification because, as a technology of aural mediation, it centred listeners' attention on *jeliw's* 'forceful speech', thereby appealing to an audience primarily tuned to orality and to the verbal performance of power. Nevertheless, this process of subjective authentification of cultural traditions remained highly exclusionary because it was limited to listeners from regions in southern Mali.

Several male farmers from one of these regions (near Kita, in Mali's southwest) who had participated in the US-RDA youth activities recalled in 1994 that listening to these songs deeply affected their self-esteem as members of the new nation. They unanimously declared that 'it was this music that made listening to the radio worthwhile' and reminisced about their feelings of pride when they realised that the oratory that related to distinctly local identities became part of a national cultural heritage.[15] Their reminiscences also suggested that they, similar to younger, male farmers in other areas of the Mande heartland, felt pride at the official celebration of *jeli* singers as emblems of an unbroken continuity with a precolonial past, a past undistorted by the corrupting effects of colonial rule. To this particular audience segment, then, *jeli* singers embodied the very possibility to *speak about* the past as an authentic source of one's social identity.

Although listeners from these areas associated *jeli* music not with a national past but with particular local social relations and identities, they gradually took for granted that their music and historical traditions had a special significance to the invocation of a national community. To listeners from other areas, in contrast, who had no emotional or cultural connection to these genres, *jeli* praise broadcast on national radio came to represent the new relations of inequality and exclusion that structured the much-celebrated national community. They, too, associated broadcasts of *jeli* performances with particularistic identities, not with an all-encompassing, national community. The indifference or lack of interest with which these listeners followed the *jeliw*'s central positioning in official imaginations echoed their resentment of their own economic and political marginalisation. Their reactions, then, point to the limits of state-orchestrated evocations of national community or, to put it differently, manifest the fact that the making of the Malian nation remained an 'unfinished business'.

Jeliw Praise Singers Patronised by the State

As a consequence of the party's conception and promotion of 'culture', *jeli* musicians and historians became *artisti*, professional artists, and clients of the state. Old and new forms of clientilistic structures coexisted: conventional ones, based on personal bonds between party members and individual artists, often overlapped with institutions of state patronage, such as the national performance groups (*ensembles*).[16] Those *jeli* musicians who consented to the new role as clients that party officials offered them became key figures in the dissemination of political information and of what the party leaders conceived of as authentic African values.

Some of them, mostly women, adapted the praise songs conventionally performed on behalf of 'great men' (*cèbaw*), that is, influential and wealthy patrons, to the new situation by portraying the president and party officials as successors of mythical heroes and thus insinuated an unbroken continuity between political traditions, past and present; that is to say, the allegoric equation of past rulers with present statesmen claimed a linear relationship between past and present times. The present was celebrated as the logical outcome of past political events, and the existence of 'state' institutions and representatives were projected into a mythical past (Cutter 1968).

The epic of Sunjata Keita, together with accounts of other heroes and 'kings' from the southern triangle of Mali, formed the pool of symbolism on which *jeliw* drew to construct this vision of a long-standing, unbroken tradition of political leadership.[17] Songs dedicated to President Keita, for instance, established a genealogical connection between him and Sunjata Keita, the legendary founder of the medieval 'empire' of Mali. More importantly, *jeliw* were officially authorised to talk about the past and to narrate the history of the new nation, based on the assumption that the relationship between politics past and present had remained unabated by colonial influence.

At first sight, the role assigned to these *jeli* singers resembles the one played by *lieux de mémoire* in the contemporary making of national histories in the Euro-American West (Nora 1989). Nora's notion of 'sites of memory' refers to symbolic places or cultural expressions of a collective memory that mediate a shared, emotional attachment and become focal points of a national heritage. As Nora argues, the recent proliferation of these sites in France indicates that the function of memory as a medium for a subjective sense of historical continuity has changed radically. In a situation in which people are both aware of and bemoan a radical rupture with the past, both collective memory and individual memory are made by creating distant symbols *of* the past. These symbols simultaneously mediate a longing for and a detachment from the past (also see Carrier 2000). Here, then, resides a crucial difference to the significance of *jeli* singers to post-independence politics. *Jeli* singers were promoted as vehicles for a sense of historical continuity and *immediacy*. Even if their contribution to the making of the nation-state was contested by various groups of listeners, it was nevertheless significant. In their role as articulators of the nation's history (and of the nation's *right to claim* a history), they helped validate its aspiration to belong to the realm of political modernity.

All this illustrates my earlier observation that, along with the transformation of the political institutional setting since colonial rule, the relevance of *jeli* performances changed, too. Post-independence state patronage of 'the arts' led to *jeliw* being treated as living emblems of an unbroken continuity with the past. By promoting and objectifying 'traditional culture', the first government of independent Mali helped standardise diverse regional musical and textual conventions. In this fashion (and similar to the dynamic identified with regard to the youth cultural festivals), the oral traditions articulated by *jeliw* were readjusted and transformed.

The representation of Maninka and Bamana *jeliw* as chief guardians of tradition not only gave them, if compared to other cultural producers, a privileged representation in a national public, it also created a particular internal hierarchy and competition among different *jeli* families from Mali's southern triangle; certain *jeli* families and their patrons' family histories were singled out, either because of their special ties to those in power or because their family histories lent themselves easily for the invocation of a glorious past. These family identities became key to the narration of the new nation's history.

The new, national history that *jeli* oral traditionists were asked to promote condensed highly diverse regional political traditions into a standardised and unified national past. They selected an imperial past from a range of past political institutions and events, and depicted historically unstable and embattled political formations such as the Mali empire as static and statist structures. The histories of the populations who lived in a historical setting characterised by fluctuating power relations between different lineages, and whose established political institutions were open to challenge, were not rendered in these official historical accounts. In this sense, *jeli* musicians did not so much 'invent' (Hobsbawm 1983) a national political tradition as reconstruct it in partial ways (see Trouillot 1995, 1997). The national community and its history, narrated by *jeli* traditionists, were from the outset based on the silencing of alternative political imaginaries.

Yet, even for listeners from the Mande heartland who tended to identify with *jeli* oral tradition, the significance of these performances changed rather swiftly. Listeners capitalised on the subversive readings inherent in praise songs to express discontent with Modibo Keita's regime. These critical readings of praise songs became particularly relevant after 1965, in a situation of growing disappointment with the effects of socialist policy and totalitarian control. Thus, whereas *jeli* performances initially offered a blueprint for collective identification, at least for specific groups of the Malian population, they turned, over the years, into a medium to question official constructions of legitimate leadership (Schulz 2001a:Chapter 5).

Listeners continued to draw on the double-edged quality of praise songs over the years of Moussa Traoré's military regime who came to power after staging a military coup in 1968. Simultaneously, major transformations occurred in the political institutional context that, under Modibo Keita, had offered *jeli* praise singers and traditionists new opportunities to gain an income and to become clients of the state. After an initial 'honeymoon' period, in which prominent *jeliw* swiftly changed their political affiliation and engaged in flattery on behalf of the new military leadership, a gradual disjuncture between praise and party politics occurred. Because listeners increasingly regarded any straightforward flattery on behalf of politicians with doubtful eyes, *jeli* singers sought to endear themselves to a variety of VIPs ranging from wealthy businessmen and -women to other figures of influence and renown who had risen to influence under the new regime.

The gradual disjuncture of praise and politics, and the growing privatisation of praise, entailed a paradoxical development. On the one hand, public praise turned into a lucrative profession in which an ever-growing number of musicians engaged. Many of these musicians were not of *jeli* origin; yet they tended to imitate the stylistics and contents of *jeli* praise, for instance, by constructing a prestigious genealogy for patrons whom they exhorted on radio to generously compensate them for their praise. These various singers thus capitalised on a process that may be described as the professionalisation of praise and that was based on a very particular form of commemorating the past: the invocation of an unbroken continuity between the past and the present.

One the other hand, and ironically, the broadcasting of praise songs led to a loss in the symbolic value and in the textual complexity of *jeli* oral traditions. In other words, the transformation of praise from a socially situated and context-dependent client service into a paid profession further eroded the (always slightly questionable) credibility of *jeli* singers and contributed to their loss in prestige. As a consequence, *jeli* praise was less effective than before in bestowing on the praised patron a nimbus of glory and legitimacy (Schulz 1998, 2001a:Chapter 6).

Another implication of the monetisation of *jeli* praise was that 'memory', embodied by *jeli* historians and once seen as the expression of a unique and personalised client service, became a commodity. The fact that any wealthy sponsor could now purchase the public declaration of an eminent family genealogy minimised its symbolic value. It weakened people's appreciation of this mode of narrating history. That is to say, these particular *jeli* singers and traditionists, as well as the oral traditions they articulated, lost their performative capacity to generate listeners' emotional identification with a past order, an order they envisioned as being superior to the present one.

As a consequence, and in spite of the continuation of a highly centralised, authoritarian cultural policy under President Traoré's single-party rule, *jeli* orators lost the privileged treatment they had received immediately after independence. They were bereaved of the nimbus they had once enjoyed in their role as guarantors of the mere possibility to render the past in an authentic way and thus to project an immediate link between the past and the future moral order.[18]

The Politics of Culture in the Era of Political Liberalisation

The onset of multiparty democracy in 1991, along with the concomitant unsettling of centralised authoritarian control, marked a significant rupture with former governmental cultural policy, in particular with established ways of invoking national community. This rupture reinforced the longer-standing erosion of *jeli* praise singers' effectiveness in evoking an unbroken continuity with Mali's 'authentic traditions'. The era was set off by the *coup d'état* that put an end to President Traoré's single-party rule in 1991 and brought the *regime de transition* under Toumani Touré to power. Political liberalisation also heralded an upsurge of politics of recognition that are variously couched in the idiom of 'Islamic' renewal and moral difference (Schulz 2004) or in a discourse of local and cultural belonging.

Especially in the country's northern triangle, conflicts over scarce resources that had been bloodily repressed under the preceding regimes flared up again, this time framed, more than ever before, as a matter of ethnic and regional marginalisation. The civil war in Mali's north that had contributed to the destabilisation of Traoré's regime and continued after President Konaré's election, often transmuting into parastatal structures (Klute and Trotha 2004), was the more immediate rationale for a major administrative reform after 1994. This *Politique de la décentralisation* was implemented under the auspices (and pressure) of Western donor organisations, in tandem with other liberalisation measures. It transformed national politics in ways that were much more far reaching than its 'peace-keeping' mission. In combination with the effects of multipartyism, the decentralisation process crucially changed the vectors (if not the logic) of political clientage and resource ap-propriation. As a pivotal element of decentralisation reform, *communes* were introduced as new local-level executive units to which a considerable measure of budgetary decision making and control was delegated. Not surprisingly, this reform measure encouraged the framing of a politics of recognition in a discourse on local belonging, partly because only those who were accepted as members of a local 'community' were entitled to participate in communal budgetary decisions. Under single-party rule, with its absolute primacy of party membership, politics had been oriented toward the capital as the centre of state power and resources. Under multiparty democracy, venues for the mobilisation of resources became more complicated and crisscrossing, and were at least partly inverted.[19] From now on, those politicians or state officials fared best who were able to mobilise support in their 'home' locality, an effort that, in turn, was primarily a function of their effectiveness in securing funds in the capital that would benefit their community back home. This means that, under the new conditions of 'democratic rule', in a situation in which the government is still unable to guarantee basic services and entitlements for its citizens, the latter pursue their interests through a politics of belonging that allows them to base their claims on membership in a local community.

Crucial to the effervescence of a vociferous politics of recognition, variously presented as cultural and/or moral difference, was that the Transition Regime's granting of civil liberties generated a highly diverse, partly privatised media landscape. Continued after 1992, under the first democratically elected president Alpha Konaré and his party ADEMA, this development resulted in a hitherto unthinkable mushrooming of media institutions, especially of local radio stations. The concomitant partial privatisation of the music and entertainment industry reinforced the disruption of the preceding regimes' highly centralised policy of promoting national culture.

With the ending of the civil war in Mali's north in 1996, governmental cultural policy shifted to another gear. To contain the centrifugal forces set free by political liberalisation, Konaré's government engaged in a project of national community making that not only recognised but celebrated cultural and regional diversity. In this, the government deliberately fostered a politics of belonging 'from above' that would give opponents less opportunity to frame their claims for political representation as a matter of cultural exclusion.

In line with the new policy of promoting Mali's '(cultural) diversity-in-unity', several television programmes were designed to portray Mali's various regional cultures for a nationwide audience, and to ensure a more equitable representation of peoples from the north. Also part of the new communication policy was a restructuring of the national broadcast station and a revision of certain programmes, so as to ensure a greater flexibility and openness to audience feedback. However, in spite of the resulting, greater diversity of topics and genres, the imbalance between the northern and southern cultural traditions on national television continues up to this day.

For *jeli* performers, the changes after 1991 yielded important consequences, both for their individual biographies and for their significance to national cultural politics. With the end of state patronage of the arts, a greater variety of musical genres and performers were popularised on state and private media.[20] *Jeli* singers' credibility was questioned more than ever before, partly because some of them had been all too eager to shift their political allegiances with the changing regimes. Also, as *jeli* praise increasingly turned into a commodity, it could not generate the same respect for patrons. A growing number of listeners took *jeli* singers' public invocation of Mali's glorious history not as a sign not of their capacity to commemorate the past, but of the very rupture between past and present, crystallising in *jeli* singers' growing venality. It is telling in this regard that in 1999, in reaction to the general disaffection with the public flattery of *jeli* singers, Konaré's government prohibited any *jeli* praise on national media. Although this measure put a brusque end to the role as articulators of the past that *jeliw* claimed for themselves, it did not thwart individual *jeli* singers' efforts to laud, albeit in a more subtle fashion, potential sponsors in songs distributed via audiotapes.

Other *jeli* performers, all of them women, found different venues to make up for the drying up of patronage relations. Since the mid-1980s, they capitalised on new opportunities in the entertainment market established by national television and a growing video industry to become trendsetters in matters of classy outfits, 'cool' body movements, and a 'modern' lifestyle. Since then, these *jeli* women, as well as other pop stars who adopted similar musical styles and demeanor, have become central to the formulation of an 'African-and-cosmopolitan' orientation for their many (female) fans (Schulz 2001b). The success of these female pop stars has significant repercussions in the international entertainment market: Here, their musical genres (among them praise songs), which are most often based on the political and historical traditions of the Mande heartland, are marketed as emblematic of Malian national culture. Their international success as articulators of Malian music thus becomes partly disconnected from their national standing where, as I intimated before, these singers have lost much of their credibility and are not taken as trustworthy guardians of their patron families' noble origins and legendary deeds.

Meanwhile, the growing privatisation of the entertainment market and the concurrent thriving of decentralised media institutions have allowed various other types of artists and musical genres, such as singers from the north, from the Wasulu region, as well as *balafon* players and the hunters (singular, *donson*) and their music, to gain in national renown. Their various regional origins allow them to compete over the role of emblematic elements of a newly conceived, 'diverse-yet-unified' national culture and simultaneously serve as a blueprint for consumers' claims to cultural difference.[21] This ambiguous potential of 'traditional' performance genres constitutes the backdrop for the popularity of the television series *Terroir,* to which I now turn.

A major reason for the popularity of this programme, I argue, stems from the fact that it displays a great range of musical genres and styles. It thereby offers consumers of different age, educational, and regional background an opportunity to claim for themselves contingent and sometimes changing, particularistic identities in a multicultural nation-state. The recent shift from *jeli* genres to a variety of performance genres as constitutive elements of national culture indicates yet another rupture. Political efforts to invoke a unified national community by staging the state's historical legitimacy have given way to the government's endeavor to perform (in the two senses of the term) the state's capacity to ensure the common good by mending internal difference within the national community. This shift manifests itself in, among other things, the changing ways 'Malian culture' is staged on national media. Rather than being celebrated by reference to its 'glorious past', national culture is identified with a notion of authenticity unambiguously defined by its rural, 'local' origins.

Envisioning 'the Land' As the Cradle of Cultural Belonging: The Programme *Terroir* and Its Reception

Various categories of spectators (among them many farmers who only rarely have the opportunity to watch the series) are eager to invite the *Terroir* production team to document their 'local tradition'. Their eagerness, and the enthusiastic reactions by those who watch their 'tradition' on national television, indicates that opportunities to show one's 'own traditional culture' to a nationwide audience yield a very special appeal. This interpretation is supported by the fact that even telespectators whose performances are less represented in the programme show a greater interest in it than in any other cultural programme and praise it for its staging of 'Mali's diverse cultures'. To be sure, *Terroir* is no living proof of a successful national integration and equal representation of regional diversity. Nevertheless, the programme's remarkable success serves as a window onto recent changes in official representations of Malian national culture and, by implication, on the specific challenges posed by multiparty democracy and its attendant liberalisation measures to the making of national community. What possibly heterogeneous, official and popular, narratives of cultural belonging emerge in the context of current politics of recognition?

The programme *Terroir* is particularly relevant to an analysis of historical transformations in the official performance of national community because it contrasts with programmes commonly produced on Malian television (and with media productions of other countries with a long-standing history of top-down broadcasting policy) in two important respects. First, the major part of production costs of individual documentaries are no longer covered by the ORTM but by those who invite the team to their 'homeland'. The weight of decision-making power thus shifts importantly to the side of various local factions who wish to disseminate their local tradition to a nationwide audience. Second, this raises the impression that the selection of specific performances is by and large the result of 'grass-roots' initiatives, that is, of those telespectators who claim a national significance for their local traditions. This, at least, would have been the dominant interpretation in the late 1980s and early 1990s, at a time when scholarly studies on popular 'resistance' to the authoritarian state, in Africa and elsewhere, abounded. The issue, then, is not only whether this perspective fully captures the complexities of the programme's production process but also whether it sufficiently takes account of the partly new ways in which power is sought and exerted under conditions of (at least nominally) post-authoritarian rule.

As a point of entry into my analysis, I choose Bayart's sophisticated notion of 'popular modes of political action', a notion he introduced to point to the various symbolic forms through which subordinate groups of society engage state politics (Bayart 1983, 1985; also see Bayart et al. 1992). Following de Certeau's (1984) attention to the political implications of seemingly apolitical 'practices of everyday life' (de Certeau 1984:1–42), Bayart asserts that subordinate groups, in expressing dissent, draw on the same cultural repertory as the elites do. This repertory consists of an 'ensemble of cultural representations . . . of gestures, symbols, aesthetic forms, cosmic, religious, moral, and sexual values'.[22] Bayart departs from de Certeau's view that the practices ('tactics') of subordinate groups take place only at the interstities of power and cannot develop an autonomous logic (Bayart 1985:356; see also de Certeau 1984: xix–xx). Although they share the same register, Bayart claims, subordinate groups appropriate and redirect the means (*dispositifs*) of power and create an autonomous sphere of action and of 'significant practices' (Bayart 1983:98, 1985:366).

Can we interpret *Terroir* along these lines? In other words, does the programme articulate a 'narrative from below' that has emerged as a result of political liberalisation and that allows to counter official constructions of national culture? Or is the distinction between constructions of culture 'from below' versus those 'from above' spurious, particularly under current political conditions that enable the making of media productions in which divisions between the production and the consumption of media narratives become occasionally blurred?

The success story of the television programme and its recent renaming from *Musique du Terroir* to *Terroir* (in 2003) highlight important changes in official understandings and ways of representing 'national culture' after the end of single-party rule. The origins of the programme date back to the times of 'state-patronised' cultural production under President Traoré. Starting with its first broadcast soon after the creation of the television station in 1983, it was initially aired only irregularly, that is, on special occasions or on request of prominent party officials. Yet because the producer's coverage of various musical performances and of local oral histories immediately generated such enthusiastic responses by various segments of the television audience, it was soon launched as a regular programme on Tuesday night.[23] Over the years, it has shifted from its focus on music to a more inclusive claim to 'document and disseminate Mali's diverse rural traditions'. As intimated by the new title, the 'land' or 'earth' (French, *terre*, from which *terroir* is derived) is envisioned as the site *par excellence* of cultural authenticity, that is, of a 'culture' that has not yet been distorted by money's corrupting effects on social relationships and moral obligations. This authentic appeal of 'the land' is directly related to the at once material and symbolic significance that local belonging has recently gained in national politics.

These shifts in the definition of 'culture' have been accompanied and reinforced by important changes in the institutional and financial set-up of the programme. The changing funding structure of *Terroir* in the course of the twenty-three years of its existence indicates that new governmental policy does not stop at celebrating regionally diverse and 'participatory' culture-making but encourages a new, 'participatory' funding structure, too. The move toward privatising the cultural sector, such as the organisation of musical performances, has translated into a broader array of financing modes.[24] A (perhaps not fully intended) consequence of this development is that state-directed displays of 'culture' are increasingly entering into competition with local understandings of, and efforts to represent, 'authentic traditions'.

Most of the present broadcasts are, with respect to the funding structure, 'coproductions' of the Ministry of Communication and the village whose performances are recorded. Yet, the major share of the costs is covered by the villagers who host the event and by their 'cousins in town', the so-called *ressortissants*. The latter are villagers who migrated to the region's capital or to Bamako and who maintain contact with their homeland through chains of reciprocity and moral obligation.

The *ressortissants* play an eminent role in financing the productions costs by finding generous sponsors (many of them politicians) or motivating villagers to make the necessary financial arrangements. Moreover, because of their geographically stretched networks of social and political connections, *ressortissants* are in the best position to establish the first contact with the producer of the programme and to 'convince' the latter, either directly or through more or less subtle pressure exerted by the director of the television station or by an influential member of the Ministry of Communication, to take on the task of documenting what the interested parties 'back home' wish to circulate as 'local tradition' in a national arena. Finally, the *ressortissants* play a key role in organising the logistics for the viewing sessions, on the night(s) when the documentary is screened on national television. These 'movie nights' turn into veritable feasts, and the urban relatives of those whose performances are televised feel under considerable pressure to provide the material infrastructure to make the evening a success. Particularly on the occasion of the first airing, inhabitants of the featured village come in flocks to town, on foot, by donkey carts and bikes, and in jointly rented bush taxis. They gather in the courtyards of their urban 'cousins' or 'sons' and comment enthusiastically on each and every element and participant in the broadcast performance. Because most of these participants sit in the audience and comment on their own contribution to the broadcast, their media engagements are infused with a sense of immediacy and of spontaneous, emotional identification that turn the reception of the broadcast into a secondary performance event. Hence, the viewing sessions constitute crucial occasions on which telespectators claim their own, specific location in a multicultural nation state by fashioning particular representations of 'local culture' to a nationwide audience.

To be sure, the views of 'local tradition', and the motivations of the different actors and 'local' sponsors to initiate their media representation, are highly diverse. Motives range from an interest in aggrandising one's individual standing (or that of one's family or family branch, or village) in a geographically circumscribed setting to the efforts by some *ressortissants* to bolster their claims to land property in their village of origin, and, finally, to the attempts by deputies and other party politicians to increase their popularity at various local, regional, and national levels. The last kind of motivation becomes pertinent in times prior to electoral campaigns.[25]

The *ressortissants* and their families are usually the driving force in the process that leads from the initial deliberations between the initiators and sponsors to an official invitation extended to the producer and his camera team. Since the 1950s, an era of intense urbanisation in southern Mali, *ressortissants* from all regions of Mali have been organising themselves in urban associations in an effort to create structures of social and financial support in town and to maintain and actively produce ties to their rural homes (for example, Meillassoux 1968). Already at this time, efforts by *ressortissants* to articulate their locally defined identities in an urban environment in which they intermingle with people from various regions of Mali centred on cultural performances. Even today, most associations of *ressortissants* regularly organise 'cultural events' in town. To make sure that these events bear a particularly 'local' flavor, they invite musicians, oral traditionists, and other representatives of 'local culture'. They are eager to participate in the performances by dressing up in costumes they consider 'typically local' attire. And they invite not only neighbors and friends to these events but, if possible, party and state officials as well as other potentially influential patrons.

The staging by *ressortissants* of 'traditional culture' in town, and the attractiveness of the image of the rural as the site of cultural authenticity, are not entirely new phenomena (for example, Austen 1992). Nor are they limited to the context of postcolonial Africa (see Handler 1988:Chapter 3). Unprecedented, however, is the extent to which the celebration of locality echoes, and feeds into, a broader politics of belonging that challenge the official storyline of a national 'unity-in-diversity'. Also, because of the changed political circumstances, *ressortissants* have stronger reasons than ever before to display their 'authentic' local culture, not just to neighbors and friends in town but also to a nationwide audience, and thereby receive a boost in standing that will positively influence their networks of financial and social transaction.[26] Their aspirations are in line with governmental attempts to perform national integration *qua* recognition of local particularity (of which *Terroir* is the living proof). Yet, this interlocking of interests simultaneously energises the centrifugal tendencies inherent in the politics of belonging.

Although individual *Terroir* documentaries are largely financed by telespectators who want to display their 'authentic traditions' to a national public, it would be misleading to interpret these productions as instances of a political culture 'from below' that is more 'democratic' or all-inclusive than state politics. After all, the producer has considerable discretionary power over the choice of represented genres, the particular content, and the sequence of images to be broadcast.[27] Moreover, the initiatives of villagers and their urban 'cousins' to represent 'authentic tradition' to a nationwide television audience frequently form part of long-standing power struggles, most often between different, locally influential clans or among different branches of the same family. Although the conflicting parties are generally, and understandably, keen on keeping their conflicts hidden from outsiders, their struggles frequently break out into the open once the camera team arrives at the site of performance. Episodes I witnessed in the period between March of 2001 and January of 2005 showed forcefully that even if disagreements among different local power figures over the broadcast coverage may have been resolved prior to the arrival of the production team, the presence of the latter will stir up old-standing dormant conflicts. The attempts by various conflict parties to bend the balance of power to their own advantage interlock with disagreements over what elements of 'local culture' should receive particular attention and coverage.

Very often, the situation is further complicated by the presence of party politicians who, as already intimated, seek to use the presence of the camera team to reconfigure local power balances to their own advantage. The joint objective of the various 'local' conflict parties to document and televise 'authentic tradition' thus often reflects and simultaneously invigorates power struggles in which local opponents need to come to terms with representatives of state institutions on one side and party politicians on the other. There is thus no coherent state presence or 'politics from above' against which local forces intervene. Rather, both 'the state' and local interest groups are characterised by internal fragmentation and a plurality of actors whose interests and strategies span the national-regional divide.

The fact that all these parties are involved, in one way or another, in fierce disputes about what elements of 'authentic local culture' should be represented and what should remain untold and invisible points to the special importance that the notion of locality gains in the current era of a politics of belonging. Closer scrutiny of these disputes reveals that the work of 'documenting' local culture involves a complex readjustment structured by two main selection processes and that 'authenticity', similar to other idioms of belonging, is an ultimately empty category whose fuzziness contrasts with the stability it celebrates (see Ceuppens and Geschiere 2005:387, 402). First, the particular performance elements that are presented to the camera team are themselves the result of a series of consultations, or of open confrontation, among local power groups. The second major selection is effected by the producer in two subsequent steps: by advising his team to focus on particular events, at the expense of others, and by selecting the ultimate version of 'local culture', in consideration of the sensitive nature of some of the recorded contents. Hence, similar to the selection effected by the hosts, the producer's re-composing of 'local culture' involves an complex process of translation suitable to the publicising of previously socially restricted or intimate knowledge.[28] In other words, the contents and the format of 'authentic culture' are readjusted in the process of recording and broadcasting. As genres originally intended for a spatially, and sometimes socially, restricted audience, the process of extending their spectatorship to a nationwide and anonymous audience transforms the function of the performance that becomes objectified as an element of 'traditional culture' (see Handler 1988:54–59).

Although the broadcast performance is clearly different from what is usually staged in the live performance, telespectators from the locality in question 're-cognise' the televised production as 'their own authentic tradition'. And they tend to view it as a blueprint for their claim to a particular, local positionality in a multicultural state and vis-à-vis an imaginary national audience.

Telespectators' enthusiastic reactions to the display of 'their authentic traditions' in *Terroir* suggests a clear disjuncture between the existence of 'objctive' markers of an 'authentic' performance and the subjective acknowledgment of a performance's unaltered and 'authentic nature' by individual spectators or entire audiences. This subjective process of authentification works through the spontaneous and sensual identification with various elements of the performance. As spectators' unprompted comments suggest, their spontaneous, sensually mediated process of identification is facilitated by visual mediation. In its simultaneous evocation of the visual and the aural senses, the television programme draws consumers sensually and aesthetically into the performance and allows them to experience it as 'genuine' and 'authentic' in the sense that it 'moves' and 'touches' them viscerally and emotionally.[29] But it seems that television, in its role as an institution, is in yet another respect crucial to the process of authentification. Whatever practices are depicted on national television as emblematic of 'traditional culture', they all receive an additional nimbus of authenticity through the very process of broadcasting them on national television and thus presenting to in a national public.

Conclusion

This article explored the particular version of 'national culture' that emerged in Mali's post-independent history at the interface of a governmental politics of culture and communication, of media technologies, and people's media engagement. I argued that the dialectical production of 'the past' as a source of cultural identity and nationalist pride was gradually transformed under the subsequent regimes of postcolonial Mali. Central parameters of claiming and validating one's past have changed, along with a shift in significance (and employment) of 'the past'. In previous decades, 'remembering the past' formed part of a hegemonic quest for a national heritage and an all-encompassing collective identity that tended to silence internal difference. This representation of national culture contrasts with more recent governmental attempts to create a sense of national unity not by reference to a common past but by acknowledging cultural diversity and celebrating the nation state's capacity to ease out the tensions arising from internal difference.

What conclusions can we draw from the shift from mass-mediated celebrations of oral traditions identified with practices of remembering an 'authentic' past to the staging of 'cultural diversity' on state television? In what sense is this shift indicative of how individuals and groups need to frame and pursue their citizenship entitlements under current political conditions shaped by the effects of multiparty 'democracy'?

The fact that forms of staging national unity and heritage in Mali have changed so drastically since the early 1990s illustrates that post-authoritarian conditions create very specific terms through which the politics of recognition are framed and played out. Throughout contemporary Africa, official efforts directed at the making of national community, and at the performance of the nation *as* community, are circumscribed by the weak normative, executive, and controlling capacity of the central state, and by the concomitant influence of values, ideals, and ideological reference points whose circulation are accelerated by transnational media institutions and images.

As part of the postcolonial predicament, the act of remembering an ethically superior past appears as crucial to citizens, in view of the historical experience of a radical rupture with past institutions and practices. In the contemporary moment, remembering is also essential to their attempts to lay claim to particular rights and entitlements predicated on their location in a plural ethnic and normative field. References to one's 'traditions' serve to bolster citizens' claims to a locally specific and particularistic identity and thereby feed into the great symbolic importance that notions of locality and of 'connectedness to the land' presently enjoy.

This change in the significance of 'tradition' operates in tandem with an expanding entertainment market. Facilitated by the mushrooming of various media technologies and institutions, genres of oral tradition that reverberate an aura of local connectedness are appropriated as elements of an individual, modern, and genuinely African identity. Various musical and oral traditions have become commodities and objects of consumption in a market of cultural authenticity the salience of which is reinforced by the present politics of cultural belonging.

How does the television programme *Terroir*, and its astounding success, fit into this development? First, it illustrates that, with the move toward representing a 'diverse-yet-unified culture' on national television, and with the attendant tendency to define 'the authentic' by its association with a locale's 'earth', the very performance traditions that are represented and objectified as 'culture' necessarily turn into standardised and 'cleaned-up' versions of unrecorded live performances. The resulting 'cultural heritage' is, very similar to the former party-promoted national culture, of a composite nature. Yet, these alterations do not seem to matter much to telespectators who claim a connection to the locality whose traditions are televised.

Can the programme *Terroir* therefore be interpreted as an instance of a 'narrative from below'? Or should it instead be seen as an extension of a 'narrative from above' that has been camouflaged as an expression of local initiative? I would argue that the programme *Terroir*, in its intricate intermingling of state cultural policy and institutional structure with various 'local' and regional interest groups and political factions, highlights the limits of the conceptual opposition of the making of politics 'from above' to those 'from below'. The success story of *Terroir* points instead to the ways in which politics are made, and narratives of belonging are constructed, in a web of intersecting connections among various local interest groups, their mediators at the regional and national levels, and state and party officials with divergent agendas.

The changing and sometimes conflicting narratives of cultural authenticity and belonging produced on national media and through consumers' media engagements thus illustrate that the hegemonic spell of this symbolic repertoire is as limited as its subversive potential. *Terroir's* reverberations are yet more multifaceted: The programme provides an at least partly successful formula for the performance of national community out of islands of cultural difference. At the same time, this mode of furthering national integration through 'locality', that is, through the acknowledgment of regional diversity, rather than through citizenship, generates its own backlash because it helps articulate the centrifugal tendencies that the government seeks to contain. In this sense, *Terroir* exemplifies the complicated and paradoxical nature of politics through which the nation, as a political community, is projected and fought over in the contemporary era of post-authoritarian rule.

Notes

1. Most of the entertainment programme on national television consists of Western imports. These are mostly U.S. and Latin American soap operas, and European, U.S.-American, and French West African music clips.
2. Usually, these admirers come from the area whose musical and performance traditions have just been shown on television.
3. Following Spitulnik (forthcoming), I use the term 'audience' to describe constituencies that come into being through their engagement with particular media (also see Barber 1997). 'Public' in contrast, refers to interlocking clusters of communication whose operation is shaped by the presence of modern state institutions.
4. My analysis of audience responses to official policy and cultural broadcasts draws primarily on the reminiscences of older listeners (almost all of them men) that I collected in the period between January 1994 and February 1996.
5. After 1985, when television was introduced, the national broadcast station was named RTM (Radiodiffusion et Télévision du Mali). In 1992, its name changed to ORTM (Office de Radiodiffusion et de Télévision du Mali).
6. For instance, a theatrical version of the epic of Sunjata, the legendary founder of the medieval Mali empire, could be read as an implicit challenge to French colonial rule. During the years Modibo Keita spent at the Ecole William Ponty in Senegal, he played in a theatrical group. On his return to Mali in 1937, he created the group 'Arts et Métiers', which, according to Diawara (1994), provided, as a cultural association, a cover for clandestine anticolonial political activities. Modibo Keita and his wife, who was an actress, performed in plays that celebrated mythical or real political heroes and often *constituted* parables of the current situation of foreign rule and oppression, such as the incident in which Sunjata, after years in exile, returns to his homestead and overthrows the 'imperialist' aggressor Sumanguru Kanté. The theatre play thus alluded to the possibility that Sundjata's empire was only a forerunner of a strong and independent nation to come. For three written versions of the Sunjata epic, see Innes (1974).
7. In anecdotes related to me in the period between 1996 and 2004, former participants in the youth festival reminisced about the ways a song they had considered to be part of local everyday 'entertainment' (*njanaje*) made its way first to the regional town and then to the capital Bamako, where it was presented as a token of a national heritage.

8. This is how several members of regional folklore groups recalled their 'patriotic attitude' in conversations with me in 1996 and 1998.
9. Several former officials of the Ministry of Culture asserted that one reason for the organisation of youth festivals at the regional and national levels was to offer folklore groups from the northern regions the opportunity to gain renown at the national level. But some of the former officials also admitted that for practical reasons, such as distance, transportation, and expenses, it was difficult to realise an equal representation of northern and southern folklore groups in Bamako at the national festival.
10. The singular form of *jeliw* (Bamana) is *jeli* (*jali* in Maninka).
11. In the scholarly literature, the women singers are often referred to as 'griots', which is the French term for *jeli* (for example, Camara 1976; Hale 1998; Keita 1995) or as *jelimusow* (= *jeli* women, for instance, Duran 1995). The term 'griot' glosses over considerable differences in the occupations and social origin of '*jeli* clients' and does not account for the fact that in some areas where no *jeliw* exist, other client families accomplish the tasks of *jeliw*. Not in all societies of Mali is praise singing and speaking the exclusive domain of *jeliw* (cf Diawara 1989, 1994). To call all women singers who perform on national radio and television 'griottes' risks creating confusion, because a growing number of the female stars are not of *jeli* origin. I refer to the singers as 'pop stars' because they have in common that they owe their success to broadcast media.
12. The same observation applies to print media as the other principal means of public communication in post-independent Mali. But given the high rate of illiteracy in this period, one can assume that the press played a comparatively minor role in representations of the new nation.
13. To be sure, farmers to whom I talked did not agree on the kind of songs or on the *jeli* singers they had appreciated most. Nor had they always approved of the praise songs performed on behalf of the new political leaders. Still, they saw praise songs as part and parcel of *jeliw*'s conventional tasks performed on behalf of powerful patrons. What mattered most about a song was whether listeners could recognise its music or lyrics and thus identify it as part of 'our truly own songs' (*an'w ka donkili yèrèyèrè*).
14. Aural broadcasting allowed women singers in particular to become a 'template' for subjective identification. Listening to female singers, farmers would experience feelings of collective belonging and identify the voice with the moral community they imagined. At the same time, the appeal of *jeli* women's songs resided in their specifically local imprint.
15. They usually described them as '*an'w ka donkili yereyere de do*' ('our genuinely own/authentic songs') or fenw korolen ('topics/things of the past').
16. Most *jeliw* who played in the national *ensembles* came from the urban area where they had to look out for new income opportunities and new sponsors because their former patrons no longer supported them. All musicians, even those who were not members of the national performance groups, were organised in a national organisation, the *Association des Artistes Traditionels*. The party maintained personal ties to many of them and invited them to perform on official occasions, such as post-election parties and campaigns.

17. Most of these southern oral traditions related to centralised political institutions. Among them were songs lauding legendary rulers, such as Da Monzon from the so-called kingdom of Segu, Sheku Hamadou, the ruler of the Fulbe 'empire' of Maasina.
18. Still, these individual *jeliw*'s loss in status and general appreciation does not preclude that until this day, publicly performed *jeli* praise still has the effect of generating prestige for the patron on whom the praise is bestowed. This is so mainly because the public interaction between patron and *jeli* client gives the former ample opportunities to display his or her generosity – a gesture that will be taken as an indication of his or her capacity to attract followers and clients and thus to rightly occupy a prominent social position (see Schulz 1999).
19. These effects of political liberalisation, imposed by the World Bank and Western donor organisations, are neither limited or unique to Mali. For an insightful discussion of the differential repercussions of these reforms on the ways in which a regime seeks to maintain authoritarian control, see Nyamnjoh and Rowlands (1998).
20. Some patronage ties between outstanding performers and individual state and party officials survived these changes, but they were effected exclusively through personal connections and no longer held the status as official, institutionalised relationships.
21. Similar to the times, when the 'monopoly' held by *jeli* singers as emblems of Malian culture was reflected in the scholarly preoccupation with *jeliw* and their 'ambiguous status' (see Conrad and Frank 1995), the recent diversification of performers and genres that are taken as representing Malian culture has generated a new body of scholarly research on music and performance genres other than those of the *jeliw*.
22. '(L')action politique se réfère à un ensemble des représentations culturelles. Elle consiste en un répertoire de gestes, de symboles, de formes esthétiques, de valeurs cosmiques, religieuses, morales ou sexuelles, de renvois historiques qui lui confèrent sens et consistance' (Bayart 1985:366, my translation).
23. The persistent success of the programme is perhaps best illustrated by the fact that most recently, the producer was unable to broadcast in due time the recordings he had already effected. In February 2006, his request to extend the broadcast time was finally granted by the director of the national broadcast station. At present, the programme is scheduled twice a week, but, as the producer told me in a conversation in July 2006, he is still unable to disseminate all productions in a timely fashion.
24. Originally, that is, under President Traoré's single-party rule, the production of *Terroir* was initiated and funded exclusively by the national broadcast station, with individual documentaries being conceived under the direct tutelage by the Ministry of Communication and, occasionally, by the Ministry of Culture. In this, the funding structure of this programme resembled that of other nationally produced 'music shows'. With the rise of the *Regime de Transition* to power in 1991, the funding of individual *Terroir* productions changed, mostly as a result of the upsurge of 'grass-roots' initiatives. A significant trend toward a reliance on 'local' initiatives and funding emerged during the two legislature periods of the first democratically elected government of Alpha Konaré and his party ADEMA. Cultural policy under the current government of President Toumani Touré (elected in 2001) has by and

large reinforced the emphasis on cultural diversity, as well as the construction of the rural 'home land' as font of cultural authenticity.
25. As I witnessed during my research in Mali between May and July of 2006, with the next legislative elections coming up in spring of 2007, deputies from various regions are eager to participate and to play as visible a role in the performance as the camera team (and hosts) allow them to do.
26. The decision to restructure the format of some ORTM programmes, particularly the attempt to make more room for audience feedback, can be seen as a response to the growing competition of national radio and television with the various local radio stations and, since 2005, the first private television station.
27. This is not to deny that those who invite him have an enormous influence on what is ultimately represented as 'authentic local culture'. But, as I argue below, villagers as well as their 'cousins' who represent their interests in town are able to influence only the first part of the process in the course of which the elements are selected that are subsequently televised as 'authentic tradition'.
28. Instances of this process of 'translation' and concomitant alteration abound. In one case, the camera team, invited to cover the work of an expert of occult knowledge, was allowed to film only particular sequences of his interventions. Another case was the famous remaking of the roof of the Kamablon, the sacred hut associated with the history of the Manding and guarded by the *jeli* family Diabaté of Kela. After a longer dispute between representatives of the Diabaté family and the family of the village chief, the camera team had to be content with shots taken from afar, so as to avoid that the screening of the hut without a roof would expose the Diabaté's 'secrets'.
29. For a more detailed discussion of how specific media technologies generate aesthetically mediated experiences of emotional identification, see Schulz (2006).

Bibliography

Askew, K. 2002. *Performing the Nation*. Chicago: The University of Chicago Press.
Austen, R. 1992. 'Tradition, Invention and History: The case of the Ngondo (Cameroun)', *Cahiers d'Etudes africaines* 126:285–309.
Barber, K. 1997. 'Preliminary Notes on Audiences in Africa', *Africa* 67(3):347–62.
Bayart, J.-F. 1983. 'La revanche des sociétés africaines', *Politique Africaine* 11 (Septembre):95–127.
———. 1985. 'L'enonciation du politique', *Revue Francaise de Science Politique* 35(3): 342–73.
———.1996. *L'illusion identitaire*. Paris: Fayard.
Bayart, J.-F., A. Mbembe, C. Toulabor (eds.). 1992. *Le politique par le bas en Afrique Noire*. Paris: Karthala.
Benjamin, W. 1963. Das Kunstwerk im Zeitalter seiner technischen Reproduzierbarkeit: Drei Studien zur Kunstsoziologie. Frankfurt: Suhrkamp.
Camara, S. 1976. *Gens de la Parole: Essai sur la condition et le rôle dans la société Malinké*. Paris, La Haye.
Carrier, P. 2000. 'Places, Politics and the Archiving of Contemporary Memory'. In *Memory and Methodology*, S. Radstone (ed.), pp. 37–58. Oxford: Berg.
Ceuppens, B., and P. Geschiere. 2005. 'Autochthony: Local or Global? New Modes in the Struggle over Citizenship and Belonging in Africa and Europe', *Annual Review of Anthropology* 34:385–407.

Comaroff, J., and J. Comaroff. 2000. 'Millenial Capitalism: First Thoughts on a Second Coming', *Public Culture* 12(2):291–344.

———. 2004. 'Criminal Obsessions, after Foucault: Postcoloniality, Policing, and the Metaphysics of Disorder', *Critical Inquiry* 30:800–24.

Conrad, D., and B. Frank (eds.). 1995. *Status and Identity in West Africa: The Nyamakalaw of Mande*. Bloomington: Indiana University Press.

Coplan, D. 1994. *In the Times of Cannibals: The Word Music of South Africa's Basotho Migrants*. Chicago: University of Chicago Press.

Corrigan, Ph., and D. Sayer. 1985. *The Great Arch: English State Formation as Cultural Revolution*. Oxford, New York: Blackwell.

Cutter, C. 1968. 'The Politics of Music in Mali', *African Arts* 1(3):38, 74–77.

Danielson, V. 1997.*The Voice of Egypt: Umm KUlthum, Arabic Song, and Egyptian society in the Twentieth Century*. Chicago: The University of Chicago Press.

de Certeau, M. 1984. *The Practice of Everyday Life*. Berkeley and Los Angeles: University of California Press.

Diawara, M. 1989. 'Women, Servitude and History: The Oral Historical Traditions of Women of Servile Condition in the Kingdom of Jaara (Mali) from the Fifteenth to the Mid-Nineteenth Century'. In *Discourse and Its Disguises, Birmingham: Centre of West African Studies*, K. Barber and P. F. de Moraes Farias (eds.), pp. 109–37. Birmingham: University of Birmingham.

———. 1994. 'Production and Reproduction: The Mande Oral Popular Culture Revisited by the Electronic Media', *Passages* 8:13–22.

Dominguez, V. 1989. *People As Subject, People As Object: Selfhood and Peoplehood in Contemporary Israel*. Madison: University of Wisconsin Press.

Englund, H., and F. Nyamnjoh (eds.). 2004. *Rights and the Politics of Recognition in Africa*. London: Zed Books.

Geschiere, P., and F. Nyamnjoh. 2001. 'Capitalism and Autochthony: The Seesaw of Mobility and Belonging'. In *Millenial Capitalism and the Culture of Neo-Liberalism*, J. Comaroff and J. L. Comaroff (eds.), pp. 159–90. Durham, NC: Duke University Press.

Hale, T. 1998. *Griots et Griottes: Masters of Words and Music*. Bloomington: Indiana University Press.

Handler, R. 1988. *Nationalism and the Politics of Culture in Quebec*. Madison: University of Wisconsin Press.

Hobsbawm, E. 1983. 'Introduction: Inventing Traditions'. In *The Invention of Tradition*, E. Hobsbawm and T. Ranger (eds.). Cambridge: Cambridge University Press.

Horkheimer, M., and T. W. Adorno. 1972. *Dialectic of Enlightenment*, J. Cumming (trans.). New York: Continuum Puiblishing.

Innes, G. 1974. *Sunjata: Three Mandinka Versions*. London: School of Oriental and African Studies, University of London.

Keita, M. C. K. 1995. 'Jaliya in the Modern World' In *Status and Identity in West Africa: The Nyamakalaw of Mande*, D. Conrad and Barbara Frank (eds.), pp. 182–96. Bloomington: Indiana University Press.

Klute, G., and T. von Trotha. 2004. 'Roads to Peace. From Small War to Parastatal Peace in the North of Mali'. In *Healing the Wounds. Essays on the Reconstruction of Societies after War*, M.-C. Foblets and T. von Trotha (eds.), pp. 109–43. Oxford: Oñati International Series in Law and Society.

Mbembe, A. 2001. 'Ways of Seeing: Beyond the New Nativism – Introduction', *African Studies Review* 44(2):1–14.
Meillassoux, C. 1968. *Urbanization of an African Community: Voluntary Associations in Bamako*. Seattle: University of Washington Press.
Meyer, B., and P. Geschiere (eds.). 1999. *Globalization and Identity: Dialectics of Flow and Closure*. Malden, MA: Blackwell.
Nora, P. 1989. 'Between Memory and History: Les lieux de mémoire', M. Roudebush (trans.), *Representations* 26:7–25.
Nyamnjoh, F., and M. Rowlands. 1998. 'Elite Associations and the Politics of Belonging in Cameroon', *Africa* 68(3):32–37.
Schulz, D. 1998. 'Morals of Praise: Broadcast Media and the Commoditization of *Jeli* Praise Performances in Mali', *Research in Economic Anthropology* 19:117–33.
———. 1999. 'Pricey Publicity, Refutable Reputations: *Jeliw* and the Economics of Honour in Mali', *Paideuma* 45:275–92.
———. 2001a. Perpetuating the Politics of Praise: *Jeli* Praise Singers, Radios and Political Mediation in Mali. Köln: Rüdiger Köppe Verlag.
———. 2001b. 'Music Videos and the Effeminate Vices of Urban Culture in Mali', *Africa* 71(3):325–71.
———. 2004. 'God Is Our Resort': Islamic Revival, Mass-Mediated Religiosity and the Moral Negotiation of Gender Relations in Urban Mali. Habilitationsschrift, Free University, Berlin.
———. 2006. 'Promises of (Im)mediate Salvation: Islam, Broadcast Media, and the Remaking of Religious Experience in Mali', *American Ethnologist* 33(2):210–29.
Simone, A. M. 2001. 'On the Worlding of African Cities', *African Studies Review* 44(2):15–43.
Snyder, F. 1967. 'The Political Thought of Modibo Keita', *Journal of Modern African Studies* 5(1):79–106.
Spitulnik, D. Forthcoming. *Media Connections and Disconnections: Radio Culture and the Public Sphere in Zambia*. Durham, NC: Duke University Press.
Steinmetz, G. 1999. 'Introduction: Culture and the State'. In *State/Culture: State-Formation after the Cultural Turn*, G. Steinmetz (ed.). Ithaca, NY: Cornell University Press.
Taylor, C. 1994. 'The Politics of Recognition'. In *Multiculturalism: Examining the Politics of Recognition*, A. Gutmann (ed.). Princeton, NJ: Princeton University Press.
Trouillot, R. 1995. *Silencing the Past: Power and the Production of History*. Boston: Beacon Press.
———. 1997. 'Silencing the Past: Layers of Meaning in the Haitian Revolution'. In *Between History and Histories: The Making of Silences and Commemorations*, G. Sider and G. Smith (eds.), pp. 31–61. Toronto: University of Toronto Press.
Turino, T. 2000. *Nationalists, Cosmopolitans, and Popular Music in Zimbabwe*. Chicago: University of Chicago Press.
Werbner, R. 2004. 'Epilogue: The New Dialogue with Post-liberalism'. In *Rights and the Politics of Recognition in Africa*, H. Englund and F. Nyamnjoh (eds.), pp. 261–74. London: Zed Books.
Young, C. 1988. 'The African Colonial State and Its Political Legacy'. In *The Precarious Balance: State and Civil Society in Africa*, D. Rotchild and N. Chazan (eds.), pp. 25–66. Boulder, CO: Westview Press.

Demystified Memories: The Politics of Heritage in Post-Socialist Guinea
Ramon Sarró

> Our society is achieved by getting rid of the failings inherited from the past: from the fetishist past, from the colonial past, and from the feudal past.
>
> Sékou Touré (1976:90, my translation)

The Baga-speaking peoples of coastal Guinea have known a long succession of violence. Almost every narrative they provide a visitor about their history as an ethnic group is linked to one form or other of violence: the violence of the Muslim *jihad* of the eighteenth century, when Muslim Fulbe herders pushed non-Muslim farmers out of the Fouta Djalon mountains and forced them to move to the coastal mangroves where their descendants live today; the violence of the coastal slave trade, which is still today remembered in the villages; the violence of French colonialism, when a bunch of Baga people were given immense power over others (normally considered their 'strangers'); the violence of an iconoclastic religious movement led by the Muslim preacher Asekou Sayon; the memories of the anticolonial movement led by the *Rassemblement Démocratique Africain*; the violence of Sékou Touré's first Republic, with its socialist 'demystification campaigns', 'cultural revolution', and oppressive policies (1958–1984). But not everything in Baga cultural history is related to disruption. Baga farmers are in fact much better known to the wider public for their impressive art and material culture than for their traumatic history. Most of the most famous pieces of African art in Western museums do come from this Guinean people, an art to which scholars are now paying a deserved attention (Berliner 2002a, 2002b; Curtis 1996; Curtis and

Sarró 1997; Lamp 1996). The entanglement among disruption, destruction, and creativity is an element not only of Baga history but also of their everyday life in today's Guinea, a daily life marked by a strong ambivalence to materiality, art, and 'tradition'. But, to understand this present-day situation, we must first recall the rudiments of Baga cultural history.

Landlords, Strangers, and Iconoclasts

Historians have identified a recurrent settlement pattern on the Upper Guinea Coast, where Baga live, based on the relationship between 'landlords' and 'strangers' (Brooks 1993; Dorjahn and Fyfe 1962; Rodney 1970). According to this pattern, people placed themselves under the aegis of a landlord who offered protection while enriching his social capital. In 2003, when discussing the relationships between landlords and strangers, Mahmoud, a 75-year-old Muslim man, told me that most of the people composing any Baga village today were late arrivals. 'Now we are outnumbered', he concluded, meaning that there were more late arrivals than landlords. And he added, 'we say we are all Baga, but in reality there are more strangers than Baga'. He also insisted that everybody in the Dabaka (the territory that Baga speakers occupy) was landlord and stranger to someone else. According to his explanations, a person in need of protection might go to a village and place him- or herself under the protection of a descent group or of a whole ward. If the people of this ward accepted the stranger, the ward's spirit would grant protection. Even if the strangers had strong enemies in their original village, or if they were escaping punishment, nobody would do anything to them once a descent group had promised protection.

It is unclear whether Baga had chiefs in precolonial times. While some documents present them as a clearly decentralised, segmentary society, oral tradition in fact speaks of a ceremony called 'to settle a chief' through which groups of landlords appointed a chief from a descent group of late arrivals. Whatever the case, since 1886 the Baga were under French rule, mediated through chiefs appointed by the French, sometimes referred to as 'Baga kings' in colonial sources. In 1922, the French created a 'Canton Baga', and until 1956 they continued to appoint elders to be 'traditional' or 'customary' chiefs of the Baga.

The institution of the traditional chieftaincy as promoted by the French soon became rather tyrannical. It reified notions of gerontocracy and patriarchy that most likely had a long history in precolonial Upper Guinea coast but had probably never been as rigid a structure as it came to be in colonial times, when it was sanctioned and enforced by French laws and officers.

Under this regime, youths had to work very hard at 'customary' celebration of marriages, funerals, and initiations as well as the occasional visits of chiefs and colonial officials. For the youth, Baga 'custom' became more and more oppressive: Not only did they have to tap massive amounts of palm wine for all the celebrations, but they were also subjected to forced labour, 'rice campaigns', and other abuses that were channelled through the customary chieftaincy and therefore perceived (and today remembered) as part of the 'Baga custom'. Under French rule, Baga were enclosed upon themselves in their Canton Baga, which to all effects worked as both a magnifying lens and as a fence; it amplified the local and provided a buffer against outside forces, particularly those of Islam, which since the early twentieth century was becoming a strong subaltern voice in many other Guinean cantons. Traditional rituals, which served to legitimate the status quo in which traditional chiefs and their relatives would enrich themselves and oppress the youths, were clearly protected by French colonialists, particularly worried about the anticolonial content of some varieties of Islam. Interestingly, among the Baga Sitem subgroup, Christianity became an unexpected ally of tradition. Many of the landowning elders converted to Christianity in order to articulate an opposition to Islam, the strongest critical voice against tradition, palm-wine drinking, secret cults, and unfair chiefs to be heard in the colonies.

After the Second World War, a refreshing wind was felt all around French West Africa. As from 1946, the anticolonial movement *Rassemblement Démocratique Africain* fought for the full citizenship of Africans, as promised by De Gaulle at the Brazzaville Conference (1944). Although at its beginning the RDA had links with European left-wing parties, in some parts of West Africa it eventually found that Islam was a secure medium to propagate the anticolonial message (Morgenthau 1964:237). In much of the West African territory, Islam became the real agent in the modernizing opening-up of the villages. Its followers denounced unfair chieftaincies as well as all those 'customs' that were keeping Africa behind: alcohol, masks, ritual elders, and secret societies. Since the early 1950s, committees of the RDA were, in every Guinean village, a parallel and antagonistic institution to the increasingly obsolete 'customary chieftaincy' endorsed by the French.

Into this volatile situation appeared in 1956, at the very end of French colonialism, the iconoclastic jihadist figure of Asekou Sayon. Sayon marked the junction between two eras in Baga history, and he is remembered as a real agent of transformation, almost as a 'trickster' figure, as Charles Jedrej kindly observed (personal communication 1999). Sayon was a Muslim converter, a witch-finder, a 'fetish' destroyer, an RDA sympathiser, an unsatisfied people's leader, among other things. Almost immediately after the work of the jihadist,

President Sékou Touré deployed the State in a forceful campaign to establish a modern Guinean nation and identity and to ban regional forms of ethnic identity and local religious cults (it was possible to be only Guinean and Muslim). Thus, the deeds of Sayon are recalled today as a turning point in the history of the Baga.

Sékou Touré and the Politics of 'Demystification'

Sayon's movement was a complex one in which there were different religious, political, and other agendas at play. It was 'destructive' in that it represented the end of some rituals and of a religious identity linked to these rituals. The very places where sacred groves existed previously were now to harbour Muslim mosques, modern schools, or cash crop plantations. The Republic of Guinea that Sayon and many others had helped to build by destroying the 'fetishes' and by creating a common Guinean public space was not going to permit such sacred groves to be reintroduced and their rituals to return. The tragedy for Sayon was that, although he helped destroy the 'fetishes', he did it from the wrong side. To Touré and other politicians, men such as Sayon were just as 'fetishistic' and obscurantist as the sorcerers they were chasing. In a modern state, there was no room for them. Sayon became a marginal nuisance and could consider himself fortunate not to have been imprisoned, as were many other *marabouts* (Kaba 1976:65). No words could express better what Sékou Touré and his party thought of the *marabouts* than this official note written as early as 1959:

> We must fight against swindler *marabouts*, fight against religious fanaticism, essentially destructing fraternity and solidarity, fight efficaciously against *maraboutage*, *maraboutisme*, charlatanism, and all the forces of exploitation linked to obscurantist entities. In sum, we must attain what we could call the *de-maraboutisation* and de-intoxication of the masses.[1]

In such a 'de-maraboutizing' context, shortly after leaving prison in 1958, unsurprisingly, Asekou Sayon tried as hard as he could to maintain a low profile and to live off peanut farming instead of the production of charms and antiwitchcraft rituals. Asekou Sayon's life and deeds represented the transition from one period to another. He was born and educated at a time and in a region of *grands marabouts*, and he used (and was used by) the RDA. He learned how to manipulate the oppression that people felt and their thirst for social change, and in so doing he collaborated in the creation of a new political order in which, however, there was no room for him.

The RDA led Guinea toward Independence (1958) and remained in power in the first Republic of Guinea (1958–1984). For RDA leaders, early proponents of the kind of ideology and social engineering James Scott has called 'high authoritarian modernism' (Scott 1998), traditional beliefs and the modernity of the state could not go hand in hand. Moreover, according to the philosophy of the RDA, these beliefs were no more than a 'mystification' by male elders to maintain control of gullible young men and women. Consequently, in independent Guinea a strong programme of grassroots 'demystification' was put to work that in many cases was as, if not more, violent than Sayon's movement. There is some confusion among scholars as to when exactly the campaign started. Rivière, who wrote what for many years was the only available source about this largely undocumented campaign (Rivière 1969), said it started in 1961. In a more recent case study, however, Michael McGovern has argued that already in early 1959 there were demystification policies in the region known as *Guinée Forestière* (McGovern 2004). Sankhon, on his part, claims that from 1960 to 1968 there were reforms aiming at putting an end to customs, but they were not taken too seriously by local populations, and therefore a proper 'campaign' started in August 1968, following the socialist cultural revolution that was launched on 2 August 1968, inspired by the Chinese example (Sankhon 1987). In writing about the Guinean Cultural Revolution, Sékou Touré explained:

> The Cultural Revolution had to attack fetishism, charlatanism, religious fanaticism, any irrational attitude, any form of mystification, any form of exploitation, with the aim to liberate the energies of the People and engage them in the consolidation of the rational bases of its development. (Touré 1978:33; my translation)

Abdoulaye Tyam has argued that the 'educative' programme of the RDA to demystify local practices and beliefs had several phases (Tyam 1975:73). By 1975, he writes, anybody found wearing amulets or practising any sort of either 'fetishism' or *maraboutism* would be sentenced to fifteen years of jail.[2] Many other practices were also deemed irrational and banned: long and expensive funerals, certain agronomic practices, and polygamy.

In these demystifying programmes, officials were sent to the villages to prove that elders were using masks, initiations, and 'irrational' beliefs to empower themselves and keep other people under their control. The men sent to the villages could not come back to their bases, as Sankhon says, without having disclosed 'the *nimba* in its true nature of man' (Sankhon 1987:42); otherwise, *they* would be in trouble vis-à-vis their superiors in town. Following a common Guinean usage, Sankhon uses the word *nimba* as a generic term for 'mask', 'cult', or 'spirit' – in any case, nothing but a disguised *man* (a male individual, not the generic human being). As Sankhon recalls, women were actually happy to be shown by the forces of the State that men had been fooling them, and they felt quite empowered by this unexpected knowledge. Neither the 'popular' iconoclasm instigated by Sayon nor the 'state' iconoclasm ordered by Touré had female cults as targets for destruction, and, as some authors have argued, this fact has actually greatly intensified the strength and importance of female cults in postcolonial Guinea (see Berliner 2005 for the Bulongic; McGovern 2004 for a similar situation among the Loma).

State-monitored iconoclasm seems to have been particularly intense and violent in the forest region neighbouring Sierra Leone and Liberia, especially among the Loma (Højbjerg 2002; McGovern 2004). Among coastal Baga, probably because of the thoroughness of Sayon's iconoclastic movement only one year before decolonisation, there was no need for the state to pursue iconoclasm. The demystification campaigns were not as strongly remembered among my interviewees as they were among interviewees of Højbjerg and McGovern.

Educational theatre was to replace ritual initiations. This theatre was to show that *marabouts* were nothing but swindlers and that traditional healers had no reason to exist, since the state had hospitals and doctors. In any case, should traditional healers have any effective secret plants or products, their duty was to deliver them to the State for scientific examiniation (Sankhon 1987:43). Masks and other ritual objects, together with dances and songs, were to be appropriated by the State with the purpose of creating a 'national' folklore, in what Wolfgang Bender has called a 'bureaucratisation of culture' (Bender 1991; for the making of Guinea's folklore see also Kaba 1976; Lamp 1996; Miller 1990). It was a folklore made up of elements from different regions, publicly displayed in National Museums and projected to an international audience via Keita Fodeba's famous company *Les Ballets Africains* (for a history of this company, see Miller 1990; Rouget 1956) and Aboubabar Demba Camara's orchestra *Bembeya Jazz National*, the country's official *griot*. Despite the iconoclasm in the villages, a new hermeneutic project arose at state level, one in which masks and other objects were going to be interpreted according to the true spirit of the Guinean people: not as representations of obscure bush spirits but as manifestations of the Peoples' struggle for cultural liberation.

If initiations and masks were one mark of the 'irrational' elements that a modern nation could not afford to live with, so was ethnicity. The constitution of the newly independent Guinea made ethnic particularism illegal.

Article 45 declared that 'every act of racial discrimination as well as all propaganda of a racial or regional character shall be punishable by law'. By 1962, President Sékou Touré wrote that:

> There is no more in the Republic of Guinea the Malinké race, the Susu race, the Fulbe race, the Guerzé race, the Landuma or Kissi race. The Susu, Malinké Toma, Guerzé, Fulbe, Landuma, or Kissi have taken up their language differentiation as a means of communication between men. Thus, every youth of Guinea, every adult of Guinea asked about his race, will reply that he is an African. (Touré cited by Mazrui and Tidy 1985:91)

For the Baga, it was impossible to revive the practice of initiation, in contrast to other Guinean groups, especially those living closer to boundaries. Loma, for instance, could continue their initiations by sending their children to their relatives' villages in Liberia, even if this was subject to legal punishment (McGovern 2004). The Bassari could go to Senegal to have their initiations, and maybe people along the Guinea Bissau border also went to their neighbours in that country. Unlike them, Baga had nowhere to go, other than their memories. At times, Baga tried to bring to life these memories. Sékou Beka Bangoura mentions and analyses a solemn sacrifice that took place in Bukor in October 1971 in which people had to perform the ritual according to 'custom' instead of Muslim sacrificial rules (Bangoura 1972:71–72). There were probably other such attempts, but they were dangerous. In Mare, roughly at the same time, some men trying to revive a cult were denounced by some vigilante neighbours, good Party fellows, and punished by the state, as one of them explained to me in 2003. If iconophilic Baga had thought they had only to hide their objects, wait for Sayon' departure, and then bring them back again, they were wrong. After Sayon's exploits, another kind of iconoclasm arrived, and it arrived to stay.

Once Were Landlords

In their effort to destroy any sort of inequality and 'feudalism', the PDG reversed the power structure of the old canton and village chiefs. Descent groups that had wielded power in colonial times (and most probably in pre-French times, too) had no saying whatsoever about who the chiefs were going to be in postcolonial days. When I asked old Mahmoud why there had been no more 'crowning' ceremonies (*kides wube*) ever since the arrival of the PGD, he replied: 'You need a [secret] place to do the *kides wube*; with colonialism we had such a place, with the RDA we did not have it anymore'.

Distinctions between 'Baga' and 'stranger', which in colonial times had been so relevant in mapping out the political field of coastal cantons, became polit-ically unsound and dangerous. All Guineans were to be seen in equal terms. Differences on the basis of ethnicity or seniority were not allowed; nor could age, gender, ethnicity, or migration narratives be used to differentiate Guinean citizens. As Sékou Touré wrote against Senghor and other *négritude* intellec-tuals, in an Africa inhabited by human beings not even colour could make people different (Touré, N.d.). The discourse against feudal prerogatives was particularly humiliating for those groups who only recently had based their ethos in ge-nealogy, land accumulation, and ethnic seniority.

Geopolitical divisions also played an important part in the delegitimization of some of these inherited privileges. The independent Guinean state accepted some of the colonial boundaries. For instance, the two *cercles* of Boffa and Boké were transformed into prefectures with the same names. 'Cantons' disappeared, however, and they were replaced by *arrondissements* whose boundaries did not match the previous cantons. Villages also disappeared and were transformed into 'districts', each one divided into sectors. In a democratic sense, each sector was to have the same form of representation, which meant a complete reversal of the power relations in Baga Sitem villages.

In colonial times, Baga Sitem lived in some fifteen villages in the 'Canton Baga'. This canton became the *arrondissement* of Bintimodia, with the capital in Bintimodia, which had been a Susu place subordinated to Baga landlords. Each Baga village was divided into *sectors*. Let us look at the village of Mare, for instance. In colonial times, this village had three wards: Kareka, Kambota, and Katengne. Each one of these wards had some adjacent inhabited territories. For instance, some people in Kareka were the owners of Dukulum (literally, 'the bush'), a place where some Susu farmers had settled, as well as of Bakiya, where Jakhanke had settled in the mid 1950s. The people of Kategne and Kabota also had their strangers' areas. These places belonged to Baga, and, to some extent, so did their inhabitants: They were strangers *of* Baga landlords. With the new political structure, however, Mare found itself divided into eight *secteurs*, of which only three were inhabited by Baga farmers (the three original wards) and the other five by Susu, Jakhanke, and other strangers whose lands had previously 'belonged' to Baga. However, such phrasing was not allowed by the new government. Baga could still think of, say, Dukulum as being part from Kareka, but the new administration made Dukulum a proper *secteur*, and its citizens had the same importance, rights, and duties as those from Kareka. The situation created by the new administration of the 1960s still prevails today. In 1994, I met a Baga man in Katako who heard me say that Mare had eight wards; we were speaking in French and following a common usage. I used the word *quartier* instead of the administrative *secteur*. He said ironically: 'Mare grew up fast; it had only three last time I was there'. I later realised that most Baga think of their village in a very different way than its Susu inhabitants do. For Baga, there are only three main divisions in Mare (with subdivisions); for Susu, there are eight. The few Baga people living in Dukulum, to stick to our example, say they live in Kareka because that is where the 'big house' of their descent group is located and because they see Dukulum as part of Kareka. Susu people living in Dukulum insist that they live in Tanene (the Susu name of Dukulum; it means 'new village') and speak of the three central *secteurs* of Mare as the *Bagatai* (in Susu, Bagaland) as though they, the Susu, were not living on the Baga territory. This example applies to all Baga Sitem villages.

As some interviewees put it, the tragedy for Baga was that they became a 'minority group' in their own villages. Furthermore, land was nationalised by a series of decrees, starting in 1959 but culminating in 1967. Baga could no longer prove that they were the landlords of the lands on which the Susu were working. One of the outcomes of the new political conjuncture was that being 'Baga' in independent Guinea was not a great advantage. If in the past there had been conversions from stranger status to Baganess and if in the colonial period being Baga meant being closer to power, in postcolonial Guinea, strangers in the Dabaka were clearly better off by remaining strangers and by accusing Baga (ex-)landlords of claiming to be their 'feudal' *seigneurs*.

The Politics of Tradition in Post-Socialist Guinea

Against the political background of Sékou Touré's repressive regime, the situation changed dramatically after the installation of the second republic by President Lansana Conté in 1984, with increasing liberalization and decentralisation. Instead of the monitoring of a national heritage from top to bottom, specific ethnic groups now became involved in claiming what they perceived as their own cultural heritages. Already in the 1980s, some groups resumed their initiations and other ritual practices that had been banned under Sékou Touré. The Landuma, for instance, who neighbour the Baga to the north, publicly celebrated the reopening of their sacred bush in the early 1990s. Another characteristic of post-Touré Guinea was the increasing involvement of *ressortissants* (urban dwellers who trace their origins to specific villages or regions) in village affairs and in reintroducing ethnic idioms that would have been unacceptable in Touré's Guinea.

Like any other Guinean people, Baga were eager to express their cultural difference by any possible means and to freely practice whatever they felt was their custom. The art historian Frederick Lamp, who conducted pioneering field research as soon as Guinea opened up to Western researchers, witnessed this cultural reinvention and its internal problems. In fact, as he was well aware (Lamp 1996:256), he unwillingly became part of the revitalization process he was observing by making Baga aware and proud of a heritage that had been despised during the previous regime. In 2003, I met a Baga Sitem carver who used Lamp's book on Baga art as a source of inspiration to recreate the lost art of his people.

However, the enthusiasm with which Baga engaged in cultural reinvention in the 1980s decreased in the mid 1990s, when I conducted my initial fieldwork. Dances, masquerades, and other celebrations were often promised by my hosts but rarely performed. Apart from some isolated cases (such as the D'mba masquerade witnessed in the village of Tolkoc in 2001, see illustration), overall the landscape I got to know was icon-free and, even, iconophobic. Baga territory seemed to me to be more thoroughly 'demystified' than any other part of Guinea, and Baga subjectivities more fully modernised than others. Thus, when I asked interviewees why Baga had not reactivated their initiation rituals after Sékou Touré's death, as had been done in other parts of Guinea, a common answer was that Baga preferred schooling to bush initiation, by and large perceived as part and parcel of a past from which modern subjects must free themselves, very much as Sékou Touré would have put it in his demystifying language.

The reluctance to bring masks, performances, and objects into the public sphere had to do not only with the perception that these things were not compatible with education and modern life but also with the initiatory logics and its age structure. The Baga ceased their initiations in the late 1950s, and, unlike the Kissi or the Loma, who continued their initiations during Sékou Touré's times by sending their youths to Liberia or to Sierra Leone, they could not continue their initiations in any other country. This meant that the generational gap between elders (*wubeki*, pl. *abeki*) and youths (*wuan*, pl. *awut*) was, and still is, frozen. *Abeki* are those who were initiated in the pre-independence times, and *awut* are those who were not. This generational divide creates competing views on what aspects of Baga material culture are accessible, and to whom. Baga materiality becomes a precious resource, and many negotiations are required to have access to it and to have it displayed. The degree to which villagers let cultural goods be displayed not only depends on villagers' age and knowledge but also differs enormously from village to village. While some villages, mostly those enclaved in the mangroves, hold on to a strict distinction between a secret sphere and a public domain, other villages, situated closer to the urban centre of Kamsar, have created *troupes de théatre* that offer a 'folklorised' display of Baga masquerades for tourists, political visitors, and filmmakers.[3]

Demystified Memories: The Politics of Heritage in Post-Socialist Guinea

Figure 9.1 'Nimba' (or d'mba) masquerade, Tolkoc, 2001 (photograph: Ramon Sarró)

Here I am using the notion of 'folklorisation' as a self-conscious objectification of what people perceive to be their folklore or tradition and its display in cultural performances. The concept was coined by the German anthropologist Herman Bausinger (Bausinger [1961] 1990). In West Africa, the analytical possibilities of the concept have been explored by Peter Mark (Mark 1994) and by Ferdinand de Jong (de Jong 1997) in their analyses of the Jola *troupes folkloriques* (not dissimilar to the Guinean *troupes de théâtre*). It is true that the Baga do not use the concept of folklore very often, although it is a well-known term in Guinea, and Catholic Baga do use it. Sometimes it is used as a synonym for theatre, and sometimes as a category explicitly opposed to notions of secrecy, as when a Catholic man told me in 1995 that all the filmmakers making films on Baga masquerades were getting only Baga 'folklore', not their 'secrets'. In fact, the existence of an objectified 'folklore' is often used by Baga interviewees not only to proudly show that Baga do have a cultural heritage but also to argue that whatever is seen in public performances is just the tip of the iceberg. In the early 1990s, for instance, I was told about a meeting in a village in which the elders were asked by the youths and the *ressortissants* to recreate *amanco ngopong* (the biggest Baga object, not seen in any village since the late 1940s or early 1950s), so that it could be displayed at a visit of President Lansana Conté to the village. Showing important masks to honour political visitors is of course a widespread African practice. Yet, in this particular case, the elders decided not to do it, and they instructed younger villagers to show the often seen *nimba* headdress instead (undoubtedly the most widely known Baga object). As I was told, the elders knew that reintroducing the *amanco ngopong* in the public arena would be to downgrade it from *tolom* to *powolsene*, two concepts that are structurally opposed. *Tolom* (pl. *molom*) may mean 'secret' (as in the secrets learnt in initiation, not to be revealed), but it is also used to refer to masks, and especially to masks to be seen only by initiated people. *Powolsene* (pl. *yowolsene*) means 'toy' and refers to masks that are mainly used to entertain, such as *nimba*, *sibondel*, and some others. To downgrade *amanco ngopong* from *tolom* to *powolsene* would imply that the elders gave it to the youths and would lose the power they have by keeping it secret.

Whether the meeting I was told about really took place or was just one way to let me know that Baga could (if they so wanted) recreate such solemn things as *amanco ngopong* is impossible to determine, but it is also beside the point. Even if the meeting was invoked only as a rhetorical device, the effect was, precisely, to create the awesome presence of *amanco ngopong* in the imagination of those who were listening to the conversation, me included. It was, in fact, a group of elders who reported to me about the meeting, and they did so in the presence of some young people who, probably, felt simultaneously proud of their elders' powerful 'secrets' and angry at their unwillingness to give them away. The cunning way Baga elders get away with *not* materializing *amanco ngopong* reinforces the theoretical point made by Elisabeth Tonkin, according to which nonmaterial masks are in many ways more effective masks than material ones: Material masks conceal through revealing something else; nonmaterial masks conceal through sheer concealment, and by doing so they evoke extremely awesome spiritual entities.[4]

The fate of Baga cultural heritage is inevitably linked to such entanglements between secrecy and display. Some members of the community, especially the *ressortissants*, would like to have a cultural heritage displayed and propagated to the wider world. Others, however, have a centripetal view of knowledge, more in tune with initiatory notions of secrecy and personhood. Accordingly, they prefer to keep things secret and to remain silent about their past and their religious convictions. In 2001, I was told by elders of one village that they had sworn an oath to *amanco ngopong* to punish any materialization of spiritual forces; whoever carved a mask or a ritual object, or reintroduced rituals in the public sphere, would be punished by death by the fearsome spirit. Sometimes, however, there are some compromises. Thus, in 1995 the *ressortissants* negotiated an agreement with the elders about which particular dances could be taught to young children to perform at a Baga football tournament (Sarró 1999). As one *ressortissant* pointed out to me, Baga will get funds from international donors only if they show that they are a minority ethnic group in danger, and they can prove this only by performing traditional dances, not by playing football.

Ressortissants are asking the elders to teach dances and performances to the youths, but teaching these would be like opening Pandora's Box. By asking elders to do things that would have been punished by the demystification campaigns of Sékou Touré, the *ressortissants* have started a process explicitly opposed to such campaigns. While in the demystification campaigns state monitors were sent to the villages to police ritual activity and to make sure that nothing 'irrational' happened, in post-socialist Guinea *ressortissants* often aim at reintroducing such practices and logics and make sure that nobody is punished for that. The national law and the international sympathies are now with them. So far, formal initiations and sacred groves have not been reintroduced, at least not in the Baga Sitem villages I know of, but in at least two of these villages there have recently been reactualizations of contracts with local spirits that had been neglected since 1958. This spiritual empowerment may be saluted, especially since Baga do have a rich heritage that they have unnecessarily despised for too long. Unfortunately, however, among his many wrongdoings, Sékou Touré was right in at least one crucial thing: In colonial times masks, rituals and spirits ('fetishes' in his Marxian language) were used as mechanisms to oppress people (mostly youths, women, and strangers) and were intertwined with local practices of landlord-ship (or 'feudalism', as he would have it). The challenge for Baga farmers is to live with their rituals and their spirits without claiming autochthony and power over youths, women, and strangers. If they do not meet this challenge, they will not be reclaiming their heritage but remystifying it. How to have one without the other is probably a challenge Baga share with many other peoples in today's Africa.

Notes

1. Circular No. 21/BMP/PDG-RDA, 16 October 1959, addressed to all the sections of the Party. Cited in Sankhon (1987:43; my translation). *Marabout* here does not mean a Muslim man of learning, as it may do in other contexts, but a Muslim who relies on magical practices and not on the strict letter of the Qur'an. Strictly Qur'anic masters were tolerated by the regime.
2. *Horoya* Num. 2200 (November 1975), p. 40.
3. For a particularly interesting documentary on Baga art and dances filmed in the mid 1990s, see Laurent Chevalier's *Aoutara* (France and Guinea, 1996) about a troupe of Baga women based in Conakry.
4. Tonkin develops her points about masks that are only 'a cry in the night' in her survey of masks and masquerades (Tonkin 1979a), a rare document that unfortunately has become difficult to get hold of and that I have not been able to consult. I am grateful to her for a recent conversation in Beucha (Germany), and I apologise for any possible misrepresentation of her views. As I understand her, the points she

makes in this paper are consistent with her other theoretical work on masks and power (Tonkin 1979b, 1988).

Bibliography

Bangoura, M. M. (ed.). n.d. [c. 1991]. 'Patmè: Traditionalisme Baga'. Conakry: La commission culturelle.

Bangoura, S. B. 1972. 'Croyances et pratiques religieuses des Baga Sitému', Mémoire de diplôme de fin d'études supérieures, pp. 71–72. Kankan: IPJN.

Bausinger, H. 1990 [first German edition 1961]. *Folk Culture in a World of Technology*. Bloomington: Indiana University Press.

Bender, W. 1991 [first German edition 1985]. *Sweet Mother: Modern African Music*. Chicago: University of Chicago Press.

Berliner, D. 2002a. 'A *callè* Never Dies: About the *bansonyi* among the Bulongic Baga (Guinea-Conakry)', *Arts et Culture* 3:99–111.

———. 2002b. '«Nous sommes les derniers Bulongic»: Sur une impossible transmission dans une société d'Afrique de l'Ouest'. PhD thesis. Free University of Brussels.

———. 2005. 'La féminisation de la coutume: Femmes possédés et transmission religieuse en pays bulongic (Guinée-Conakry)', *Cahiers d'Études Africaines* 45(1):15–38.

Brooks, G. E. 1993. *Landlords and Strangers: Ecology, Society, and Trade in Western Africa, 1000–1630*. Boulder, CO: Westview Press.

Camara K. 1998. *Dans la Guinée de Sékou Touré: Cela a bien eu lieu*. Paris: L'Harmattan.

Curtis, M. Y. 1996. 'L'art nalu, l'art baga de Guinée: Approches comparatives'. PhD thesis, University of Paris.

Curtis, M. Y., and R. Sarró. 1997. 'The *nimba* Headdress: Art, Ritual and History of the Baga and Nalu peoples of Guinea', *Museum Studies* 23(2):121–33.

de Jong, F. 1997. 'The Power of a Mask: A Contextual Analysis of the Senegalese *Kumpo* Mask Performance', *Focaal* 29:37–56.

Dorjahn, V. R., and C. Fyfe. 1962. 'Landlord and Stranger: Change in Tenancy Relations in Sierra Leone', *Journal of African History* 3(3):391–97.

Højbjerg, C. 2002. 'Inner Iconoclasm: Forms of Reflexivity in Loma Rituals of Sacrifice', *Social Anthropology* 10(1):57–75.

Kaba L. 1976. 'The Cultural Revolution, Artistic Creativity, and Freedom of Expression in Guinea', *The Journal of African Studies*, 14(2):201–18.

Lamp, F. 1996. *Art of the Baga: A Drama of Cultural Reinvention*. New York and Munich: The Museum for African Art & Prestel Verlag.

Mark, P. 1994. 'Art, Ritual and Folklore: Dance and Cultural Identity among the Peoples of the Casamance'. *Cahiers d'Études Africaines*, 34(36):563–84.

Mazrui A. A., and M. Tidy. 1985. *Nationalism and New States in Africa*. Nairobi: Heinemann Kenya.

McGovern, M. 2004. 'Unmasking the State: Developing Modern Political Subjectivities in Ttwentieth Century Guinea'. PhD thesis, Emory University.

Miller, C. L. 1990. *Theories of Africans: Francophone Literature and Anthropology in Africa*. Chicago: University of Chicago Press.

Morgenthau, R. S. 1964. *Political Parties in French-Speaking West Africa*. Oxford: Clarendon Press.

Rivière, C. 1969. 'Fétichisme et déemystification: L'example guinéen', *Afrique Documents*: 131–68.
Rodney, W. 1970. *A History of the Upper Guinea Coast, 1545 to 1800*. Oxford: Oxford University Press.
Rouget, G. 1956. 'Les Ballets Africains de Keita Fodéba', *Présence africaine*:7.
Sankhon, A. 1987. 'Contribution à l'histoire des Baga de Conakry', Mémoire de diplôme de fin d'études supérieures, University of Conakry.
Sarró, R. 1999. 'Football et mobilisation identitaire en Guinée La «réinvention de la tradition» des jeunes bagas', *Politique Africaine* 27:153–171.
Scott, J. C. 1998. *Seeing Like a State: How Certain Schemes to Improve the Human Condition Have Failed*, New Haven, CT: Yale University Press.
Tonkin, E. 1979. 'Masking and Masquerading with Examples from West Africa', *University of Birmingham Discussion Papers*, Series C, Sociology and Politics, no 36.
Touré, S. 1976. 'Dire la vérité et dénoncer nos défauts', *Revue du Parti-État de Guinée* 98:83–103.
———. 1978. 'Discours d'ouverture' : Colloque idéologique international de Conakry sur le thème l'Afrique en marche, *Parti-Etat de Guinée*, vol. 24, Conakry: Bureau de Presse de la Présidence de la République: 21–46.
———. N.d. 'Au sujet de la "negritude"', in *L'Afrique et la Révolution*. Conakry: Bureau de la Présidence de la République.
Tyam, A, 1975. 'Les rites funéraires en pays baga (Baga Forè de Boffa)', Mémoire de diplôme de fin d'études supérieures, Conakry: IPGAN.

Palimpsest Memoryscapes: Materializing and Mediating War and Peace in Sierra Leone
Paul Basu

The anthropology of West Africa has recently benefited from two particularly nuanced Sierra Leonean ethnographies, both of which are concerned with the relationships among local memory practices, an often violent past, and landscapes in which material and immaterial traces of that past may be encountered (Ferme 2001; Shaw 2002). Working among Mende-speakers in the southeast of the country, Mariane Ferme explains that she is interested in exploring the modalities through which 'material objects, language, and social relations become sites where a sometimes violent historical memory is sedimented and critically reappropriated' (2001:5). In Sierra Leone, Ferme notes, 'collective memory and landscape are replete with evidence of military, political, and social advancement followed by reversals, and of crises turning into moments of opportunity' (ibid.:225). Relics of the colonial state and its modernizing project have thus been allowed to decay and be swallowed up by vegetation: paved roads have reverted to dirt tracks, commercial signs have rusted away, and buildings have fallen into ruin as such sites have been purposefully neglected by postcolonial authorities (ibid.:23). The forest environment, in contrast, although illegible to the uninitiated, continues to be a resonant and living memoryscape for those able to discern its secrets. A cluster of kola trees in second-growth forest or the appropriate undulations in the forest floor thus tell of a settlement abandoned by the living but perhaps not by memory, nor by the ancestral spirits. In this way, suggests Ferme, trees and other features of the 'natural' landscape 'can be read as ruins ... as much as decaying, destroyed buildings' (ibid.:25).

Researching with Temne-speakers further north, Rosalind Shaw's concern is with the apparent absence of 'discursive memories' of slavery in the region – a curious silence given the huge significance of both the Atlantic and the domestic slave trade in Sierra Leonean history (2002). Following Bourdieu (1990) and Connerton (1989), Shaw thus searches for evidence of this ostensibly missing past in embodied, 'practical' memory and in ritual. She concludes that although 'the slave trade is forgotten as history', it is remembered 'as spirits, as a menacing landscape, as images in divination, as marriage, as witchcraft, and as postcolonial politicians' (2002:9). In contrast to early accounts of the Temne living securely under the protection of town-dwelling spirits, Shaw's informants warn of a landscape inhabited by roaming, predatory spirits who lurk along bush paths, ready to seize unlucky and unprotected victims (ibid.:55–56). Shaw's argument is that the Temne landscape has been metamorphosed into a sinister memoryscape, which 'condenses historical experiences of raiding and warfare, siege and ambush, death and capture, down the centuries and beyond recorded number' (ibid.:56).

Both ethnographies display a sensitivity to local 'regimes of memory' (Radstone and Hodgkin 2003) in which the 'realm of truth' is rarely manifest on the surface of verbal or facial expressions, or on the surface of the visible landscape, but rather remains implicit, waiting to be divined, often literally, in 'the underneath of things' (Ferme 2001:7; Shaw 2002:2). In a West African context that does not necessarily share Western 'ideals of transparency' (Ferme 2001:6), the past and the ambiguity of its material traces participate in a broader culture of dissimulation in which being adept in the 'arts of interpretation' confers power and prestige (ibid.:26–27). Here, then, stories of the past are both elusive and allusive, displaying a 'chronological heterogeneity' that challenges straightforward 'presentist' interpretations of the 'politics of the past in the present' (Shaw 2002:15; cf Halbwachs 1992) and, resisting any singular, definitive telling, provides the skilled narrator with an array of possibilities for the shaping of meaning (Ferme 2001:26).

Concerned primarily with rural contexts, these ethnographies present a mnemonic world that seems radically 'other' to the monuments, memorials, and museums associated with Western and urban modernity. Indeed, by stressing the alterity of Sierra Leonean memory practices, one can easily forget that, no matter how desperately underresourced, Sierra Leone also has its Monuments and Relics Commission, its National Museum, National Archive, and, in the aftermath of civil war, other modern 'technologies of memory', such as a Truth and Reconciliation Commission and a war crimes tribunal (the Special Court for Sierra Leone). On the one hand, such institutions are, of course, indicative of a colonial historical legacy – part of its modernizing project – and their neglect may therefore be as purposeful as that meted out on those other relics of the colonial state discussed by Ferme (ibid.:23). On the other hand, such technologies of memory are also locally appropriated and incorporated into a more profoundly 'creolised' (and 'creolising') culture, contributing to what Paul Richards describes as a 'heritage of cultural compromise forged over many centuries of social and economic flux' (1996:69–70).

It is not only Sierra Leone's Creole (locally, *Krio*) communities whose identity has been defined by this long history of flux: 'Everyone', suggests Richards, 'has complex cultural origins' here, and 'to be firmly flagged as having "age-old" roots simply makes for difficulties when it is time to adjust to new neighbours, or move on' (1996:69). Consequently, in Sierra Leone,

> there are many articulate ideas in local cultures about the importance of forgetting the past, the danger of over defining the present ... and the positive virtues of political compromise, religious syncretism, and hybridization of material culture. (ibid.:70)

For Richards, it is *this* cultural heritage that provides Sierra Leone with the greatest hope for the sustenance of a lasting peace.

Whilst it is tempting to employ an image of conflicting regimes of memory in Sierra Leone, drawing imaginary battle lines between 'indigenous' and 'colonizing' forms, it is this process of creolization – *mnemonic* creolization – that I am interested in exploring in this chapter. Thus, rather than characterizing and contrasting these regimes along such lines as social forgetting versus social remembering, immaterial versus material traces, unreflected upon everyday practices versus self-consciously iconic *lieux de mémoire* (memory versus history, tradition versus modernity, incorporation versus inscription – the list goes on), my interest is with how different mnemonic worlds articulate with and mediate one another. Such an approach recognises that, as with linguistic creolization, mnemonic creolization is a process 'invoked by endogenous as well as exogenous factors' (ibid.:74).

And yet, the metaphor of creolization is not wholly satisfactory either insofar as it suggests that there is a *synthesis* of diverse influences, whereas it is perhaps more appropriate to think of these regimes of memory as coexistent, overlapping, and intersecting, whereby one form may sometimes obscure another but without completely erasing it. A more suitable metaphor might therefore be that of the palimpsest, in which the 'memory' of prior memory practices is retained and can even dominate. In this conceptualization, Pierre Nora's *milieux de mémoire* are not supplanted by *lieux de mémoire* with the ingress of modernity (1989:7); rather, as Ferme argues of the Mende memoryscape, 'new elements map onto older forces grounded in regional history and culture, and do so on the same terrain, so that modernity reinforces their magic and potentiality' (2001:5). In this respect 'memory' and 'history' are coincident: They share the same space.

Drawing on Jan Vansina's conception of 'palimpsest tradition' (1974:320), Shaw herself uses the phrase 'palimpsest memories' to describe how practical and discursive memories from different periods become intermeshed, such that one period is remembered through the lens of another (for example, so that experiences of the recent conflict are layered with memories of the Atlantic slave trade) (2002:15). In subsequent work, however, Shaw appears to resort to a more oppositional framework, arguing, for instance, that the effectiveness of Sierra Leone's Truth and Reconciliation Commission was compromised because it valorized a particular kind of Western memory practice that was 'at odds' with local practices predicated on 'social forgetting' (2005:2–3). This argument seems to essentialize both Sierra Leonean and Western memory practices, prioritizing the authenticity of local practices and consequently valorizing another particularly Western sensibility, this time concerned with purity and moral order.

In what follows, then, my intention is to explore the 'impure' mix of convergences, intersections, and interactions of different regimes of memory in Sierra Leone, and to do so by considering a number of sites associated with its recent conflict and ongoing peace process. As Young notes of Holocaust remembrance, so also are the 'sites of memory' of Sierra Leone's conflict 'many and diverse', and in this far-from-exhaustive discussion I shall be concerned with, among other things, species of trees, banknotes, and *noms de guerre*, as well as more obviously recognizable mnemonic forms such as murals, memorials, and gravesites (cf Young 1993:viii).[1]

Under the Cotton Tree

The interface between Sierra Leone's mnemonic worlds is manifest materially and spatially at the very centre of Freetown in the juxtaposition of the National Museum of Sierra Leone and one of the city's most famous landmarks, the 'Cotton Tree'. Established in 1957, the museum is housed in a low building – the former Cotton Tree Station – which is literally sheltered under the enormous boughs of the tree (indeed, the postal address of the National Museum is 'Cotton Tree, Freetown').[2] Freetown's Cotton Tree and the National Museum bookend a recent gazetteer of Sierra Leonean heritage sites compiled under the supervision of the Krio historian Akintola Wyse and funded by the U.S. Ambassador's Fund for Cultural Preservation (Wyse 2002). In this booklet, Freetown's 'majestic Cotton Tree' is described as standing,

> like a colossus, in the middle of the city keeping watch, and 'protecting', the capital, as it has done for over two hundred years. Its gnarled and spiky trunks, sturdy bole and massive shady branches also give it the look of a sentinel, 'standing in the centre of the oldest part of Freetown, surrounded by, yet dominating the principal buildings of Church, Law, and Government'. (ibid.:10)

According to legend (and there are many such legends), Freetown's Cotton Tree is said to have sheltered the first freed slaves who were sent to settle in the Sierra Leone Colony in 1787. Other stories state that, earlier, a slave market was held in the shade of the tree, and others still, that the tree was planted by freed slaves who had brought the seed with them from the Caribbean where the species is also found. Predating and dominating the structures of nation and state, Freetown's Cotton Tree is thus an important site of memory of Sierra Leone's slave heritage (a foundational narrative for Sierra Leone's Krio population). The tree both acts as a witness to the violent uprooting of people from their homeland in the image of the slave market and provides a symbol of sanctuary and protection for the freed slaves on their 'return' to Africa. Furthermore, in the story of the cotton tree being planted by exslaves, the tree itself shares in their experience and provides a literal motif for the rerooting of the slave diaspora in African soil.

Indeed, as JoAnn D'Alisera has recently observed, Freetown's Cotton Tree also features prominently as a resonant symbol of homeland and 'icon of longing' for a more recent Sierra Leonean diaspora in the United States, its photographic representation serving as a 'mediator' for a set of negotiations that emerge at the intersections of past and present, here and there, and indi-vidual and communal memory that, in part, define the diasporic experience (D'Alisera 2002). The iconic nature of the tree is similarly evident in the work of visual artists at home in Sierra Leone, not least in their responses to the conflict. Simeon Benedict Sesay's painting, *Handiwork of Child Combatants* (2000), for example, depicts the January 1999 rebel invasion of Freetown (Figure 10.1). At the bottom right of Sesay's composite image, the rebels can be seen entering the city, leaving a trail of carnage in their wake; at the top right of the picture, those citizens fortunate enough to escape are shown making their way to a refugee camp. Meanwhile, depicted on the left half of the painting, Freetown's Cotton Tree stands as a lone witness, towering above streets emptied save for dogs and vultures picking over the corpses of victims, while the Law Courts

Figure 10.1 *Handiwork of Child Combatants*, Simeon Benedict Sesay, 2000 (source: Muana and Corcoran 2005, plate 24)

Building (the 'Gran Kot') and the National Museum have been abandoned. Confronted by this image, one thinks of the words penned in 1947 by the British colonial administrator and ethnographer, E. F. Sayers:

> How many human joys and human sorrows has our Freetown Cotton Tree not seen, and how many tragedies and comedies must have been enacted within the sight of it and within its sight? . . . Freetown's Cotton Tree stands today for a sense of continuity in our corporate life, a symbolic link between our past and our future. (Sayers 1961:133–34)[3]

Colossal though Freetown's famous specimen may be, the cotton tree has much deeper roots in the Sierra Leonean memoryscape. Some of the earliest European accounts of Sierra Leone mention the special place of cotton trees in local cosmologies; as well as boundary markers, they are described as being regarded as 'idols', as 'symbols of power and might', and as sacred places under whose shade ceremonies are held and carved wooden statues set up (Alvares 1990:2, Chapter 1:7, Chapter 10:2, Chapter 12:2). Indeed, the silk cotton or kapok tree (*ceiba pentandra*) is a significant species throughout West Africa. Highly venerated, these trees frequently form the centre of village social life (Gottlieb 1992). Cotton trees were often planted to mark the establishment of new settlements and are associated with, and sometimes named after, founding ancestors (Fairhead and Leach 1996:89). The kapok tree is 'the beginning of all things in the village', one of Gottlieb's Beng informants explains to her; another adds that the tree itself is 'the head of the village' (1992:19). Referencing the earlier ethnographic work of E. F. Sayers in northeast Sierra Leone, Michael Jackson cites a standard Koranko lament sung at the funerals of high-ranking elders, which explicitly links the greatness of the cotton tree with the greatness of the deceased:

> *This year oh, a gold cotton tree has fallen, oh sorrow, a great cotton tree has fallen this year oh.*
> *A great cotton tree – that reached to heaven – has fallen. Where shall we find support and shade again?*
> *Lie down, lie down Mara [name of a ruling clan], the war chief has gone.* (Jackson 1989:70; see also Sayers 1925:22)

As many commentators have described, fences of living cotton trees were also planted as part of the sometime elaborate fortifications erected around towns and villages at times of war in Sierra Leone (Alldridge 1901:56; Malcolm 1939). Although these 'war fences' were prohibited by the British colonial government after 1896, remnants nevertheless survive, and the sight of the much-matured rings of cotton trees rising above second-growth forest often indicates the location of long-deserted settlements: ruinlike 'inscriptions', suggests Ferme, telling 'of violent encounters or at least of abandonment of a once-inhabited site' (2001:25; see also DeCorse 1980:51).

The Cotton Tree, the Dove and the Le10,000 Note

Given the place of the cotton tree in both urban and rural mnemonic consciousness, and therefore its capacity to act as a unifying symbol, one is likely not surprised that it has been incorporated into Sierra Leone's national iconography. The Freetown tree appeared, for instance, on the first issue of Sierra Leone's own banknotes in 1964, only later to be joined and subsequently replaced by the head of the head of state. Banknotes are, of course, not only carriers of monetary value, they are also a particularly interesting medium for the expression of what Michael Billig (1995) terms 'banal nationalism': those unnoticed, everyday 'flaggings' of national identity and heritage. Unlike flags or anthems, however, banknotes have the peculiar characteristic of needing to be redesigned relatively frequently in order to counter the efforts of counterfeiters. As Jacques Hymans has recently observed, this fact 'forces states every decade or two to confront anew the question of how to portray the nation and its values' (Hymans 2005:317).

Figure 10.2 Obverse and reverse of the 2004 Bank of Sierra Leone 10,000 Leone note

In 2004, two years after Sierra Leone's civil conflict had officially ended, the Bank of Sierra Leone introduced a new 10,000 Leone note (Figure 10.2). According to a speech made by J. D. Rogers, the Governor of the Bank, at the launch of the note, the theme of its design – 'National cohesion leading to peace and prosperity' (the words are printed on the note's obverse) – was proposed by President Kabbah himself (Rogers 2004). In addition to this inscription, the obverse of the banknote also features the Sierra Leonean national flag and a white dove with an olive branch in its beak flying over the territory of Sierra Leone as represented in the form of a map. After a fifteen-year absence from Sierra Leonean banknote designs, an image of the cotton tree returns to feature prominently on the reverse side of the bill, although it is interesting to note that it is no longer specifically identifiable as *Freetown's* Cotton Tree. In the background design of the reverse, framing the representation of the tree, is Sierra Leone's national coat of arms and the repeating motif of the dove with olive branch.

The values promoted in the iconography of this banknote seem unequivocal. For a bankrupt, so-called failed state emerging from over a decade of civil war and engaged in various transitional justice mechanisms, there is a clearly articulated aspiration to see the spirit of peace as a reunifying force reigning over the nation – a desire to see the dove of peace come to roost, as it were, in the nation's cotton tree. But it is also interesting to observe how this aspiration is expressed on the banknote through the juxtaposition of the autochthonous symbol of the cotton tree – an emblem literally rooted in the soil of Sierra Leone – alongside a symbol of Judaeo-Christian origins, the olive-branch-bearing white dove, which was adopted as a symbol of the International Peace Congress held in Paris in 1949. Indeed, the inherently Eurocentric internationalism of this symbol of peace would seem to speak to a critique of truth and reconciliation commissions, pursued in a Sierra Leonean context by Shaw (2005), which challenges their universalist assumptions about trauma and recovery, their anthropomorphizations of the nation-state, and their foundations in Western psychotherapeutic practice (Hamber and Wilson 2002). As previously noted, Shaw's argument is framed through opposing a Western, globalizing concept of memory, which valorises the 'social remembering' of traumic events, with an indigenous Sierra Leonean memory culture 'based on the *social forgetting* of violence' (2005:3; italics in original).[4] Thus, although an explicit objective of Sierra Leone's TRC was to create 'an impartial historical record' of the conflict, Shaw maintains that its implicit mandate was 'to bring about an ideological or cultural transformation by turning a population who, for the most part, sought to forget, into truth-telling, nation-building subjects' (ibid.:8).

Although the report of the TRC may indeed be read as an exercise in nation-building myth-making, one doubts that this image of a dominant regime of memory effectively colonizing subaltern minds is born out in practice. Despite much rhetoric, there is little evidence to suggest that the TRC has effected anything like this kind of 'ideological or cultural transformation' in Sierra Leone's population. On the contrary, the activities of the TRC seem often to have been met with suspicion and indifference, and one suspects that ultimately the TRC will have little direct influence on whether peace will hold in Sierra Leone. Nevertheless, the '*Learn from Yesterday for a Better Tomorrow*' slogans of the TRC *are* graffitied onto the palimpsest of Sierra Leone's contemporary memoryscape, entering the consciousness of Sierra Leoneans through dis-trict hearings (Kelsall 2005) and popular radio programmes (Rashid 2006), as well as through the materializing practices that are the concern of this chapter. But in 'over-writing', such exogenous influences do not necessarily erase underlying practices so much as add another layer to their complexity – a process of incorporation that is apparent in the juxtaposition of the dove and the cotton tree on the Le10,000 note. The point is that just as the conflict localized in Sierra Leone throughout the 1990s had a 'global range of symbolic and dramaturgical references' (Richards 1996:xvii), so Sierra Leone's peace process is also bound up in the 'media flows and cultural hybridizations that make up globalized modernity' (ibid.).

In the Name of Bai Bureh

Such global flows and hybridizations are evident, for example, in the *noms de guerre* assumed by fighters on all sides of Sierra Leone's conflict: the names of Hollywood heroes such as 'Superman', 'Rambo', 'Terminator', and 'Rocky', for instance, whose exceptional qualities are transferred, by association, to the bearer. But even pseudonyms taken from indigenous Sierra Leonean heroes have more complex global genealogies. Take 'Colonel Bai Bureh', for example: This was the *nom de guerre* adopted by, among others, Abubakar Jalloh, a commander of the Revolutionary United Front (RUF), the main rebel force during the conflict.

Bai Bureh of Kasseh (c. 1840–1908), Jalloh's namesake and another of the sites of memory I want to consider here, was a famous Temne warrior and leader who, in 1898, led an uprising against the British colonial power in what has become known as the 'Hut Tax War' (see Abraham 1974; Denzer 1971). Employing guerrilla tactics against British regiments inexperienced in bush warfare, Bai Bureh succeeded in evading capture for many months and was said to have supernatural powers, to be bulletproof and to have the ability to become invisible or stay under water for long periods (Kabba 1988:42).[5] Although a cultural memory of Bai Bureh no doubt survives locally (see Shaw 2002:64-66, for example), it is interesting to observe how this Temne chief has entered into the Sierra Leonean national iconography, not least through the agency of two American Peace Corps volunteers.

A life-sized representation of Bai Bureh is displayed in the National Museum of Sierra Leone. On an official tourism website, a caption explains that the statue 'is dressed in the . . . guerrilla leader's own clothes and holds the cutlass with which he fought in the Hut Tax War of 1898' (www.visitsierraleone. org/thingstodo.asp, accessed 20 July 2006). Significantly, however, it was an American secondary-school history teacher and Peace Corps volunteer named Gary Schulze who, as acting curator of the museum in 1962, argued that the story of Bai Bureh and the Hut Tax War ought to be included in the museum's displays (Gary Schulze pers. comm.). The earlier absence of what has become a key historical narrative celebrating Sierra Leone's resistance to colonial oppression is itself telling insofar as the museum hitherto presented a more 'Kriocentric' view of Sierra Leonean national heritage, and the Hut Tax War and subsequent Mende uprising of 1898 are ambiguous episodes in this heritage, not least because the majority of the victims of these insurrections were in fact Krios (Fyfe 1962:571–74; Hargreaves 1956:71).

Under Schulze's temporary management, however, the story was duly incorporated into the museum's exhibitions, and, indeed, it was Schulze who commissioned a Freetown-based sculptor to make the statue of Bai Bureh that would form the centrepiece of the display. Since there was no record of Bai Bureh's appearance other than a single drawing, made in profile, by a Lt H. E. Green of the 1st West Africa Regiment after he was captured, it was left to the sculptor's imagination to fashion the face; and although the *ronko* gown and cutlass were authentic to the region and period, they were merely samples taken from the museum's collections and did not belong to Bai Bureh himself as is popularly claimed (Gary Schulze pers. comm.). Indeed, whereas Green's drawing shows Bai Bureh wearing the conical white hat typical of West African Muslim elders of the late nineteenth century, Schulze dressed the museum statue in a red tricorn, which is associated with Mande hunters but, significantly, not with the Temne. Despite the improvised nature of the statue, Schulze explains that, in the months following the statue's installation, thousands of people visited the museum to see Bai Bureh, and, in subsequent years, photographs of the figure began to appear in Sierra Leonean history books (for example, Alie 1990:140). The statue has subsequently been paraded at agricultural shows and other events throughout the country and has come to define Bai Bureh's image in the popular imagination (Gary Schulze pers. comm.).

It was, however, another Peace Corps volunteer, the anthropologist Joseph Opala, who enshrined Bai Bureh, alongside other historical figures, such as Sengbe Pieh, the leader of the 1839 Amistad slave revolt, in what amounts to a national hagiography: a volume entitled *Sierra Leone Heroes* (Kabba 1988). As a Peace Corps volunteer, Opala was attached to the National Museum between 1974 and 1978; staying on in Sierra Leone, he later became a lecturer at Fourah Bay College in Freetown. In 1986, conscious of the absence of patriotic imagery in the country, Opala wrote a series of articles for the Freetown-based *Daily Mail* newspaper on what he termed Sierra Leone's 'neglected heroes' (Opala 1994:201). Around the same time he urged the Momoh government of the day to produce a book on these historical figures, which he hoped would be distributed freely to schools throughout the country. In 1987, the book was given the go ahead, and Opala was appointed to the editorial board. Opala notes that, when compiling and commissioning illustrations for the book, he was 'keenly aware' that he was involved in the creation of 'patriotic icons' and 'took pains to place the heroes in memorable poses' (ibid.). *Sierra Leone Heroes* – the first edition of which features a more militant representation of Bai Bureh on its cover – was not distributed freely to schools, but sold commercially. Although sales were good, Opala explains that it was his use of it as a textbook for a course he taught on Art, Anthropology, and National Consciousness at Fourah Bay College that led to it being adopted by an increasingly politicised student body as a source book of emblems for Sierra Leonean cultural nationalism (ibid.). Indeed, the significance of Opala's role in promoting a more nationalistic mnemonic consciousness in Sierra Leone is evident when he describes how he would assign 'students the task of memorializing a hero in a painting, sculpture, song, poem, or play' (ibid.; see also Christensen 2005).[6]

Amid an escalating rebel war, the corrupt Momoh regime was deposed in a military coup in 1992, and it was the fabricated face and apparel of the museum statue of Bai Bureh that displaced Momoh's on the Le1,000 banknote introduced by the National Provisional Ruling Council (NPRC) government in 1993.[7] More recently, this same visage has been brought to life in the Sierra Leonean/Nigerian coproduction of a video film entitled *Bai Bureh Goes to War*. As the late Abu Noah, the writer and executive producer of the film, was keen to stress to me, although ostensibly about an historical leader and war, the film has much relevance for contemporary African politics: 'Today's leaders need to tap into the fountain of unsullied leadership qualities of our forebears', he explained.

> Contemporary world events buttress the foregoing . . . As we strive to make the African Union a viable one, the story of Bai Bureh couldn't have been more timely. It challenges both leadership and followership in the modern African society. The quality of leadership enjoyed by Africans before the advent of the colonial masters must be revisited. (Noah 2004)

Mediated by American ideas of patriotic iconography, the imagination of a Krio sculptor, the political ambitions of the NPRC regime, and idealizations of precolonial African polities – such is the nature of the making of an 'indigenous' Sierra Leonean hero (a malleable site of memory and ancestor capable of being claimed by all sides in a civil war).[8]

War Memorials and Peace Monuments

Unlike previous regimes, the NPRC was conscious of the power of patriotic monuments and street art, and, in 1992 and 1993, statues and murals depicting

Bai Bureh and Sengbe Pieh were erected and painted alongside those celebrating the heroic officers of the 1992 coup. In his 1994 article describing this popular movement and his own involvement in it through the *Sierra Leone Heroes* book, Opala notes that images of Captain Valentine Strasser and other leaders of the NPRC were intentionally associated with depictions of these historical figures, thereby incorporating them into an evolving national pantheon (1994:205). There are still a few decaying examples of the murals to be seen in Freetown – for instance, those on Howe Street depicting Captain Prince Ben-Hirsh and Lieutenant Samuel S. Sandy, two NPRC 'martyrs' who were killed during the coup. Lieutenant Sandy is shown dressed in camouflage jacket and beret under the inscription 'Even the Dead Lead Us Through', suggesting that, like Bai Bureh before him, he was claimed by the NPRC as an 'ancestor': not a figure of the past, but one who has gone on ahead and in whose footsteps others will follow – an active presence in contemporary events (Last 2000:380).

The initial popularity of the NPRC was largely due to its resolve to put an end to the rebel war that had been plaguing the country. One way in which this militancy was materialised and made visible was in the installation of street side statues celebrating the new government's victories against rebel forces. One such statue was erected in 1994 to commemorate a skirmish in the town of Bo, in the Southern Province of Sierra Leone, at a road junction that became

Figure 10.3 Remains of the 'Soldier Kill Rebel' monument erected by the NPRC in 1994 in Bo (photograph: Paul Basu)

known as 'Soja Kill Rebel Corner'. The toppled remains of the statue survive, partially hidden behind advertising placards and under a tangle of tree branches that have been thrown over it (Figure 10.3). Although the statue now lies in a number of pieces, one can see that it graphically depicted a government soldier about to bayonet a cornered rebel. An inscription on its plinth reads:

> This monument... symbolizes the improved rebel war in Sierra Leone. It is dedicated to all our loyal and gallant soldiers of the NPRC Government.

It was not until 2002, six years after the NPRC itself was toppled from power, that the conflict was officially declared over and the process of reconstruction was begun in earnest. During the district hearings of the ensuing Truth and Reconciliation Commission, the Commission staged what it termed 'traditional reconciliation ceremonies' at sites where massacres or other atrocities had taken place. These ceremonies included the performance of cleansing rituals and pouring of libations, as well as prayers and religious ceremonies. According to the report of the TRC, such activities were regarded as being particularly important for local communities 'because they serve as recognition of the suffering of victims as well as the collective memory of the past' (TRC 2004a, vol. 3b:475).

Such events were sometimes marked by the erection of memorials, thus leaving material traces of the peace process throughout the country in an attempt to counter the more abundant traces of the conflict. In Bo, for instance, on the closing day of the local TRC hearings, a ceremony was held at Soja Kill Rebel Corner in which the intersection was itself renamed 'Peace Junction' and a memorial sign board erected to signal the fact. Although this might seem like a classic enunciative act, which brings about the reality it announces and thus transforms the commemoration of war into a celebration of peace, the reality on the ground is, of course, that the junction is still remembered by its more vivid *nom de guerre*.

This attempt to overwrite conflict and leave an itinerary of peace monuments rather than war memorials in its wake was repeated by the TRC in other towns throughout Sierra Leone. Perhaps the most significant example is the renaming, in August 2003, of Freetown's Congo Cross Bridge as 'Peace Bridge' (Figure 10.4). This bridge marked the extent of the rebel incursion into Freetown in January 1999 and was the site of particularly fierce fighting. The bridge was renamed as part of a larger event marking the end of the TRC hearings, a National Reconciliation Procession, in which representatives of all the major factions marched together across the bridge on their way to

Figure 10.4 Signboard advertising the 2003 renaming of Freetown's Congo Cross Bridge as 'Peace Bridge' (photograph: Paul Basu).

the National Stadium, where speeches and formal apologies were delivered. A special 'child-friendly' version of the TRC report draws out some of the symbolic resonance intended in the act of renaming: 'The Peace Bridge reminds the people of Sierra Leone that the war was overcome. And it gives hope that peace will become the bridge to the future' (TRC 2004b:31).

With the support of President Kabbah, a National War Memorial Committee was established in 2002, and a competition was held to elicit designs for memorials in Freetown, Bo, Kenema, and Makeni. Despite an announcement in February 2006 that the President had also called for the erection of a commemorative monument in Bomaru, the town on the Sierra Leone/Liberia border where 'the first shots which started the long and protracted senseless war were fired' (www.statehouse-sl.org/archives/feb-2006.html, accessed 10 August 2006), to the best of my knowledge, none of these has yet been constructed, owing to lack of resources. These government initiatives were encouraged by the TRC, and a section of one of the appendices to its report is devoted to the issue of 'Memorials and Transitional Justice'. This section of the report was compiled along with a series of recommendations for the establishment of 'successful memorials' in Sierra Leone by Artemis Christodulou, a graduate student from Yale University who was serving as an intern at the TRC at the time. Christodulou stresses the need to integrate 'traditional and cultural methods of memorialization' into any proposal and provides some suggestions made by various Sierra Leonean 'stakeholders' with whom she had consulted.

In the context of my earlier discussion regarding the cotton tree as a complex site of memory in Sierra Leone, it is interesting to note a suggestion for a memorial proposed by a group of excombatants, which involved leaving imprints of their hands in a cement wall encircling the Freetown tree. This was intended to signify 'a tacit agreement with themselves, with other perpetrators, and with the nation and the world that they will never use these hands again to pick up a weapon and strike a fellow human being' (TRC 2004a, app. 4, pt. 1:7). Given that the amputation of civilians' hands was one of the 'signature tactics' of the Sierra Leone conflict, this proposal had especial resonance, and, despite misgivings, some amputee groups were evidently supportive of the idea. Christodolou recommended that a forum be established so that perpetrators and victims could meet together to discuss the proposed memorial, suggesting that this would 'serve as a powerful space for healing and reconciliation' (ibid.).

No matter how well-meaning such interventions, it is significant that the report of the TRC fails to properly identify what form local 'methods of memorialization' might take or how such methods might be integrated with models imported from elsewhere. More fundamentally, as Shaw (2005) argues, the TRC does not consider the possibility that commemoration might be an inappropriate tool for reconciliation in the first place. It is not that war memorials are unknown in Sierra Leone, of course, but their connotative associations are ambiguous, to say the least. A prominent example is the memorial that lists the names of the Sierra Leoneans who were killed fighting for the British in the First and Second World Wars. Located in front of the old Secretariat Building in Freetown, the one-time hub of colonial government in Sierra Leone, this colonial relic, one suspects, brings to mind an altogether different, postcolonial narrative from that it was intended to commemorate. Indeed, the old Secretariat Building was attacked during the May 1997 coup staged by the Armed Forces Revolutionary Council (AFRC), and, although it is now being renovated, its gutted shell stood for several years as yet another kind of monument of warfare.

If the war memorial or peace monument remains a peripheral (and, in the case of the TRC's commemorative sign boards, an ephemeral) artefact in the Sierra Leonean memoryscape, there is one final category of site that I should like to consider at which 'indigenous' and 'non-indigenous' regimes of memory intersect more complexly: the site, that is, of mass graves associated with Sierra Leone's conflict.

Concerning the Dead in Mass Graves

The mass grave occupies a particular place in the Western imagination as an emblem of atrocity. As well as having associations with appalling violence and the dangerous, polluting power of dead bodies (Hallam, Hockey, and Howarth 1999), mass graves, it is argued, inspire fear because they also involve the burial of social memory and identity (Ferrándiz 2006; Sanford 2003). Not only are mass graves often intentionally hidden and left unmarked by perpetrators – at once amplifying terror through secrecy, concealing evidence, and denying survivors a body to mourn – but in their carelessly cast jumbles of corpses is entailed an effacement of individual identity, which is especially unsettling for societies used to commemorative practices that preserve an individual's identity to the grave (for instance, the indexical relationship between an inscribed headstone and the identity of the body below it).

As part of a wider interdisciplinary fascination with cultural trauma, violence, and memory, an increasing number of anthropologists have begun exploring

Investigators find evidence about what actually happened during the conflict.

Figure 10.5 Illustration from *Wetin Na Di Speshal Kot: The Special Court Made Simple*, a booklet produced by the Special Court's Outreach Section in 2002 and distributed to Sierra Leonean schoolchildren; note the depiction of the mass grave – its association with memory, with evidence, and with the investigation of 'what *actually* happened during the conflict'.

the social and political significance of mass burials. In contexts ranging from Argentina (Crossland 2002; Robben 2000) and Guatemala (Sanford 2003) to Spain (Ferrándiz 2006), Cyprus (Sant Cassia 2005), and Eastern Europe (Verdery 1999), researchers have been considering the implications of exhuming both bodies and memories when such sites undergo forensic excavation as part of truth commissions or other investigations. As Crossland (2002) observes of the excavation of mass graves outside Buenos Aires, the physical uncovering of bodies at these sites constitutes a reappearance of the 'disappeared', which again makes visible the 'crimes of the juntas' and revivifies memories of state violence and oppression. Anthropologists have also explored the politics of preserving mass gravesites and their transformation into memorials of genocide (Cook 2005; Hughes 2005; Jarvis 2002; Williams 2004). Hughes, for example, contrasts the memorial activities of the Cambodian state at Choeung Ek with local-level memorial practices elsewhere in Cambodia; she observes how the memorialization of gravesites reflects contestations between multiple actors, meanings, and values, 'including Cambodian party-politics, Khmer Buddhist beliefs about death, and local and internationalised discourses of justice, education, and memory' (Hughes 2005:286). With advances in DNA identification techniques, the forensic examination of mass graves has now become a standard part of the toolkit of transitional justice mechanisms and human rights interventions across the world (Figure 10.5).

In 2001, human rights officers of the United Nations Mission in Sierra Leone began receiving information from local NGOs regarding discoveries of graves and other sites of atrocities related to Sierra Leone's conflict. The following year the Argentine Forensic Anthropology Team (EAAF) was funded by the UN Office of the High Commissioner for Human Rights to conduct a preliminary survey of these sites and to advise the TRC and other organisations regarding future investigations. In the course of a month, members of the EAAF team visited fifty-five sites located in five districts in the east and centre of the country. With permission from local authorities and chiefs, interviews with witnesses were conducted and the sites inspected, planned, and recorded. Although no exhumations were carried out, the EAAF made recommendations for the preservation of the sites so that evidence would remain intact should excavation be deemed of interest to the TRC or judicial inquiry (EAAF 2002). Details of the EAAF's activities and its discoveries of mass graves were reported widely in the Freetown press.

Following the EAAF's preliminary survey, the TRC embarked on its own programme of investigations of mass graves, extending its remit to include other sites 'that have a story to tell' – for example, 'mass killing sites, execution sites, torture sites, and amputation sites' (TRC 2004a, app. 4, pt. 2:1–2).

TRC investigators were sent into the field with the following objectives:

a. to identify as many 'mass graves' and 'other sites' as possible in all districts,
b. to photograph the identified sites,
c. to identify the number of victims,
d. to reveal the identity of the victims,
e. to identify the types of [human rights] violations committed at the site,
f. to identify the perpetrators,
g. to identify and locate the tools and instruments used in committing the violations,
h. to identify the persons and institutions responsible for the management of the sites,
i. to determine the current uses of the sites (if any),
j. to advise the local community on the protection, preservation and security of the site. (ibid.:2)

It is clear from its report that the TRC encountered a number of difficulties in relation to these tasks, not least the lack of time and financial resources to properly conduct the research, which meant that coverage was rather patchy and the districts of Kambia, Western Area and Port Loko were not included at all. A more complex difficulty, which had far wider implications for the success of the TRC, is described in the TRC report as 'some confusion on the part of the local populace between the TRC and the Special Court' (ibid.). The problem of simultaneously conducting a truth commission, which promoted amnesty, and a war crimes tribunal, which sought to prosecute perpetrators of the more serious human rights violations, is discussed at some length in the TRC report itself (TRC 2004a, vol. 3b:363–430). One result was that potential informants were reluctant to participate in TRC investigations because they were afraid that they would be called as witnesses or prosecuted by the Special Court: thus, detailed information relating to mass burials, even if known, was often not forthcoming.

Despite these limitations, the TRC compiled a database of some 99 mass gravesites, the majority containing fewer than 20 bodies, but a significant number reputedly containing in excess of 100 bodies each (two sites in Bonthe District were reported to contain 450 and 600 bodies, respectively). A table in an appendix of the TRC report provides details of the location of each of these sites, together with the number and the identity of victims (where known), the alleged cause of death (usually gunshot wounds), the date of the killings, date of burial, and the alleged perpetrators (usually RUF and AFRC, but instances of killings by the Sierra Leone Army [SLA] and Kamajor Civil Defence Force are also recorded). Graves were often dug hurriedly and without ceremony after an attack on a village; in other cases, bodies were not buried until a number of years after the killings took place (for instance, when a village that had been abandoned after an attack was later resettled). As the report states: 'Behind every mass grave there is a tragic story' (TRC 2004a, app. 4, pt. 2:1). An example of one such story, gathered by TRC investigators working in Pujehun District, follows:

> At Bumpeh Pejeh chiefdom two mass graves were discovered. As the burial took place three years following the killings in 1996, the remains could not be identified. According to eyewitnesses, Bumpeh Pejeh was the only chiefdom in the Pujehun district that had a heavy presence of SLA soldiers. As a result, many people from other areas came to this town for security. The RUF attacked the chiefdom causing heavy casualties and resulting in the dispersal of the population. When displaced persons returned after three years they discovered that many of the original inhabitants were missing. When the residents of the chiefdom returned the entire village had become overgrown. It was during the time when the bushes were being cleared ('under-brushing') that many of the remains were discovered. Most of the remains were collected from the township and some others were retrieved from the nearby bush. The first set of remains that was discovered was buried in a hole near a cotton tree at the southern end of the township. When the first site was full, the people dumped the remains at a second mass gravesite between the roots of the cotton tree. (TRC 2004a, app. 4, pt. 2:19)

In contrast to the ephemeral efforts of the TRC to displace the memory of war through the erection of peace monuments, this account – typical of similar descriptions recorded throughout the country – provides a vivid and disturbing illustration of how the landscape of Sierra Leone continues to be transformed into a memoryscape of conflict, and not necessarily through intentionally commemorative practices.[9]

At the time of its investigations, the TRC found that, in most cases, the mass gravesites it visited were in a state of neglect, and their future preservation was in danger. The TRC recommended that, because they 'serve as powerful reminders of the abuses of the past and the need to ensure that they never occur again', steps must be taken to preserve and mark the most significant sites in all districts (ibid.:21). Whereas the TRC proposed the erection of 'shrines and monuments' over the graves, consultation with local people demonstrated that there was a preference for more '"community oriented" ways of remembering and commemorating the dead' (ibid.:20) – for instance, the erection of hospitals, schools, and other community facilities that have a more immediate use value in the present and that 'remember' in another sense insofar as they call to mind a quality of life lost in the years of conflict. This preference calls to mind a debate that took place in Britain in the aftermath of the First World War between those who favoured commemorating the dead with schemes that served some utility for the living and those who felt 'a noble piece of sculpture' was a more fitting tribute (King 1998:86–105). In the Sierra Leonean context, the divergence between these approaches underlines the TRC's concern that the gravesites must remain *visible* reminders of past abuses and reveals its blindness to the fact that many of these sites were already 'marked' (or not) in locally meaningful ways – it is surely no coincidence, for example, that the mass graves in Bumpeh Pejeh chiefdom were located under a cotton tree.[10]

If the mass grave is a particularly terrifying spectre that haunts the Western (and international humanitarian) imagination, the question arises as to what other layers of meanings accrue at these sites. How, for instance, are they perceived according to local cosmologies in which different attitudes toward the dead may prevail? This is not the place to detail the mortuary customs of the various ethnolinguistic populations of Sierra Leone; however, as in other regions in West Africa, it is clear that the circumstances in which a person dies, as well as the person's status, affect the ceremonies performed, the location and nature of the burial, and the fate of the person's 'spirit' in the afterlife. Some sense of this may be discerned in an excerpt from a poem by Josaya Bangali entitled 'Elegy: For the Dead in Mass Graves':

> *Ancestors of new death*
> *Take this message*
> *To ancestors of old death*
> *Among whom was Sengbe Pieh*
> *Not forgetting Mama Yoko and Bai Bureh.*
> *Tell them that the children of Nyagua*
> *Have opened each others' stomachs*
> *And fought over their entrails.*
> *They've been laid to rest*
> *On top of each other.*
> *No side-bands are worn*
> *To pronounce them dead*
> *And the ceremonies of the spirit-house*
> *Cannot be looked after.*

Although Bangali writes in English, he is a Mende-speaker, born in Tikonko Chiefdom, south of Bo. He was educated at Christ the King College, Bo, and at Njala University, where he studied Literature and Linguistics. The imagery Bangali uses in his 'Elegy' combines a nationalistic sensibility with more traditional motifs in a manner that, as I have been arguing, is quite characteristic. Bangali explained to me that he wrote the poem as a response to the hopeless situation that Sierra Leoneans had, he thought, brought upon themselves because they no longer heeded the wisdom of their cultural heritage and traditions (a heritage mediated through the very processes I have been describing).

The following interpretation is based on Bangali's own comments. In the poem, Bangali contrasts those who have been killed fighting in Sierra Leone's recent civil conflict – the 'ancestors of new death' – with legendary figures from Sierra Leone's past who fought against slavery and oppression (Sengbe Pieh, Bai Bureh, Madam Yoko, Nyagua – the 'ancestors of old death'). Whereas Bangali argues that the ancestors of new death will soon be forgotten, he claims that the ancestors of old death 'are immortal and cannot be extinguished from memory' and that 'their deeds are worth emulating' (pers. comm.). The recent dead are thus told to carry a message to these ancestral heroes of old, that Sierra Leoneans – the 'children of Nyagua' – instead of uniting against common foes, are fighting one another in a most hideous manner. Those killed in the conflict are dumped into mass graves, their corpses piled on top of one another. Bangali explains that 'among the Mendes, the blood relatives of the deceased wear white side-bands to differentiate themselves from ordinary sympathizers; and it is by wearing side-bands that outsiders know that the wearer has lost a dear one' (pers. comm.). According to the poem (and, indeed, this is corroborated by the TRC investigations), the dead in the mass graves go unmourned, and the appropriate funeral ceremonies – the 'ceremonies of the spirit-house' – are not observed.

According to traditional Mende belief, this last point is of particular significance, for it is through the *tenjamɛi* ceremony, performed three days after the death of a woman, or four days after that of a man, that the dead are enabled to 'cross over the water' and properly join the community of the ancestors (Gittins 1987:57). If the *tenjamɛi* ceremony is not performed, then the dead person is destined to remain a liminal earth-bound spirit, or *ndɔubla*, 'not properly integrated either with the living or with the ancestors' (ibid.:61, fn.33). Such spirits are thought to linger around their place of burial and are regarded as being discontented, capricious, and sometimes 'a threat to the living' (ibid.:57).

Rebirthing the Nation?

The sites of memory, which have been the concern of this essay, are also sites of mediation. Not only are they the material mediators through which coexistent regimes of memory are brought into relation with one another, and through which multiple meanings of war and peace in Sierra Leone are shaped, but – as Sayers remarked of Freetown's Cotton Tree – they are also sites that mediate between the past and the future. The master trope articulated in the report of the Truth and Reconciliation Commission is, of course, that of 'rebirth'. By seeking to create 'an impartial historical record' of Sierra Leone's conflict (TRC 2004a, vol. 1:10), the TRC hopes that the 'lessons of the past' can be learned, and out of the crisis of civil war can be born a new, peaceful, and just nation-state. Such an ambition is expressed in the many essays, poems, and paintings submitted by 'men and women of all ages, backgrounds, religions, and regions' in response to the TRC's invitation to Sierra Leoneans to contribute to the shaping of a 'National Vision' for the future of the country (TRC 2004a, vol. 3b:i, 503). Examples of these submissions were reproduced in the final chapter of the report of the TRC, and they were also made into an exhibition that was displayed at Sierra Leone's National Museum between December 2003 and June 2004. Alongside images of reconciliation and hope painted in the colours of Sierra Leone's flag or superimposed on the cutout shape of the national territory, a contribution from Bishop Joseph Humper, the chairman of the TRC, articulates this trope of rebirth most explicitly. Under the title of 'A Sierra Leonean Renaissance', Humper's message states that he envisions 'a revived Sierra Leone, born out of the ashes of a reckless and senseless civil conflict, [which] shall become active and committed to the establishment of genuine peace'.

Humper's words resonate with a broader vision of African Renaissance, associated in its most recent formulation with the pronouncements of Thabo Mbeki (Ajulu 2001). However, rebirth is not the only trope discernable in the palimpsest of Sierra Leone's memoryscape. If the desire of local communities to commemorate the victims of civil war with schools and hospitals, rather than with monuments and mausolea, suggests a future-orientated attitude that serves the living and not the dead, it is as well to remember the lingering discontent that haunts Sierra Leone's mass graves. Indeed, barely concealed beneath the optimistic rhetoric of the TRC is a more pessimistic observation: that many of the characteristics identified as antecedents to the conflict continue to persist in Sierra Leone, and, hence, there is considerable doubt as to whether the 'lessons of the past' will in fact be learned (TRC 2004a, vol. 3a:149). Thus, rather than prematurely celebrating the rebirth of a nation, we might heed the still-potent underlying layers of Sierra Leone's palimpsest memoryscape and, with some justification, fear that which is undead and which cannot yet be properly laid to rest (cf De Boeck 1998).

The authors of Sierra Leone's TRC report are not, of course, alone in seeking to construct a myth of the past that serves the perceived imperatives and aspirations of the present. This is, in part, my point: that there are multiple entities, each differently positioned in the social, cultural, and political landscape, each committed to a particular engagement with the past in the light of present needs, hopes, and future-oriented agendas. What is interesting to observe in this familiar, 'presentist' interpretation, is the way in which the same historical 'motifs' are, more or less strategically, reappropriated by differently positioned entities to serve very different ends (see my discussion of Bai Bureh, for instance). The past, no less than the present, thus becomes a contested ground. What this interpretation fails to capture, however, is the sense that it is not only the *use* of the past in the present that is contested but also the very nature of 'pastness' and its 'presence'.

Too often this contest is characterized as an opposition between competing regimes of memory, such that traditional mnemonic practices are regarded as being suppressed by modern historicizing ones, and local conceptualizations as being displaced by globalizing hegemonies. As this chapter has sought to argue in a Sierra Leonean context, the relationship between these regimes is more complex. Rather than reductive dichotomies, we need a more nuanced understanding of the 'synchronic heterogeneity' of diachronic processes in a given context (Cole 2001:289). Whereas the mnemonic practices of any one individual or social body might entail a synthesis of some of the diverse influences co-existent at a particular time and place, at a more general level these heterogeneous elements do not necessarily cohere into a new creolised form. Rather, the memoryscape is continually 'overwritten', resulting in an accretion of forms. But, unlike an ideal type of stratified archaeological contexts, whereby successive strata overlay one another neatly, this accretion occurs in an uneven manner and, to pursue the archaeological metaphor, is constantly being excavated and reburied, mixing up the layers, exposing unexpected juxtapositions, and generating unanticipated interactions. Such is the medium of the palimpsest memoryscape.

Acknowledgments

The fieldwork from which this essay is drawn was funded by a Nuffield Foundation grant for which I am extremely grateful. I should also like to thank

Palimpsest Memoryscapes: Materializing and Mediating War and Peace ◉ 255

Mike Rowlands and Ferdinand de Jong for their invitation to contribute to this book, James Fairhead for his comments on an earlier draft of the chapter, Josaya Bangali for permission to reproduce his poem 'Elegy: For the Dead in Mass Graves', and James Vincent for his invaluable research assistance.

Notes

1. No attempt is made to provide a history of Sierra Leone's conflict. For recent analyses, see Abdullah (2004) and Keen (2005).
2. A fuller history of Sierra Leone's National Museum and cultural heritage legislation is currently in preparation. In the present context, however, it is worth noting that the establishment of the Museum should be seen in the context of a broader movement across colonial British West Africa. In 1944, having visited the region as a member of the Commission on Higher Education in West Africa, Julian Huxley sent a detailed memorandum to the Colonial Office arguing that there was an urgent need to establish museums in each of Britain's four West African colonies. This memorandum was supported in a 1946 report commissioned by the Colonial Office and prepared by Hermann Braunholtz, then Keeper of Oriental Antiquities and Ethnography at the British Museum. Given the straitened conditions in the immediate aftermath of the Second World War, the colonial governments did not, however, consider this a high priority, and the recommendations were slow to be taken up. In Sierra Leone, it was not until 1954 that Governor Robert de Zouche Hall, who had a personal enthusiasm for cultural heritage matters, pushed for the creation of a museum under the management of the newly reconstituted Sierra Leone Society. M. C. F. Easmon, a retired Krio medical doctor and chairman of the Sierra Leone Monuments and Relics Commission, was appointed as its first curator.
3. In relation to his use of the possessive pronoun, '*our* Freetown Cotton Tree', it is interesting to note that Sayers was regarded by his peers in the colonial service as somewhat having 'gone native' (John Hargreaves pers. comm.). A Temne and Koranko speaker, Sayers was a frequent contributor to *Sierra Leone Studies* in the 1920s and 1930s on ethnographic topics, and he also served on the Monuments and Relics Commission from its inception, in 1947, until his death in 1954.
4. Shaw makes a distinction between 'social' and 'individual' forgetting, arguing that, although people still have personal memories of violence, it is the voicing of this memory in public that is avoided, since this is viewed as encouraging its return (2005:9).
5. In the context of the more recent conflict, Bai Bureh's supernatural powers resonate with those associated with the 'hunter-warrior' *kamajors* of the Civil Defence Force, who, through '"contractual" associations with specific bush spirits' were believed to be able to make themselves 'invisible and impermeable to bullets' (Ferme 2001:27; Leach 2000:588).
6. Opala's involvement in Sierra Leonean cultural heritage issues continues in his support of a campaign to have the 'slave fort' of Bunce Island in the Sierra Leone River designated as a UNESCO World Heritage Site (see http://freetown.usembassy.gov/bunce_island_preservation.html, accessed 21 July 2006).

7. In addition to Bai Bureh, other historical Sierra Leonean 'heroes' to be represented on the new issue of Sierra Leonean banknotes during the NPRC rule included Sengbe Pieh (Le5,000) and Kai Londo (Le500). Each represents a different ethnic/language group within Sierra Leone (respectively, Temne, Mende, and Kissi); it was not until 2002 that a Krio national hero was added, with a portrait of Isaac T. A. Wallace appearing on a new Le 2,000 note. All of these figures feature in the *Sierra Leone Heroes* book.
8. As well as being Abubakar Jalloh's *nom de guerre*, Bai Bureh lends his name to the 'Bai Bureh Star' (a medal awarded by the government 'for military gallantry of the highest degree'), the 'Bai Bureh Warriors' (Port Loko's main football team), and the 'indigenous political ideology' of 'Burehism' promoted by the People's Democratic League, which draws its principles from the 'teachings, preachings, ideas, beliefs, and practices' of the nineteenth-century chief. Citing an unpublished article by Joseph Opala, Christensen notes that, during Siaka Stevens' presidency, a group of actors was jailed for staging a play about Bai Bureh on the grounds of 'inciting rebellion' (2005:17, fn.10).
9. This account also resonates strikingly with Thomas Alldridge's late nineteenth-century descriptions of the devastated Sierra Leonean landscape in the aftermath of what he refers to as 'a long and serious tribal war', attesting to the palimpsest-like accretions of violent associations in place:

> We had not gone far into the Krim country before, as I went along, I saw many white objects on the ground which at first I hardly noticed, but which upon inspection I found to be bleached skulls.
>
> In the line of destruction extending over many miles, not a town was to be seen, the sites that they had occupied being then overgrown wildernesses; banana plants and kola trees alone testifying to the fact that here, not long since, had been human habitations. (Alldridge 1901:166)

The 'tribal war' to which Alldridge refers was actually provoked by the expansion of colonial trade in the region (see Caulker 1981).
10. See David Bunn's fascinating discussion of the politics of the changing visibility of Xhosa graves and the 'evolution of an intricate reciprocity between British monumentality and Xhosa grave practices' in the Colonial Eastern Cape (Bunn 2002).

Bibliography

Abdullah, I. (ed.). 2004. *Between Democracy and Terror: The Sierra Leone Civil War*. Dakar: Council for the Development of Social Science Research in Africa.

Abraham, A. 1974. 'Bai Bureh, the British, and the Hut Tax War', *The International Journal of African Historical Studies* 7(1):99–106.

Ajulu, R. 2001. 'Thabo Mbeki's African Renaissance in a Globalising World Economy: The Struggle for the Soul of the Continent', *Review of African Political Economy* 87:27–42.

Alie, J. A. 1990. *A New History of Sierra Leone*. Oxford: Macmillan.

Alldridge, T. J. 1901. *The Sherbro and Its Hinterland*. London: Macmillan.

Alvares, M. 1990 [c.1615]. 'Ethiopia Minor and a Geographical Account of the Province of Sierra Leone', P. E. H. Hair (ed. and trans.). http://digicoll.library.wisc.edu/Africana/.
Billig, M. 1995. *Banal Nationalism*. London: Sage.
Bourdieu, P. 1990. *The Logic of Practice*. Palo Alto, CA: Stanford University Press.
Bunn, D. 2002. 'The Sleep of the Brave: Graves as Sites and Signs in the Colonial Eastern Cape'. In *Images and Empires: Visuality in Colonial and Postcolonial Africa*, P. S. Landau and D. D. Kaspin (eds.). Berkeley and Los Angeles: University of California Press.
Caulker, P. S. 1981. 'Legitimate Commerce and Statecraft: A Study of the Hinterland Adjacent to Nineteenth-Century Sierra Leone', *Journal of Black Studies* 11(4): 397–419.
Christensen, M. J. 2005. 'Cannibals in the Postcolony: Sierra Leone's Intersecting Hegemonies in Charlie Haffner's Slave Revolt Drama Amistad Kata-Kata', *Research in African Literatures* 36(1):1–19.
Cole, J. 2001. *Forget Colonialism? Sacrifice and the Art of Memory in Madagascar*. Berkeley and Los Angeles: University of California Press.
Connerton, P. 1989. *How Societies Remember*. Cambridge: Cambridge University Press.
Cook, S. E. 2005. 'The Politics of Preservation in Rwanda'. In *Genocide in Cambodia and Rwanda: New Perspectives*, S. E. Cook (ed.). Piscataway, NJ: Transaction.
Crossland, Z. 2002. 'Violent Spaces: Conflict Over the Reappearance of Argentina's Disappeared'. In *Matériel Culture: The Archaeology of Twentieth-century Conflict*, J. Schofield, W. G. Johnson, and C. M. Beck (eds.). London: Routledge.
D'Alisera, J. 2002. 'Icons of Longing: Homeland and Memory in the Sierra Leonean Diaspora', *Political and Legal Anthropology Review* 25(2):73–89.
De Boeck, F. 1998. 'Beyond the Grave: History, Memory and Death in Postcolonial Congo/Zaïre'. In *Memory and the Postcolony: African Anthropology and the Critique of Power*, R. Werbner (ed.). London: Zed Books.
DeCorse, C. R. 1980. 'An Archaeological Survey of Protohistoric Defensive Sites in Sierra Leone', *Nyame Akuma* 17:48–53.
Denzer, L. R. 1971. 'Sierra Leone – Bai Bureh'. In *West African Resistance: The Military Response to Colonial Occupation*, M. Crowder (ed.). London: Hutchinson.
EAAF (Equipo Argentino de Antropología Forense). 2002. Annual Report.
Fairhead, J., and M. Leach. 1996. *Misreading the African Landscape: Society and Ecology in a Forest-Savanna Mosaic*. Cambridge: Cambridge University Press.
Ferme, M. C. 2001. *The Underneath of Things: Violence, History, and the Everyday in Sierra Leone*. Berkeley and Los Angeles: University of California Press.
Ferrándiz, F. 2006. 'The Return of Civil War Ghosts: The Ethnography of Exhumations in Contemporary Spain', *Anthropology Today* 22(3):7–12.
Fyfe, C. 1962. *A History of Sierra Leone*. London: Oxford University Press.
Gittins, A. J. 1987. *Mende Religion: Aspects of Belief and Thought in Sierra Leone*. Studia Instituti Anthropos No. 41. Nettetal (Germany): Steyler Verlag-Vort und Werk.
Gottlieb, A. 1992. *Under the Kapok Tree: Identity and Difference in Beng Thought*. Bloomington: Indiana University Press.
Halbwachs, M. 1992. *On Collective Memory*, introduction by L. A. Coser (ed. and trans.). Chicago: Chicago University Press.
Hallam, E., J. Hockey, and G. Howarth. 1999. *Beyond the Body: Death and Social Identity*. London: Routledge.

Hamber, B., and R. A. Wilson. 2002 'Symbolic Closure Through Memory, Reparation and Revenge in Post-Conflict Societies', *Journal of Human Rights* 1(1):35–53.

Hargreaves, J. D. 1956. 'The Establishment of the Sierra Leone Protectorate and the Insurrection of 1898', *Cambridge Historical Journal* 12(1):56–80.

Hughes, R. 2005. 'Memory and Sovereignty in Post-1979 Cambodia: Choeung Ek and Local Genocide Memorials'. In *Genocide in Cambodia and Rwanda: New Perspectives*. S. E. Cook (ed.). Piscataway, NJ: Transaction.

Hymans, J. E. C. 2005. 'International Patterns in National Identity Content: The Case of Japanese Banknote Iconography', *Journal of East Asian Studies* 5:315–46.

Jackson, M. 1989. *Paths Toward a Clearing: Radical Empiricism and Ethnographic Enquiry*. Bloomington: Indiana University Press.

Jarvis, H. 2002. 'Mapping Cambodia's "Killing Fields"'. In *Matériel Culture: The Archaeology of Twentieth-century Conflict*, J. Schofield, W. G. Johnson, and C. M. Beck (eds.). London: Routledge.

Kabba, M. R. A. (ed.). 1988. *Sierra Leonean Heroes: Fifty Great Men and Women Who Helped to Build Our Nation*, 2nd ed. Freetown: Government of Sierra Leone.

Keen, D. 2005. *Conflict and Collusion in Sierra Leone*. Oxford: James Currey.

Kelsall, T. 2005. 'Truth, Lies, Ritual: Preliminary Reflections on the Truth and Reconciliation Commission in Sierra Leone', *Human Rights Quarterly* 27:361–91.

King, A. 1998. *Memorials of the Great War in Britain*. Oxford: Berg.

Last, M. 2000. 'Healing the Social Wounds of War', *Medicine, Conflict and Survival* 16:370–82.

Leach, M. 2000. 'New Shapes to Shift: War, Parks and the Hunting Person in Modern West Africa', *Journal of the Royal Anthropological Institute* (N.S.) 6:577–95.

Malcolm, J. M. 1939. 'Mende Warfare', *Sierra Leone Studies* (O.S.) 21:47–52.

Muana, P. K., and C. Corcoran (eds.). 2005. *Representations of Violence: Art about the Sierra Leone Civil War*. Madison, WI: 21st Century African Youth Movement.

Noah, A. 2004. 'Bai Bureh Goes to War: Movie Overview'.

Nora, P. 1989. 'Between Memory and History: *Les lieux de mémoire*', *Representations* 26:725.

Opala, J. A. 1994. '"Ecstatic Renovation!": Street Art Celebrating Sierra Leone's 1992 Revolution', *African Affairs* 93:195–218.

Radstone, S. and K. Hodgkin. 2003. 'Regimes of Memory: An Introduction'. In *Regimes of Memory*, S. Radstone and K. Hodgkin (eds.). London: Routledge.

Rashid, I. 2006. 'Silent Guns and Talking Drums: War, Radio and Youth Social Healing in Sierra Leone'. In *Postconflict Reconstruction in Africa*, A. Sikainga and O. Alidou (eds.), Trenton, NJ: Africa World Press.

Richards, P. 1996. *Fighting for the Rain Forest: War, Youth and Resources in Sierra Leone*. London: The International African Institute, in association with James Currey and Heinemann.

Robben, A C. G. M. 2000. 'State Terror in the Netherworld: Disappearance and Reburial in Argentina'. In *Death Squad: The Anthropology of State Terror*, J. A. Sluka (ed.). Philadelphia: University of Pennsylvania Press.

Rogers, J. D. 2004. 'Launching of Le10,000 Note and Le500 Coin – The Governor's Address'.

Sanford, V. 2003. *Buried Secrets: Truth and Human Rights in Guatemala*. New York: Basingstoke.

Sant Cassia, P. 2005. *Bodies of Evidence: Burial, Memory and the Recovery of Missing Persons in Cyprus*. Oxford: Berghahn.
Sayers, E. F. 1925. 'The Funeral of a Koranko Chief', *Sierra Leone Studies* (O.S.) 7:19–29.
———. 1961. 'Our Cotton Tree', *Sierra Leone Studies* (N.S.) 15:131–34.
Shaw, R. 2002. *Memories of the Slave Trade: Ritual and the Historical Imagination in Sierra Leone*. Chicago: Chicago University Press.
———. 2005. 'Rethinking Truth and Reconciliation Commissions: Lessons from Sierra Leone', United States Institute of Peace, Special Report No. 130.
TRC (Truth and Reconciliation Commission). 2004a. 'Witness To Truth: Report of the Sierra Leone Truth and Reconciliation Commission'.
———. 2004b. 'Truth and Reconciliation Commission Report for the Children of Sierra Leone'.
Vansina, J. 1974. 'Comment: Traditions of Genesis', *Journal of African History* 15(2): 317–22.
Verdery, K. 1999. *The Political Lives of Dead Bodies: Reburial and Postsocialist Change*. New York: Columbia University Press.
Williams, P. 2004. 'Witnessing Genocide: Vigilance and Remembrance at Tuol Sleg and Choeung Ek', *Holocaust and Genocide Studies* 18(2):234–54.
Wyse, A. J. G. (ed.). 2002. *Vistas of the Heritage of Sierra Leone*. Freetown: Fourah Bay College and Sierra Leone National Museum.
Young, J. E. 1993. *The Texture of Memory: Holocaust Memorials and Meaning*. New Haven, CT: Yale University Press.

About the Contributors

Paul Basu
Paul Basu is a Senior Lecturer at the Department of Anthropology, University of Sussex. His recent publications include *Highland Homecomings: Genealogy and Heritage Tourism in the Scottish Diaspora* (2007) and *Exhibition Experiments* (edited with Sharon Macdonald, 2007). Specialising in cultural heritage and museological issues, he is currently consulting on a major museum development initiative in Sierra Leone.

Beverley Butler
Beverley Butler coordinates an MA in cultural heritage studies and lectures in cultural heritage studies, museology, and cultural memory at the Institute of Archaeology, University College London. She has a specialist focus on North Africa and Eastern Mediterranean and on Alexandrian/Egyptian and Palestinian cultural heritage. Her interests include the theorisation and reconceptualisation of cultural heritage studies and the development of cultural heritage ethnographies. Her most recent research, an ethnographic study of the revival of Bibliotheca Alexandrina, Egypt, is *Return to Alexandria – Cultural Heritage Revivalism and Museum Memory* (Left Coast Press 2008).

Ferdinand de Jong
Ferdinand de Jong is Lecturer in anthropology at the School of World Art Studies and Museology of the University of East Anglia. He has conducted research on masked performances and initiation ceremonies in Senegal. His book *Masquerades of Modernity: Power and Secrecy in Casamance, Senegal* has just been published by Edinburgh University Press (2007). He has also co-edited a special issue of the *Canadian Journal of African Studies* on the civil war in Senegal. His current research focuses on the memory and heritage of the slave trade and colonialism in postcolonial Senegal.

Charlotte Joy

Charlotte Joy is completing an ESRC-funded PhD in anthropology at University College London. She carried out ten months fieldwork in Djenné, Mali, and spent two months at UNESCO's Intangible Heritage Department in Paris. She is specialising in developing a comparative ethnographic approach to the study of cultural heritage politics and its relation to development issues.

Peter Probst

Peter Probst is Associate Professor of African art history and visual culture at Tufts University in Boston, USA. He has done field research in Cameroon, Malawi, and Nigeria and has published widely on issues of modernity (*African Modernities*, James Currey, 2002), the notion of local vitality (*Between Resistance and Expansion*, Lit Verlag, 2004), and the dynamics of locality and Nyau masked performance in Malawi (*Kalumbas Fest*, Lit Verlag, 2005). His new book on art, politics, and the making of heritage in Osogbo is due in 2008.

Michael Rowlands

Michael Rowlands is Professor of anthropology at UCL. His research has focused on material culture and cultural heritage studies in West and Central Africa, on new technologies and collections, and the comparative study of long-term historical change. Recent publications include *A Handbook of Material Culture* (2006) and articles on material culture, cultural property and rights, and heritage and modernity.

Ramon Sarró

Ramon Sarró is a Senior Research Fellow at the Institute of Social Sciences, University of Lisbon. He holds a PhD in anthropology (University College London, 1999) and has been the Ioma Evans-Pritchard Junior Research Fellow at St Anne's College, Oxford (2000–2002). Since 1992, he has conducted fieldwork on coastal Guinea, mainly on an iconoclastic movement that took place in 1956 among the Baga-speaking people and its legacies and memories today. His book *Surviving Iconoclasm: The Politics of Religious Change on the Upper Guinea Coast* will be published by the International African Institute in 2008. He has coedited, with David Berliner, the volume *Learning Religion: Anthropological Approaches* (Berghahn Books, 2007).

Katharina Schramm

Katharina Schramm is a postdoctoral research fellow at the Martin-Luther-Universität Halle-Wittenberg. She received her PhD in social anthropology from the Freie Universität in Berlin. She has written a number of articles on issues of tourism, memory, and race. Her book *Struggling over the Past: The Politics of Heritage and Homecoming in Ghana* is forthcoming with Left Coast Press. She is co-editor of *Remembering Violence: Anthropological Perspectives on Intergenerational Transmission* (Berghahn Books, 2008). Her current research focuses on the interface between diaspora-identity, new genetics, and citizenship.

Dorothea Schulz
Dorothea Schulz teaches at the Department of Religious Studies, Indiana University. She received her PhD in sociocultural anthropology from Yale University (1996) and her *Habilitation* from the Freie Universität, Berlin (2005). Her research, publications, and teaching centre on Islam in Africa, the anthropology of religion, gender studies, media studies, public culture, and the anthropology of the state. She is currently finalising a book manuscript entitled 'Embarking on the Path to God: Islamic Renewal and Mass-Mediated Religiosity in Urban Mali'.

Index

Abdullah, I., 255n1
abolition, 80–81. *See also* slave trade
Abraham, A., 240
Accra Declaration, 78
Adepegba, C., 105, 112
Adorno, T. W., 188
Africa: import-dependency of, 71; post-colonial, 19, 203, 206
African Charter on Human and Peoples Rights, 18. *See also* Banjul charter
African Diaspora, 73–74, 81–82
Afrocentrist theses, 21
Ahmadou, C., 139, 141
Ajulu, R., 253
Akpabli, K., 75, 76
Akurang-Parry, K. O., 84, 95n45
Akyeampong, E., 78, 96n47
Alexandrina Museum, 20
Alie, J. A., 241
Alldridge, T. J., 237, 256n9
Alvares, M., 236
Anderson, B., 100–101, 116, 119, 121n14
anticolonialism, 21
antimonument movement, 27
Antze, P., 14
Aofolaju, B., 108, 112
Appadurai, A., 162
Apter, A., 22, 121n11
architectural landscape, 15. *See also* monuments

Argenti, N., 22
Arnoldi, M.-J., 128
Askew, K. M., 22, 188
Austen, R., 203
authentic traditions, 186, 187, 192, 204, 205, 206, 211n27. *See also* tradition
autochthony, 186

banalisation, 174–175
Bangoura, S. B., 221
Barber, K., 173, 208n3
Barthes, R., 100, 120n2
Basu, P., 23, 27
Bausinger, H., 225
Bayart, J.-F., 186, 201, 210n22
Bedaux, R., 18, 149
Beier, U., 121n5
Bell, D., 129
Bender, W., 220
Benjamin, W., 101, 162, 165, 166, 181, 188
Berliner, D., 215, 220
Bierman, I. A., 141
Billig, M., 237
Blake, J., 146
Blier, S., 118
Boahen, A. A., 76
Bodnar, J., 72
Bourdieu, P., 232
Boyer, C., 100
Boym, S., 130
Brent, M., 148

Brooks, G. E., 216
Brown, M. F., 162
Bruner, E. M., 76, 95n26, 161, 181
Brunet-Jailly, J., 149
Bryant, R., 182
Bunn, D., 256n10
Burnham, P., 14
Butler, B., 20–21, 25

Camara, S., 209n11
Caroll, K., 121n6
Carrier, P., 194
Castaldi, F., 22
Caulker, P. S., 256n9
Ceuppens, B., 186, 205
Chami, F., 17
Chéroux, C., 115
Chesi, G., 103, 122n21
Christensen, M. J., 242, 256n8
civil rights, 18. *See also* cultural rights
Cleere, H., 129, 147
Clifford, J., 16, 162
Coe, C., 95n40
Cole, J., 14, 72, 254
colonialism, 18, 121n7, 130; French, 215–218; in Sierra Leone, 232–233, 241
Comaroff, J. L., 186, 187
Comaroff, J., 186, 187
commodification, 178, 182n8, 196. *See also* tourism
Connerton, P., 19, 232
Conrad, D., 210n21
conservation, 17; of cultural practice, 162
Cook, S. E., 248
Coombes, A. E., 15, 99
Coplan, D., 192
Corrigan, P.R.D., 187
Cosentino, D., 121n5
Cotton Tree, 234–235; symbolism of, 236–238; as unifying symbol, 237–238
Crary, J., 100
Crossland, Z., 248
Cube, A. von, 121n7
cultural heritage, 79, 207; as a discursive tradition, 20; globalisation of, 18; performance and, 128, 190–199,
202; preservation of, 16, 162; and the State, 127, 131, 150, 203; and UNESCO, 146–147
cultural patrimony, 18
cultural reinvention, 224
cultural revolution, in Guinea, 219–221
cultural rights, 18; and the State, 19. *See also* civil rights
culture: bureaucratization of, 220; traditional, 203. *See also* national culture
Curtis, M. Y., 215, 216
Cutter, C., 193

D'Alisera, J., 235
D'Entremont, D., 150
Danielson, V., 188
De Boeck, F., 254
de Certeau, M., 201
De Cuéllar, J. P., 91
de Jong, F., 19, 25, 164, 167, 168, 173, 182n4, 225
De Jorio, R., 15, 99, 128, 132, 133
De Witte, M., 81
Debray, R., 99, 115
decolonization, of African history, 17
DeCorse, C. R., 237
Denzer, L. R., 240
Der, B. G., 75
Derrida, J., 31–33
Diabey, B., 133, 138, 148
Diawara, M., 208n6, 209n11
Diène, D., 77
Diop, C. A., 21
Diouf, M., 22
Dippie, B., 100
Djenné: masons in, 151–153; restoration of, 133–139; as World Heritage Site, 145–157
Dominguez, V., 187
Dorjahn, V. R., 216
Doutremépuich, E., 165
Drewal, M., 115

Ebron, P. A., 93n8, 175
Eltis, D., 93n11
Englund, H., 186
Eriksen, H., 16

Errington, S., 161
ethnic groups, 170, 215, 218, 226
Eurocentrism, 79

Fabian, J., 14, 22, 175
Fairhead, J., 237
Falade, S. A., 110
Falola, T., 109, 111
Fanon, F., 21
Ferme, M. C., 231, 232, 233, 237, 255n5
Ferrándiz, F., 247, 248
Festival of Mankinko Heritage, 171–173, 182n3, n4
Fleming, P., 100
Fort, J., 89
Fortes, M., 119
Foster, J., 121n17
Frank, B., 210n21
Fraser, N., 96n46
Freud, S., 32
Fyfe, C., 216, 241

Geschiere, P., 186, 205
Gilroy, P., 79
Ginsburg, F., 181
Gittins, A. J., 252
Gizo, M. A., 93n5
Gottlieb, A., 236, 237
graves, mass, in Sierra Leone, 247–250; as memorials, 248, 250–251
Guinea: French rule in, 215–218; rule of S. Touré, 218–221
Guyer, J. I., 14
Gyase, K. F., 85, 86, 87

Habermas, J., 100
Halbwachs, M., 232
Hale, T., 209n11
Hallam, E., 247
Hamber, B., 239
Handler, R., 15, 161, 187, 203, 205
Hargreaves, J. D., 241, 255n3
Hartog, F., 100
Hasty, J., 94n20
heritage memory, 76–77, 99–100; and performance, 32–33, 191–199, 224–226; sanitization of, 99, 119; Westernization of, 20, 31, 234, 239

heritage technologies, 13, 143
heritage: discourse, 19, 111–113; globalization of, 101, 186; healing nature of, 138–139; immaterial, 24, 147–148; material, 24, 128, 142; and tourism, 18, 75–76, 224–226. *See also* heritage memory, heritage technologies, sacred heritage
Herzfeld, M., 79, 161
Hirsch, M., 19
Hobsbawm, E., 187, 195
Hockey, J., 247
Hodgkin, K., 232
Højbjerg, C., 220
Holiday, A., 80
Holocaust memorials, 27
Horkheimer, M., 188
Howarth, G., 247
Hughes, R., 248
Huyssen, A., 15, 99, 100
Hylland Eriksen, T., 129, 147, 162
Hymans, J. E. C., 237

ICOM, 72
identity politics, 14
Ingold, T., 17
Innes, G., 208n6
intangible heritage, 161, 173–182, 232
International Council of Museums. *See* ICOM

Jackson, M., 237
Jäger, J., 100, 121n17
Jarvis, H., 248
jeli, 191–199, 209n11, n13, n16, 210n18, n21
jihad, 215, 217
Johnson, S., 109
Joseph Project, 23, 73, 80–90
Joy, C., 24, 138

Kaba, L., 218, 220
Kabba, M. R. A., 240, 241
Kankurang masquerade, 162–182; occult power, 167; recontextualisation of, 172–173
Kasfir, S., 121n5, 168
Kaspin, D., 101

Kayode, A., 113
Keen, D., 255n1
Keita, M. C. K., 209n11
Keita, M., 26, 128, 132, 189, 190, 193, 195, 208n6
Keita, S., 127, 128, 132, 149, 193
Kelsall, T., 239
Kennedy, J., 121n5
King, A., 251
Klute, G., 197
Koita, H., 128
Konaré, A. O., 127–128, 132, 149, 197, 198
Küchler, Susanne, 121n4
Kuper, A., 162

Lambek, M., 14–15, 22
Lamp, F., 216, 220, 223–224
Landau, P., 101
Last, M., 243
Law, R., 112
Lawal, B., 118, 121n5
Leach, M., 236, 255n5
Limann, K. B., 89
Lipsitz, G., 93n1
Lovejoy, P., 94n25
Lowenthal, D., 17, 91, 99, 100
Luhmann, N., 122n23
Luskey, J., 100

Maas, P., 150
Mack, J., 21
MacKevitt, C., 95n28
MacMillan, A., 110
Maffesoli, M., 122n22
Malcolm, J. M., 237
Mali: diversity in, 187; politics in, 187
Mamdani, M., 18
maraboutism, 219–220
Marchand, T., 151
Mark, P., 173, 225
Matanmi II, 114–115, *114*
Matanmi III, 106, 107, 116
material culture, memory and, 14–15, 24–25, 142
Mayor, F., 77
Mazrui, A. A., 221

Mbembe, A., 13, 99, 186
McGovern, M., 219, 220, 221
McIntosh, R. J., 148
McIntosh, S. K., 148
media: effects on tradition, 188, 190–196, 203, 207; in Mali, 185–210; role of, 188, 242; in Sierra Leone, 242–243, *247*; state-controlled, 190–199, 201
Meillassoux, C., 203
memorials, 248, 250–251; Holocaust, 27
memories: collective, 14, 15, 77, 100, 114, 128–129, 132; personal, 14, 15, 132
memory, 13, 19; demystified, 215–228; heritage vs., 16–17, 106; and history, 233–234; popular, 72, 128
Meyer, B., 122n22, 186
Miller, C. L., 220
Mitchell, T., 181
modernization, 27, 135–136, 142
Mommersteeg, G., 150
monumental architecture, 21, 27, 99, 101, 118–119, 129–130, 133–135, 145–157
monumental heritage, 15, 79, 118, 128, 133
monuments, 79, 121n4, 128, 133, 236–237, 242–246, 250–251. *See also* sculpture
Morgenthau, R. S., 217
museums, 90, 128, 237
Musil, R., 100
Myers, F. M., 25
Myers, F. R., 162
myth, 112, 128, 236–237. *See also* tradition

Naas, M., 31, 32, 33
Nas, P. J. M., 15, 161
national culture, 204–206
national heritage, 173, 187, 194, 206. *See also* national culture
national identity, 15, 116, 127, 129–133, 175
nationalism, 15, 132, 135, 223; European-derived models of, 13
nation-building, 19, 131–132, 139, 239, 253–254
Noah, A., 242
Nooter, M., 99

Nora, P., 17, 19, 100, 130, 132, 142, 194
Nyamnjoh, F., 14, 186, 210n18

Oakdale, S., 162
Obetsebi-Lamptey, J. O., 80, 81, 94n22, n24, 95n29
objectification, 24–25, 162, 177, 178, 181; of folklore, 226; of memory, 25
Oguibe, O., 110
Ogungbile, D., 121n9
Ojuade, J. S., 112
Okeke, C., 121n5
Okofo, I. N., 93n10
Olugonna, D., 111
Opala, J. A., 241–242, 255n6
Osogbo Heritage Council, 101, 105, 108–109, 111, 112, 120

Panafest, 73–74
Patterson, T., 17
Peel, J., 109
Perbi, A. A., 75
pharmakon, 57, 58, 62, 175
photography, as part of heritage, 99–122. *See also* media
pilgrimage, 82, 93n8, n10. *See also* tourism
Pinney, C., 101
Plumpe, G., 122n20
politics: of belonging, 14; of demystification, 27; in heritage practices, 108; of recognition, 186; of remembering, 19, 91; of tradition, 223–224
postcolonial Africa, 13, 14, 99; Guinea, 221–222
Probst, P., 22–23, 24, 121n5
Prussin, L., 135

Radstone, S., 232
Ranger, T., 187
Rashid, I., 239
recognition, 26
reconciliation, 26
religious influence on heritage practices, 107–108, 117, 120, 122n22, 139–140
Renan, E., 131
restoration, 17, 133–137; vs. conservation, 133–134

Richards, P., 233, 240
Richardson, D., 93n11
Riegl, A., 100, 121n4, 133–134
Rivière, C., 219
Robben, A. C. G. M., 248
Roberts, A. F., 22
Roberts, A., 99
Roberts, M., 22
Rodney, W., 216
Rogers, J. D., 238
Rouget, G., 220
Rowlands, M., 14, 18, 24, 129, 153, 210n18

sacred heritage, 103–104
Saho, B., 182n8
Sanford, V., 247, 248
Sankhon, A., 219, 220
Sant Cassia, P., 248
Sarró, R., 27, 216
Sayer, D., 187
Sayers, E. F., 236, 237
Sayon, A., 217–218, 220, 221
Schmidt, P., 17
Schramm, K., 23, 76, 78, 82, 93n6, n8, n9, 94n12, n19, 95n37
Schulz, D., 25, 26, 128, 191, 195, 196, 199, 210n18, 211n29
Schulze, Gary, 240, 241
sculpture, 102–104, 118. *See also* monuments
Senghor, Léopold, 176
Sesay, S. B., 235, 236
Shaw, R., 22, 78, 231, 232, 233, 239, 240, 246, 255n4
Shelton, A., 129
Shohat, E., 101
Sidibé, M., 127, 149
Siebert, U., 94n17
Sierra Leone, 231–256; corruption in, 242–243
Simmel, G., 100
Simone, A. M., 186
Slave Route Project, 73, 74, 77–80, 87, 90
slave trade: African, 87–89; transatlantic, 71, 80, 84–90, 91, 232, 234. *See also* abolition

slavery: African slave market, 76, 84–90, 85; in Ghana, 72, 80, 84–86
Smith, A. D., 129
Sontag, S., 100
Soures, B., 140
Spitulnik, D., 208n3
Sprague, S., 115
Spyer, P., 166
Squires, C. R., 96n46
Stahl, A., 17
Stam, R., 101
Steinmetz, G., 187
Stoller, P., 22
Svalensen, L., 94n15
Sylvain, R., 162

Taussig, M., 180
Taylor, C., 186
Terdiman, R., 130
Thompson, F., 115
Thornton, J., 79
Tidy, M., 221
Tilley, C., 129
Titchen, S. M., 147
Todorov, T., 128
Tonkin, E., 226, 228n4
Touré, S., 27, 215, 218–221, 222, 223, 227
Touré, T., 189, 210n24
tourism: cultural, 77–78, 84, 150–151, 175, 224; pilgrimage, 74–75, 89–92; religious, 107
tradition, 170, 178, 182n4; authentic, 186–188, 192, 204, 205, 206, 207, 211n27; created, 189–190; local, 185, 186, 190, 200, 203, 205, 208, 219–220, 224, 240; media effects on, 188, 190–196, 203, 207; preservation of, 170. *See also* media, national culture, national heritage
Traoré, A., 127
Traoré, M., 195, 196, 197, 201, 210n24
Trotha, T. von, 197
Trouillot, R., 195
Truth and Reconciliation Commission (Sierra Leone), 234, 239, 244, 246, 249–251, 253

Turino, T., 188
Tyam, A., 219

UNESCO, 13, 24, 145; African policies, 15, 18–20, 90–91, 145; and cultural heritage, 146–147, 156–157; world heritage policy, 16, 20, 129, 133, 161
Urry, J., 84

Van der Waal, J. D., 149
Vansina, J., 233
Verdery, K., 248
Verger, P., 119

Waldman, M., 141
Ward, W. E. F., 75, 82
Weil, P., 182n8
Wendl, T., 115
Wenger, S., 103, 111, 115, 117, 120, 122n21
Werbner, R., 13, 14, 72, 99, 186
Westermann, D., 122n19
Western concepts of heritage, 146, 247, 251
Westernization: of heritage memory, 20, 31, 234, 239
Williams, E. V., 71
Williams, P., 248
Wilson, R. A., 239
World Heritage Convention, 146
World Heritage Site, 73, 79, 104, 129, 133, 146–147, 255n6. *See also* UNESCO
Wyse, A. J. G., 233

Yai, O., 111
Yates, F. A., 33
Young, C., 189
Young, J. E., 27, 233

Zeleza, P. T., 93n2